THE
SPIRITUAL EXERCISES
OF
Saint
Ignatius

1. The Gospel of St. Thomas
   by: Richard Valantasis
   Publisher - Routhedge - Ky

2. The Gospel of Thomas
   "The hidden sayings of Christ"
   Interpreter: Marvin Meyer
   Publisher: Harper Collins

THE
SPIRITUAL EXERCISES
OF
Saint
Ignatius

Translated and with Commentary by
PIERRE WOLFF

Triumph
Liguori, Missouri

Published by Triumph
Liguori, Missouri
An Imprint of Liguori Publications

Scriptural citations have been taken from the *New American Bible*, Confrater-
nity of Christian Doctrine, Washington, D.C., 1970; *The Jerusalem Bible*, Darton,
Longman & Todd, Ltd, and Doubleday, Inc., 1966; *The Catholic Study Bible*:
The New American Bible, Oxford University Press, Inc., New York, 1990; and
the Greek Text of the New Testament, from D. Eberhard Nestle, Editio Vicesima
Prima, Württembergische Bibelanstalt, Stuttgart, Germany, 1962.

Library of Congress Cataloging-in-Publication Data

Ignatius, of Loyola, Saint, 1491–1556.
    [Exercitia spiritualia. English]
    The spiritual exercises of Saint Ignatius / translated and with commentary
by Pierre Wolff. — 1st ed.
        p.   cm.
    Includes bibliographical references.
    ISBN 0-7648-0028-0; ISBN 0-7648-0142-2 (pbk.): (alk. paper)
    1. Spiritual exercises. 2. Ignatius, of Loyola, Saint, 1491–1556. Exercitia
spiritualia. I. Wolff, Pierre, 1929– . II. Title.
BX2179.L7E5   1997
248.3—dc21   96–54825

All rights reserved. No part of this publication may be reproduced, stored in a
retrieval system, or transmitted in any form or by any means—electronic,
mechanical, photocopy, recording, or any other—except for brief quotations
in printed reviews, without the prior permission of the publisher.

Copyright © 1997 by Pierre Wolff
Printed in the United States of America
01 00 99 98 97   5 4 3 2 1
First Edition

Table of Contents

---

* Bold characters indicate corresponding pages in the Commentary.

Preface

I have written commentary on *The Spiritual Exercises* of Saint Ignatius not as a theorist, but as one who has decades of experience both in making the Spiritual Exercises and as retreat master, in giving them to many people in several countries. So, rather than use this Preface to give an extensive history of the Exercises, which many other books have already done, I am going to offer a few words on the translation and then a capsule history of the Spiritual Exercises.

This text is *the official text* of the Exercises.* Three versions of the Exercises exist. The first one, called "Autograph" (A), is believed to be a copy of an original text in Spanish; the second, *"Versio Prima"* (P), is a Latin translation of the Autograph, probably made around 1534 by Ignatius himself for readers who could not understand Spanish; eventually the *Versio Vulgata* (V), a new text in classical Latin, was commissioned by Ignatius, who wanted the Exercises approved by the pope, from a French Jesuit, Father André des Freux. Both P and V were sent to the Roman Curia, which recognized and blessed them in 1548, with the approval of Pope Paul III. Ignatius then decided that *only* V would be printed and used, even by himself. Thus, V was the official text until 1835, when a new general superior of the Jesuits "rediscovered" A and made it the text people would translate and work with most frequently, both inside and outside of the Society of Jesus, right up to the present day. Indeed, V has rarely been published in an American edition; the last American version of V,

---

*The basis of our translation is the text most Jesuits have in their hands, the one found in the *Thesaurus Spiritualis Societatis Jesu*, Typis Polyglottis Vaticanis, 1948.

which was published in 1968, was more of a paraphrase than a direct translation.

The desire to deal with Ignatius' thoughts as close as possible to their origin favored recourse to the Autograph. However, this has put Ignatius' will, based on his faith in the value of the Church's recognition, too much aside. The present translation is produced in order to help reestablish some equilibrium by giving people access to a translation of the official text (V) that could be used concurrently with A and P, and that sometimes differs interestingly from them.

What we offer here *is* a translation. Most everybody knows the Italian saying "*Traduttori, traditori*" ("Translators, betrayers"); however, a text may be betrayed to a greater or lesser extent. Therefore, we have tried to be as literal as possible, even though this meant retaining some archaic or ponderous language; we did not want to give users a paraphrase in which Ignatius would have a problem recognizing himself. Rather, we want to treat readers and retreatants as intelligent people, remembering that the text of the Exercises was never intended to be used all by itself, but always under the supervision of a retreat master, who would offer appropriate commentary and direction. In fact, the Exercises were first of all written for retreat masters, who are supposed to adjust the Exercises to the individual retreatant.

Let us briefly revisit the story of Ignatius and the Exercises. Born in 1491 in Loyola, Spain, Ignatius is living the easy life of the European aristocracy; for example, he often serves as a diplomat without portfolio at the court of Navarre during this period (1506–1521). Wounded in 1521 in Pamplona, which is being besieged by French troops, he ends a military career of a few days and enters into a long convalescence. As distraction, he reads books, both tales about chivalry and the lives of the saints. Soon he notices a difference in the impact of these two types of reading. The exaltation given him by the knights' stories quickly ends in a kind of sadness, while the joy he experiences with the saints is profound and lasts. This is the beginning of his conversion, of discernment, and even, mysteriously, of the Exercises. Ignatius decides to change his lifestyle and spends nine months, at the abbey of Montserrat and at Manresa, in a sort of long retreat;

then he starts to give spiritual help to people where he is, drawing on what he has personally experienced and noticed. Problems with Church authorities (eight lawsuits in twelve years!) impel him to study in different universities in Spain and finally in Paris, and to become a priest. During those years, he gives the Exercises to many people, always correcting and refining the text according to the discoveries he's made in himself or with others. He says "that he had not composed the Exercises all at once, but that when he noticed some things in his soul and found them useful, he thought they might also be useful to others, and so he put them in writing" (*Autobiography*, n. 99). Some of these early retreatants become his friends and the companions with whom he makes vows of poverty and chastity in Paris in 1534. All these men travel to many places in Europe and minister to people at all levels of society, particularly giving the Exercises. In 1539, the first ten companions found the Society of Jesus, whose members quickly become numerous and famous in Europe, chiefly for their answer to the crisis of the Reformation and their spirituality. In 1548, the pope approves the Exercises. Ignatius dies in Rome, as superior of the Society of Jesus, in 1556, leaving behind him approximately one thousand Jesuits (including some in Brazil, India, and Ethiopia) shaped by the Exercises, the basis of their yearly retreat and of their two thirty-day retreats (one in the novitiate and one during the last year of their training, called "tertianship").

This history shows that the Exercises come from Ignatius' spiritual journey, characterized by following Jesus, practicing discernment, and acquiring a sense of service. The writing of the Exercises benefited from the fact that Ignatius gave them to many other persons. We can presume that the text of V took into account the knowledge accumulated by Ignatius through the years. Indeed, this is sometimes clearly evident.

From time to time, there appeared in the Society of Jesus "Directories." Ignatius himself left some notes for one of them. These directories were commentary about the text of the *Spiritual Exercises* in order to help retreat masters in their task. In some fashion, this book is also such a directory. However, it can help people other than retreat masters as well, especially retreatants, because today they are frequently given the book of the Exercises for their

retreat (and this book may help them after they have made the
Exercises). Hopefully, this volume can also be valuable for any
spiritual helper, because the efficacy of the Jesuits' spirituality has
been proved over centuries, not only for Jesuits, but for people
from all walks of life. I have given talks to appreciative audiences
about the meaning of the steps of the Exercises for spiritual growth,
about the systematic and short description of the Rules of discernment, and about the decision-making process. The reaction
of those audiences confirms for me the abiding relevance of
Ignatius' spiritual insight.

PIERRE WOLFF
JULY 31, 1996
EXACTLY 440 YEARS AFTER IGNATIUS' DEATH

Acknowledgments

The Exercises are rooted in gratitude, and I would like to start this book in the same manner, by thanking those to whom I owe the content of the following pages. First, my thanks to all Jesuits who formed me with Ignatius' tool: to retreat masters like my master of novices and my instructor of tertianship; to commentators like Father Gaston Fessard and some of his disciples; and to others through their articles and books. I also learned a lot through people who made the Exercises with me, for one week, thirty days, or in daily life—men and women, lay or religious, ministers, from diverse countries and Christian denominations. I am grateful for what I discovered through retreatants, even in shorter Ignatian retreats; I have especially in my mind some inmates incarcerated for long sentences in American prisons. This book would not exist without all of them, and I am thankful for this phrase here, that example there, that brought back to my heart a face seen in Liberia or Italy, a voice heard in Sweden or Belgium, a wound healed in India or France, a decision admired in Japan or the United States. Nor would it exist without my friend Giorgio Pinton, who helped me to translate the Exercises with his expertise in the Latin of Ignatius' time; or without Pat, Joan, and Mary, to whom I also offer grateful thanks.

Foreword

I t would be impossible to measure the enormous impact which Ignatius Loyola has made on the Christian world over the past four centuries through the text of his Spiritual Exercises. Countless retreats have been shaped in one way or another according to that text, and God only knows how many men and women have matured spiritually under the impulse of those retreats. While the full four weeks of the Exercises have frequently been adapted in response to the backgrounds and circumstances of individual retreatants, Ignatius' charism has continued to attract and guide people through all those adaptations and modifications. One of Ignatius' first companions confidently observed that Pope Paul III's solemn approval of the text of the Exercises in 1548 was both a rare privilege and an extraordinary honor for an individual writing; the pronouncement bordered on being infallible! And one early adversary noted in his copy of the text that such papal approval was "astonishing." It was, he thought, theologically appalling that a text which came down so strongly on the side of the individual's direct experience of God should have won the endorsement of the Holy See.* Nevertheless, the efficacy of the Spiritual Exercises in everyday life had been confirmed over and over again. For many people, the Exercises had paved the way to deep holiness and union with God. As a result of making the Exercises, they had acquired the grace of finding God in all things.

Anyone wishing to understand both the Spiritual Exercises and

---

* See John W. O'Malley, *The First Jesuits* (Cambridge: Harvard University Press, 1993), 302. Also Candido de Dalmases, *Ignatius of Loyola: Founder of the Jesuits* (Saint Louis: Institute of Jesuit Sources, 1985), 206.

the charism which lies beneath them would do well to read closely Ignatius' spiritual testament or "autobiography."[*] There he reveals the intense religious experience which gave birth to the plan of the Exercises. Ignatius had discovered the way of the Spirit through trial and error. The will of God—God's ongoing project both in his own life and in the lives of others—was, he realized, the pearl of great price. Indeed, the history behind the Exercises is the story of one person's discovery of that great treasure of which the gospel speaks, for the sake of which one parts with absolutely everything (Mt 13:44).

Actually living the gospel, however, is neither simple nor easy. One soon finds oneself doing battle with all sorts of opposing forces and desires. Just as bodily exercise would be meaningless if our bodies encountered no physical resistance, so also we would not profit from exercises of the spirit if we never encountered tension and resistance of another sort. Not every desire leads to God, not every pious thought originates in the Spirit, and not every prayer is consoling. Sometimes the reality of God seems ever more remote, and the immediacy of earthly attractions ever more desirable. One learns that seeking and putting into practice the will of God requires daily attentiveness to the word of God revealed in the world and in one's life. It also requires learning to notice key movements within one's heart and soul, movements which often slip by because we have not learned how to discern the subtle yet ordinary disclosures of the divine mystery in daily life.

Living out the gospel, freely and joyfully, depends upon the ability to recognize the features of the crucified and risen Jesus in one's life and in our world. The legacy of Ignatius in the Spiritual Exercises has been that of leading a person through the dynamics of discipleship. Loving Jesus ardently and following him closely will be impeded unless one is also growing resolutely in humility and self-knowledge, which accounts for why the Ignatian view of discipleship places heavy stress on spiritual direction.

---

[*] Several recent versions are available. For example: *A Pilgrim's Testament: The Memoirs of St. Ignatius Loyola*, trans. Parmananda Divarkar (Saint Louis: Institute of Jesuit Sources, 1995). Also, *Reminiscences or Autobiography of Ignatius Loyola*, trans. Philip Endean, in *Saint Ignatius of Loyola: Personal Writings* (New York and London: Penguin Books, 1996).

Ignatius was, it must not be forgotten, a man of his time. Anyone studying the text of the Spiritual Exercises at the close of the twentieth century will realize soon enough that we do not share at all points the same theological perspective as Ignatius. In fact, we probably do not share the same ascetical discipline at all points either. Nevertheless, the Exercises provide a way of entering into the world of the gospel and coming to the startling yet wonderful conclusion that, first, the world of the gospel is exactly where one wants to be and, second, that one cannot remain there forever. In the end, we must live in our own world and in our own times, and learn how to contemplate that world with gospel eyes. Ignatius once believed that it was God's will that he go to the Holy Land, and he believed further that it was God's will that he live and work there. But when he was ordered by ecclesiastical authority to leave the Holy Land, he recognized that instruction as coming from God; nor did he ever return. He had to imagine his own Galilee and recreate the Holy Land for himself.

The Exercises, of course, are only an instrument for steeping oneself in the story of Jesus. But instruments of the spirit serve a valuable purpose. Not all those who profess to be Christian have actually embraced the gospel. For some people, and perhaps for too many, the gospel provides no more than the symbols and motifs of a reassuring religious mythology, a "sacred canopy." It offers them a framework within which they can interpret history and create meaningfulness within their own lives. As mythology, the gospel even makes comprehensible the great human drama of sin and grace. In the end, however, the gospel is not really their story; it is merely the story of Jesus: what he did, how he died, and the happy ending of his being raised from the dead. When reduced to mythology, the gospel never actually engages us directly and immediately. We welcome Jesus' moral example. We watch Jesus do his redemptive thing, as it were; he was born to suffer and die. We become grateful but passive spectators to the divine drama which once unfolded in our history.

But the gospel can become our story, too; this is what Ignatius discovered. The divine action in and through Jesus was not a one-time display, an event from a culturally and historically distant age ever to be devoutly recalled and passively observed on our mental stages. One can really encounter and be with that Jesus of Nazareth in every time and place; such, of course, was the conviction of the evangelists themselves. Through the four weeks of the Exercises, Ignatius drew many others along the interior path God had shown him. Absolutely convinced that God had called him and placed him with his Son, Ignatius appears from behind the pages of his text to sound like the great apostle Paul as "one untimely born" (1 Cor 15:8), for Ignatius knew the risen Lord. Presumptuous as it sounds, Ignatius' zeal and love for Christ would not have run second even to that of Paul himself. Yet Ignatius seems to have been convinced that this was the quintessential Christian grace intended for all of us: to be placed by the Father alongside the Son. And for what purpose? Was it merely a private consolation? No; for Ignatius the aim was always "to help souls." Or as we might say, to share the grace of apostleship, to be companions of Jesus.

It is probably no coincidence that the enormous resurgence of interest in Ignatian retreats and spiritual direction which we have witnessed since Vatican II has been taking place at a time when there is such an intense desire to know more and more about the gospels and the person of Jesus. Modern biblical studies and research into every conceivable aspect of the New Testament records about Jesus point, I believe, to an extraordinary action of the Spirit in our time. Future generations will look back at this moment and marvel at our recovery of the human, historical Jesus.

Salvation obviously is not a matter of scholarship; we are not going to win eternal life on the basis of our intellectual accomplishments alone. Thus there needs to be an appropriation of the fruits of so much historical and textual research. Ignatius would have welcomed with delight the opportunity to read and study what is so readily available to us in biblical commentaries. But he would also have reminded us that the imagination has to steep itself in the gospel story, and that we need to give that story a chance to fill our senses. He knew quite well the risks involved when great stress is laid upon individual experience; enthusiasm could go wild and cause considerable spiritual and even bodily harm. Yet Ignatius trusted the power of the gospel story to work its way through the whole of a person's life and to free that person to say yes to God's call in Christ.

In short, the Exercises represent Ignatius' deep love of the gospels and his desire to help others awaken to that same love. This splendid edition of the Spiritual Exercises and its wise, insightful commentary puts me in mind of the gospel text: "Therefore every scribe who has been trained for the kingdom of heaven is like the master of a household who brings out of his treasure what is new and what is old" (Mt 13:52). The book you hold in your hands indeed comes from a scribe trained for the kingdom of God.

WILLIAM REISER, S.J.
DEPARTMENT OF RELIGIOUS STUDIES
COLLEGE OF THE HOLY CROSS

THE
SPIRITUAL
EXERCISES

Official Text, 1548

Annotations

[1]* **Some annotations that bring an understanding
of the following Spiritual Exercises,
and that might help the one who gives
them as well as the one who makes them**

First Annotation: By the words "Spiritual Exercises," we should understand any method of examining our own conscience, and also of meditating, contemplating, praying mentally and orally, and finally of dealing with any other spiritual activities, that will be referred to later on. In the same way that walking, traveling, and running are corporal exercises, so preparing and disposing the soul to remove all inordinate attachments and, after they have been removed, searching and finding the will of God about the management of one's life and the salvation of the soul are spiritual exercises.

[2] *Second Annotation:* The person who gives to another a method and order for meditation or contemplation must faithfully narrate the story to be meditated on or contemplated by merely passing through the principal points and adding only brief clarifications; so that the one who is going to meditate, after having first accepted the basis of the historical truth, will then go over it and consider it by himself. Thus it would happen that when he finds something that would offer a greater elucidation or apprehension of the story (whether it happens through his own reflection or a divine inspiration in his mind), he will harvest a more delightful taste and more abundant fruit than if the same thing had

---

* Note numbers are reproduced as they are now used by the Society of Jesus for *The Spiritual Exercises*.

been more extensively narrated and explained by someone else. It is not, indeed, the abundance of knowledge, but the interior sense and taste of things, that usually satisfies the desire of the soul.

[3] *Third Annotation:* Because, in all the following Spiritual Exercises, we use acts of intellect when we reflect and acts of will when we react affectively, we should be aware that, especially in the activity of the will, when we are vocally or mentally in conversation with God, the Lord, or His saints, a greater reverence is demanded from us than when we remain speculating by the use of the intellect.

[4] *Fourth Annotation:* Four Weeks are given to the Exercises that follow, each one corresponding to each part of the Exercises. Namely, the Consideration of Sins is made during the First Week, that of the Life of Jesus Christ our Lord up to His entrance into Jerusalem for Palm Sunday during the Second Week, that of the Passion during the Third, and that of Resurrection and Ascension in the Fourth Week with the Three Methods of Praying. However, although these four parts are called Weeks, they do not necessarily have to be seven or eight days long. It may happen that some individuals are slower or faster than others to reach what they are looking for (such as contrition, sorrow, and tears for their sins during the First Week), and also some individuals are more or less moved or tried by different spirits. It would be convenient, then, to extend or shorten any Week according to the matter that is proposed. However, the total length of the Exercises in time is usually thirty days, or nearly so.

[5] *Fifth Annotation:* It would greatly help him who accepts the Exercises to enter into them with a great and generous spirit, and to offer all his striving and free will to his Creator that he might decide what to do with himself and all his possessions, to best serve Him according to His pleasure.

[6] *Sixth Annotation:* If the one who gives the Exercises realizes that, for the person accepting them, neither spiritual motions, such as consolations or sadness, nor any agitations by diverse spirits, happen, he must carefully question him whether he practices

his Exercises at the scheduled times and in what manner, and also if he observes diligently all additions; an account for each of those things will be asked. Concerning consolations and desolations, the matter will be treated in the first Rules for the discernment of spirits. Additions will be addressed at the end of the First Week.

[7] *Seventh Annotation:* If the one who accompanies another person through the Exercises sees him afflicted by desolation or temptation, he must be careful not to show himself as harsh or severe, but rather as gentle and kind, encouraging the other's spirit to act courageously in the future; and, the stratagems of our enemy having been uncovered, he must work to prepare him for the consolation that will come soon.

[8] *Eighth Annotation:* For matters concerning the consolations and desolations of the one who is making the Exercises and the cunning of the enemy, the Rules that are found for the first two Weeks for the discernment of different spirits can be used.

[9] *Ninth Annotation:* When the person who is making the Exercises is inexperienced in spiritual matters, so that it happens that he is disturbed by gross and clear temptations during the First Week that present obstacles to him for continuing in God's service (like annoyance, anxiety, shame, fear because of human respect), the one who is teaching him to make the Exercises should postpone the use of the Rules for the Discernment of Spirits related to the Second Week, and instead use the Rules of the First Week only. For as much as that retreatant may derive benefits from the Rules of the First Week, so he may derive harm from those of the Second, because the subtlety and sublimity of their object is over his head.

[10] *Tenth Annotation:* If the one who is exercising is disturbed by temptations under the appearance of good, he should be fortified with the so-called Rules of the Second Week. Truly, the enemy of humankind ordinarily most often attacks under the appearance of good those who have been rather in that way of life called illuminative, which corresponds to the Exercises of the Second Week, and not so much in the other one usually

called purgative, which is included in the Exercises of the First
Week.

[11] *Eleventh Annotation:* It is advantageous for the one doing
the First Week not to know what he will be doing in the Second
Week. He should instead labor vigorously for what he is looking
for at present, as if he would find nothing good thereafter.

[12] *Twelfth Annotation:* The one who makes the Exercises must
be advised that, since he must spend an hour in each of the five
daily Exercises, which will be described later on, he should take
care to maintain his soul's peace by being conscious of giving
them more rather than less time. In fact, frequently the evil one
acts so that the predetermined time for meditation or oration is
cut short.

[13] *Thirteenth Annotation:* It is easy and light to complete a
contemplation for an entire hour when consolation abounds. On
the contrary, it is very difficult when desolation occurs. Thus it is
always necessary to combat this temptation and this desolation
in order to prevail, by extending the Exercise beyond the decided
hour. In this manner, we learn not only to resist the adversary but
also to defeat him.

[14] *Fourteenth Annotation:* If the one who is giving time to the
Exercises is seen as carried away by great consolation and fervor,
he must be prevented from binding himself with any promise or
vow in any inconsiderate or precipitous manner; he should be
advised even more diligently if he is perceived as being of an unstable nature. In fact, though a person may rightly advise another
to enter a religious order, in which the vows of obedience, poverty, and chastity are made, and though it is more meritorious to
do something with a vow than without a vow, nevertheless it is
extremely important to take into consideration the situation of
each person. It is necessary also to consider very carefully what
benefit or inconvenience may be produced by the accomplish-
ment of what one would promise.

[15] *Fifteenth Annotation*: The one who gives the Exercises should
not push the other toward poverty or the promise of poverty rather

than its opposite, nor toward one state of life rather than another. Though at any time outside of the Exercises it is licit and even meritorious to counsel all those who may be apt to embrace celibacy, religious life, or any other evangelical perfection, according to their individual nature and situation, it is preferable and more convenient during the Exercises themselves not to try to do so. It is better to search for God's will and wait for the moment when our Creator and Lord will communicate Himself to the soul devoted to Him and, embracing it, will dispose it to His love, praise, and service, just as He knows to be most advantageous for it. Thus the one giving the Exercises must keep himself in a kind of equilibrium and let the Creator Himself manage the matter with His creature, and the creature, in its turn, with Him without any mediator.

[16] *Sixteenth Annotation*: In order that our Creator and Lord Himself can act more surely in His creature, if it happens that the soul is influenced by and inclined to something less than proper, it must make all efforts with all its strength in the opposite direction. For example, if someone wishes for a position or benefit not for the glory of God or the common salvation of souls, but only for his own advantage and material profit, then his attachment must be directed to the contrary by assiduous prayers and other pious exercises in which he would ask for the opposite from God's clemency. This means that, in order to offer himself to God, he would not look for any position or benefit or anything else if he has not yet changed his previous attachment, so that he would no longer desire or possess anything for any reason other than for divine worship and honor.

[17] *Seventeenth Annotation* is most useful. The one who gives the Exercises should not want to inquire and know the personal thoughts and sins of the other; however, he has to be faithfully informed about the thoughts inspired by the different spirits, and which attract to a greater or a lesser good, in order to be able to prescribe some specific Spiritual Exercises adapted to the actual needs of the soul.

[18] *Eighteenth Annotation*: The Exercises must be adapted to the condition of the person who is making them, for example, according to his age, his education, and his aptitude, in order not to demand from someone who is uneducated, of weak spirit, or in poor health more than what he can handle without inconvenience and can assume for his profit. Equally, just as anyone becomes interiorly better disposed, that which will help him the most must be offered to him. Therefore, if someone asks only to be instructed and led to a certain level where his spirit finds rest, he could be given first the Particular Examination and then the General Examination, together with instruction on the Modes of Praying for half an hour in the morning, on God's commandments, and on mortal sins, as it is found farther. It would be necessary to suggest to him to confess his sins every eight days and receive, if he feels moved to it, the sacrament of the Eucharist every fifteen or, even better, every eight days. This method of exercising is particularly suited to people who are uneducated or illiterate; each commandment of God and of the Church, the mortal sins, the five senses, and the works of mercy will also be explained to them. Likewise, if he who gives the Exercises sees that someone is of a feeble nature and limited in his capacities, so that only mediocre progress and fruits could be expected from him, then it would be more than enough to prescribe to this one some of the above lighter Exercises up to the confession of sins; after that he can give him some examinations of conscience and a method for a more frequent confession through which he will be able to keep the progress or gain for his soul that has been already acquired. But it would not be necessary to go further, either up to the matters about the Elections or up to Exercises other than the ones of the First Week, especially when other persons are present who are able to exercise more fruitfully and limitations of time do not allow one to offer everything to everyone.

[19] *Nineteenth Annotation*: If a gifted and cultured man, who is involved in public affairs or has other obligations, disposes each day of one and a half hours for some Exercises, he should be exposed at first to the end why man has been created; then, for a half hour, he may be given the Particular Examination and the

General Examination together with an explanation of the manner of making confession and receiving the holy Sacrament. He will be counseled also to make, for one hour in the morning over three days, the meditation on the first, second, and third sin, as it is instructed further. Then, during another three days, at the same hour, he should make the meditation on the census of sins, and, during the next three days, the meditation on the punishments that correspond to the sins. He should also be told, during the time reserved for these three meditations, about the ten Additions found at the end of the First Week. The same method of meditating will be used for the Mysteries [of the Life] of Our Lord Jesus Christ that are explained later within these Exercises.

[20] *Twentieth Annotation:* If someone is freer from usual business and wishes to obtain the greatest possible spiritual fruit, then he should be offered all the Exercises in their correct order (and it will be convenient to use written records of the essential in order to keep it better in memory). As it happens most usually in these Exercises, he will derive all the greater benefit in his spiritual life because he will separate himself more from his friends and acquaintances and from all human concerns, for example, by leaving his home for another one or a more retired room where he will be freely and safely able to attend holy Mass or Vespers as he desires, without being prevented by any person of his acquaintance. This retreat will offer, among many others, the following three advantages. First, by separating himself from his friends and acquaintances, and from business less directly relevant to God's worship, he merits no small favor from God. Second, in this retreat, his mind being less distracted in all directions than before but all his thought concentrating and reflecting upon only one matter, which is to honor God his Creator and to care for the salvation of his soul, he can apply his natural energies more freely and faster for whatever he desires so much to achieve. Third, the more the soul finds itself free from things and in solitude, the more it finds itself capable of searching and reaching for its Creator and Lord; thus, the nearer the soul comes to Him, the better it becomes disposed to receive the gifts of Divine Goodness.

[21] Some Spiritual Exercises

by which man is led to the possibility
of conquering himself and deciding
on a way of conducting his life
that is free from harmful attachments

PRESUPPOSITION

[22] First of all, in order that through these Exercises both the one who is giving them and the one who is receiving them can be helped, it should be presupposed that a devout Christian would be more eagerly disposed to interpret another's obscure opinion or expression in a benevolent way, rather than condemning it. If he truly cannot defend that position in any reasonable way, then he should ask what it was that the speaker intended to say. If the latter feels or understands less correctly, then the former should kindly correct him. If this, too, is not sufficient, he should try by every suitable way to make him sound of mind and free from error.

[23]   Principle or Foundation

M an has been created to this end: to praise the Lord his God, and revere Him, and by serving Him be finally saved. All other things on earth, then, have been created because of man himself, in order to help him reach the end of his creation. It follows, therefore, that man may use them, or abstain from them, only so far as they contribute to the achievement of that end or hinder it. Consequently, we must harbor no difference among all created things (as far as they are subject to our free will, and not forbidden). Therefore, as far as it belongs to us, we should not look for health more than for sickness, nor should we prefer wealth to poverty, honor to contempt, a long life to a short one. But, from all these things, it is convenient to choose and desire those that contribute to the achievement of the end.

[23] Particular and Daily Examination

**covering three different times for disposing oneself
and twice for examination**

The first time takes place in the morning, as soon as someone awakes, when he must propose to guard himself diligently about a particular sin or vice of which he would like to correct himself.

[25] *The second time* is the afternoon, when he should ask from God the grace of being able to remember how many times he has fallen into that particular sin or defect and to be more watchful afterward. Then he should make a first examination, asking himself about the sin or vice in question, going through all the past moments of that day, starting from his awakening to now, how many times he committed it, and should put as many marks on the first line of the chart [on page 13]. This being done, he should again propose to conduct himself better for the rest of the day.

[26] *The third time* is that of the evening, after supper, when he will do a second examination, going through each hour that went by from the last examination to the present. While in the same manner remembering and counting the times he failed, he shall mark a corresponding number of signs on the second line of the chart more or less like the one prepared for that purpose.

[27] *Four useful additions in order to extirpate more easily and quickly any sin or vice.*

The first: Whenever we have committed a sin or any kind of fault, touching our chest with the hand, we will repent of the fall—and this can be done in the company of other people without their noticing it.

[28] *The second:* When evening comes and we have counted the marks on the lines and have compared those of the first examination with the ones of the second, we should check if there has been any improvement from the time of the first examination to the second.

[29] *The third:* We must compare the examinations of the day with those of the day before in order to consider if there has been an improvement.

[30] *The fourth:* In the same manner, we should compare the examinations of two weeks together in order to see if there was a correction or not.

[31] Notice also that the first of the following lines is the longest and must be used for the first day, let us say Sunday; the second line is a little shorter and is for Monday, and so on, because normally the number of transgressions will decrease each day.

```
_____      D _____

_____        _____

_____      d _____

_____         _____

_____        d _____

_____            _____

_____          d _____

_____              _____

_____            d _____

_____                _____

_____              d _____

_____                  _____

_____                d _____

_____                    _____

_____                  d _____

_____                      _____
```

[32] **GENERAL EXAMINATION OF CONSCIENCE**

which is very useful for the purification
of the soul and for the confession of sins

It is generally agreed that there are three kinds of thoughts that come to the mind of man: One kind rises from within man himself, the other two come from outside, suggested by the good spirit or by the evil spirit.

[33]   ABOUT THINKING

There are two ways to gain merit from evil thought in the matter of mortal sin, about which this can be said.

First, when the thought of committing a mortal sin comes to mind and it is vanquished because it is immediately rejected.

[34] Second, when we continue to resist such an evil suggestion, which has been again and again rejected though insistently returning, until it is totally defeated. This kind of victory is of greater merit than the previous one.

[35] We sin in a lighter or venial manner when a thought of a mortal sin arises and we indulge a short while, almost as if we were listening to it, and also when we feel incidentally some sensual satisfaction or show negligence in rejecting it.

[36] A mortal sin in thought is committed in two ways.

First, when for whatever reason one gives consent to a thought of sinning.

[37] Second, when the sin in question is in fact accomplished. And this is more grievous for three reasons: because it takes more time; because the act is more intense; finally, because more people are affected by scandal or injury.

[38]   ABOUT SPEAKING

God may be offended also through words in many ways, as for example, blasphemies and curses. We should never swear either by the Creator or by any creature, except when three conditions occur together: truth, necessity, and reverence. Furthermore, necessity should be understood as relating not to the affirmation of any truth whatsoever, but only to one of no small importance for a spiritual, corporal, or even temporal good. We mean that there is reverence when he who uses the divine name expresses it in a manner that attributes to God, Creator and Lord, the honor due to Him.

[39] We should know that though a rash or vain oath taken in the name of the Creator is a sin more serious than the one taken in the name of the creature, nevertheless it is more difficult to licitly swear by a creature than by the Creator and observe the three conditions described.

First, because in swearing by reference to a creature, we are less eager or careful to pay attention to whether or not we are swearing according to truth and necessity as we would in the name of the Creator of all things.

Second, because we are less concerned to give God due honor and respect when we refer to a creature than when we directly refer to God the Creator Himself. Also, it is more allowable to swear by a creature for those who are perfect than for those who are untrained and uneducated. The perfect ones, indeed, by their continuous practice of contemplation and their enlightenment of intellect, consider God most intimately and perceive Him in His essence, presence, and power in each single creature. Thus they are more prepared than others who have not reached such perfection to give God the reverence due to Him in their oaths.

Third, because referring too often to creatures in order to confirm an oath would create a danger of idolatry more easily for imperfect people than for perfect ones.

[40] Among the other sins committed through speaking are useless words; that is, which are of no benefit to the one who says them or anybody else, or that are said without any intention of usefulness. On the other hand, no word should be considered useless that can be of some benefit to our own soul or to someone else's, or to our own body or even to a temporal thing, or at least intended in that way by the person who says it, even if he speaks

of matters that are outside his state of life, e.g., for a person in religious life to speak about warfare or commerce. Moreover, there is merit in any conversation intended for a good goal, while the one done with bad intention or out of idleness gives way to sin.

[41] To lie, to give false witness, and to denigrate someone are also sins committed through speaking, because we should neither criticize nor calumniate. In fact, by disclosing a mortal sin committed by another that is not public, with evil intention or with serious damage to his reputation, we commit a similar mortal sin; but when it is a venial sin, then we commit a venial sin only. Moreover, every time we publicize another's vice or defect, we show our own. In truth, whenever the intention is honest, it is allowable to speak about someone else's defect in two different situations.

First, when the defect is public, like, for example, prostitution or something condemned by justice or a dangerous public error that may corrupt the minds of those dealing with it. Second, each time the hidden fault of a person is revealed to a third party who could help that person to free himself from sin, provided there is sufficient probability of obtaining such result.

Among the sins committed by speaking, also worth mentioning are mockery, slander, and other faults of this kind, which the one who gives the Exercises may list whenever he judges it necessary.

[42]   ABOUT ACTING

Looking at the Ten Commandments of God, the Precepts of the Church, and the commands of authorities or superiors, we must realize that whatever we do that goes against them is sin; it can be more or less serious depending on variations in the importance of each sin and in the habits of the sinner. Also we consider as commands of superiors the documents or indults that the popes customarily grant or publish for expulsion of the unfaithful or for peace among Christians, by which the faithful are invited to confess their own sins and receive the holy Eucharist. He who dares to scorn or transgress such pious exhortations and decisions of the leaders of the Church does not sin lightly.

[43]   MODEL OF A GENERAL EXAMINATION
        MADE OF FIVE ELEMENTS OR POINTS

1. To give thanks to God, our Lord, for all the benefits received
2. To ask for His grace to know and expel our sins
3. To question our soul about the sins committed during this same day, examining ourselves hour after hour from the time of our awakening, in thoughts, words, and actions, in the order given in the Particular Examination
4. To ask forgiveness for the faults committed
5. To propose with God's help to correct ourselves; then, afterward, to recite the Our Father

[44]   ABOUT THE USE OF
        GENERAL CONFESSION AND COMMUNION

From the general confession voluntarily made, among many others, the three following benefits may be harvested:

First, even though he who confesses once a year is not obliged to this kind of general confession, nevertheless the one who does it would derive from it a great profit and merit, because of the more intense pain that he thus feels for the sins and the malice of his past life.

Second, because of the Spiritual Exercises, the nature and malice of sins become better known than previously, and therefore one would derive much more profit and merit.

Third, it follows naturally that a man so well confessed and disposed will be better prepared to receive the Eucharist, which helps us so much to avoid sin and to both conserve and increase the grace received.

Also, it will be most opportune to make this general confession after the Exercises of the First Week.

First Week

[45]   **FIRST EXERCISE**

of meditating about the threefold sin,
with the three faculties of our soul

It comprises a preparatory prayer, two preludes, three principal
points, and one colloquy.

[46] *The preparatory prayer* is the one in which we ask from the
Lord the grace that all our energies and activities be sincerely directed to His glory and worship.

[47] *The first prelude* consists of a certain mental re-creation of the
place. It should be observed in this regard that during any meditation or contemplation of a corporal entity, for example of Christ,
we shall see with a sort of imaginary vision a physical place repre-
senting what we are contemplating, for instance a temple or a
mountain where we could find Christ Jesus or the Virgin Mary,
and everything else that is related to the theme of our contemplation.

If, on the contrary, the pondered subject is an incorporal entity, like the consideration on sin offered here, the composition
of the place could be such that, through the imagination, we would
perceive our soul chained in this corruptible body as if in prison,
and man himself exiled, in this valley of miseries, among irrational
animals.

[48] *The second prelude* will be to ask God for what I desire according to the subject of the suggested contemplation: That means
that, if I am going to meditate on Christ's Resurrection, I should

ask for joy in order to rejoice with the rejoicing Christ; if, on the contrary, it is on the Passion, I should ask for tears, pain, and anguish in order to suffer with the suffering Christ. So, in this present meditation, I must beg for shame and confusion about myself, considering how many human beings, even for only one mortal sin, were damned, and that I have also merited damnation for sinning so many times.

[49] It must be noticed in connection with the above that the preparatory prayer and the two preludes must come before every meditation or contemplation; but, if the prayer is always made in the same manner, the two preludes are different according to the diversity of the topics.

[50] *The first point* will be to exercise my memory about the first of all sins, the one committed by the angels; applying immediately the discourse of the intellect, and moved by the instigation of the will, I will reflect upon and try to understand what will put all of me to shame and embarrassment, through the comparison of that single sin of the angels with the multiplicity of my own sins. Then it might be concluded that if they, for one single crime, had deserved hell, how much more often have I merited such a torment. Thus we say that it should be brought to memory how the angels, created at first in a state of grace, but (which was necessary for the achievement of happiness) unwilling through their free will to revere and obey their Creator, grew insolent against Him, were changed from grace to wickedness and thrown from heaven to hell. Thereafter, we should consider at length these things very carefully with the intellect, and at the same time strongly insist on rousing up all possible emotions of the will.

[51] *The second point* consists in exercising those same three faculties while considering the sin of our first parents (which we'll name the second sin), remembering what a long penance they suffered because of it, how much corruption penetrated within humankind, how many thousands of human beings were driven into hell. It should be clearly remembered how Adam was made of clay on the plain of Damascus and put in the earthly paradise, how Eve was made from one of his ribs, how they had been for-

bidden to eat of the fruit of the Tree of Knowledge of Good and Evil, and how nevertheless, they ate it; how after that sin they were immediately thrown out of paradise; how, dressed in clothing made of skins and deprived of their original righteousness, they repented for the remaining time of their life in the greatest hardship and tribulation. As before, one should go over these recollections with the reasoning of the intellect and the affections of the will.

[52] *The third point* is for us to exercise the mind in a similar manner about a mortal and particular sin (we'll call this one the third sin, in order to distinguish it from the other two), considering that for such a sin, even when committed only once, many perhaps have been thrown down into hell; maybe an almost uncountable number are tortured with everlasting sufferings because of crimes that are less in number and gravity than mine. Therefore, memory should turn back to consider how great is the gravity and the wickedness of sin, which offends the Maker and Lord of all things. It should also be rationally considered that an eternal punishment is justly assigned to sin, inasmuch as it is committed against the infinite goodness of God. Finally, affections have to be aroused, as it has already been said.

[53] The colloquy will be made by imagining Jesus Christ in front of me, attached to the cross. Then I should look within myself for the reason why the infinite Creator Himself became a creature, and deemed it worthy to come from life eternal to a temporal death for my sins. Moreover, I will blame myself, questioning: What worthy of being mentioned have I done thus far for Christ? What will I do eventually, or what must I do? Looking at Him fixed on the cross, I will say all the things that my mind and heart will bring forth.

[54] Furthermore, the characteristic of the colloquy is to be like the conversation of a friend with a friend, or of a servant with his lord, at one time asking for a grace, at another accusing myself of a fault, sometimes communicating my own affairs and asking for counsel or help concerning them. At the end, the Our Father will be said.

SECOND EXERCISE

**is a meditation about sins that,
with the preparatory prayer and two preludes,
includes five articles or points,
and a colloquy at the end.**

The preparatory prayer is the same as above.

The first prelude requires the same mental re-creation of the place as in the previous meditation.

The second prelude will be made by asking for what we are looking for here; that is, an intense sorrow because of sins, and abundant tears.

[56] *The first point* consists in a process by which the sins of the whole life are recalled to memory, going step by step through each year and period of time. In this process, we are helped in three ways, by considering the places where we lived; then, the ways we related to others; finally, the different kinds of jobs, businesses, or occupations we had.

[57] *The second point* is to weigh carefully the sins themselves, how much ugliness and wickedness each one of them possesses by its own nature, even if they were not forbidden.

[58] *The third point* is to consider myself, who and what I am, using examples that would bring me to a greater contempt of myself. For example, if I am reflecting upon myself, of how little value I am in comparison to the assembly of all human beings; then, what is the multitude of all mortal beings in comparison with all angels and blessed ones; finally, of what value can anything really be that has been created when compared to God the Creator Himself. So, what kind of poor man could I really be? I could, at the end, inspect the corruption of all my being, the depravity of my soul, the filthiness of my body, and consider that I am like an ulcer or an abcess, from which a great fluid of sins, like diseased blood, and a huge torrent of vices have come out.

[59] *The fourth point* is to ponder who God is whom I have offended, bringing together all the perfections that pertain to God

as justly His own, comparing and contrasting them to my vices and defects, comparing, for example, His absolute power, wisdom, goodness, and justice with my great feebleness, ignorance, wickedness, and iniquity.

[60] In *the fifth part*, I should burst out in an exclamation, due to a vehement commotion of emotions, wondering deeply at how all creatures (mentioning each singularly) have sustained me for so long and have kept me alive until this exact moment; how the angels, carrying the sword of divine justice, have supported me without quivering, have protected me and even helped me with their intercessions; how the saints have interceded for me; how the sky, the sun, the moon, the stars, all the elements and all living things, all fruits of the earth, instead of rightly taking revenge on me, have served me; finally, how the earth did not open itself up to swallow me, revealing a thousand hells where I would be submitted to eternal pains.

[61] This meditation will end with a colloquy praising the infinite mercy of God, giving Him thanks for sustaining my life until this day; consequently, after having decided to correct myself in the future, I will recite once the Our Father.

[62]   **THIRD EXERCISE**

**will be nothing other than a repetition
of the first and second exercises,
together with three colloquies.**

After we have made the preparatory prayer and the two preludes, we shall repeat the two previous Exercises, having noticed those points and places within which we have felt consolation, desolation, or any other spiritual impression, on which we must dwell longer and more diligently. Then, following the spiritual motion in us, we will come to the three following colloquies.

[63] *The first colloquy* is addressed to Our Lady, the Mother of Christ, imploring her to intercede with her Son and to obtain the grace necessary for us in three ways: first, that we experience an inte-

rior knowledge of our faults and feel abhorrence toward them; second, that acknowledging the perverse order of our own deeds and abhorring it, we correct it and start rightly to set ourselves in order according to God; third, that having perceived and condemned the depravity of the world, we withdraw from all mundane and vain things. This being done, we should recite once the Hail Mary.

The second colloquy is in the same manner addressed to Christ, Our Lord and Mediator, so that He will obtain for us the same things from the Eternal Father. At the end, the prayer that starts with *Anima Christi* will be added.

The third colloquy will be made according to the same process and directed to God the Father in order that He will grant us that threefold grace, and the Our Father will be recited once at the end.

[64] FOURTH EXERCISE

consists in the repetition of the Third Exercise.

A repetition has to be made of the previous Exercises, as a kind of rumination over the same subjects on which I meditated previously, so that, by this exercise of memory, my intellect can reflect more easily about them without digressions. The same three colloquies have to be added as well.

[65] FIFTH EXERCISE

is a contemplation of hell,
and contains the preparatory prayer,
the two preludes, five points, and one colloquy.

The preparatory prayer is not different from the one above.

In *the first prelude*, the mental re-creation of the place is made by submitting to the eyes of the imagination the length, the width, and the depth of hell.

The second prelude consists of asking for an intimate apprehension of the pains undergone by the damned, so that, if by chance I should start to forget divine love, I would at least be kept from sinning by the fear of that punishment.

[66] *The first point* is to see with the imagination the large fires burning in hell, and there the souls as if locked in burning bodies like in prison.

[67] *The second point*: To hear with the imagination lamentations, cries, screams, and blasphemies against Christ and the saints coming out of that place.

[68] *Third*: Also with the imagination, to smell smoke, sulfur, the stink of excrement, and the foulness of decay.

[69] *Fourth*: In a similar imaginative manner, to taste the most sour things, like tears, bitterness, and the worm of conscience.

[70] *Fifth*: With the sense of touch to feel those same fires that consume souls enveloped in them.

[71] Meanwhile, having a colloquy with Christ, we should remember all those souls that were condemned to the punishments of hell, either because they did not want to believe in Christ's coming, or, in the cases where they did believe, they did not conform their lives to the precepts of His life, whether this was before Christ came, during the time in which Christ lived in this world, or after it. The greatest thanks shall be given to Christ Himself, because He has not permitted that I fall so utterly low, but rather He has walked with me to this day with the greatest compassion and mercy. At the end, I will say the Our Father.

If it seems to the one who gives the Exercises that it would be good for those who are making them to add other meditations on death and on other punishments for sin, on the Judgment, etc., he should not think that it is prohibited, even though they are not added here.

[72] The schedule of the Exercises should be as follows: The first one should be practiced in the middle of the night; the second one in the morning, as soon as we get up; the third one before or

after Mass, before we have taken any food; the fourth one around Vespers; the fifth one, one hour before supper. This schedule is applicable to all four Weeks. However, it can be changed, increased or diminished according to each individual making the five Exercises explained above, in concordance with age, spiritual and physical disposition, and personality.

[73]   **ADDITIONS**

**most useful for a better practice of the Exercises
and for achieving what we hope for**

The first is that after I have lain down, but before I fall asleep, for a short time (the time needed to say one Hail Mary), I should think of the hour when I must awake and about the Exercise to be done then.

[74] *The second:* As I wake up, I shall immediately put aside any other thought and apply my spirit to what I will contemplate during the First Exercise of the middle of the night. To increase my shame and confusion, I should also propose to myself an example such as that of a common soldier remaining in the presence of his king and the court, blushing, anxious, and confused, after the conviction of having committed serious transgressions against the king himself, from whom he had previously received many and great favors and gifts. For the Second Exercise, pondering how much I have sinned, I might imagine myself chained before the highest Judge and, like one worthy of death, conducted to the tribunal with irons on my legs. Then, impregnating myself with these or similar thoughts, according to the subject of the meditation to be practiced, I shall dress myself.

[75] *The third*: As I am a few steps away from the place where I am going to meditate, for as long as it takes to recite the Lord's Prayer, I should raise my spirit and picture my Lord Jesus as present and looking at what I am on the point of doing, and I shall acknowledge Him with a reverent humble gesture.

[76] *The fourth:* As I begin my contemplation, prostrating myself on the ground, faceup or facedown, either sitting or standing up, I choose the position through which I hope to attain most easily whatever at that moment I desire. For this purpose, we must be attentive to these two things: The first is that if I have obtained what I wish while on my knees, or in any other position, I should not look for anything more. The second, where I have obtained the desired devotion, I should remain and rest there, without any anxiety about moving ahead as long as I feel satisfied.

[77] *The fifth:* After completing the Exercise, I review, either sitting or walking, for about fifteen minutes how my meditation or contemplation succeeded: if badly, then I shall investigate the reasons why, with sorrow and the intention of correcting it; if well, I shall give thanks to God and plan to use the same method again.

[78] *The sixth:* I avoid all thoughts that may bring me joy, like the one on the glorious Resurrection of Christ, because such thoughts would hinder the flow of tears and sorrow for my sins, which are the things I should look for at this time. It would be better to think about death and Judgment.

[79] *The seventh:* For the same reason as above, I deprive myself of the brightness of the light, keeping the windows and doors of the room shut while I am in it, except when I have to read or eat.

[80] *The eighth:* I absolutely refrain from laughing and from words that would cause any laughter.

[81] *The ninth:* I do not fix my eyes on anyone, except when the situation demands some kind of greeting or a good-bye.

[82] *The tenth:* I add some kind of reparation or penance. This can be exterior or interior. The interior penance consists in the sorrow that we feel for our own sins, with the firm resolution of staying away in the future from these and from all other sins. The exterior penance is the fruit of the interior one and consists in chastising ourselves for the sins committed, which can be done essentially in three ways.

[83] *The first* is about food. One may give up not only superfluous food (which is proper for temperance rather than penance), but also part of the normal quantity. And the more we cut down on food the better, provided that we take care not to endanger or weaken too much our health.

[84] *The second* is about sleep and the manner of sleeping. Concerning them, not only may we remove soft and pleasing things but also some ordinary ones, guarding however against serious danger to life and health. Therefore, one should not reduce the necessary sleeping time, except for a little bit when it is necessary to moderate it (if someone sleeps too much).

[85] *The third* is about flesh itself. It should feel the pain inflicted by wearing hair shirts, ropes, or chains, or when scourged or plagued or submitted to other kinds of austerity.

[86] However, in all these things, it would be far better to suffer pain only in the flesh, making sure that it does not penetrate into the bones with a risk of injury. For this reason, for a flagellation we highly recommend the use of very thin strings, which will affect the body externally and not internally, where a notable wound could be produced.

[87] Moreover, four things should be noticed.

The first is about penance, and specifically that exterior penance has three uses or fruits: to make modest amends for the crimes of the past; for someone to conquer himself by submitting his inferior part, called sensuality, to the higher one, reason; finally, for asking for and obtaining a gift of the divine grace that we wish, as, for example, an intimate contrition of heart for our sins and an abundance of tears, either for those sins or for the sufferings and sorrows of Christ's Passion or for the resolution of some doubt that torments us deeply.

[88] *The second* is about the first two Additions: They are applicable only to the Exercises done at midnight and dawn. The fourth should never be practiced in church or before others, but only at home and secretly.

[89] *The third:* When the person who is making the Exercises does not obtain the desired effect, such as the feeling of sorrow or of consolation, then it is expedient to modify the pattern of eating and sleeping, and to do other kinds of penance. For example, we may practice one kind of penance for three days and then abandon it for two or three days. Because each of us is different, some of us should do greater penance and some lesser. Furthermore, just as we often omit corporal penance out of attachment to our flesh, or because we judge wrongly that our physical condition will not tolerate it without endangering our health, on the other hand, we often exceed the right amount of penance, having too much confidence in the strength of our body. When we alternate the different manners of doing penance, doing them or abandoning them as explained above, it very often happens that the compassionate Lord, who knows our nature perfectly, would reveal to each one what is uniquely appropriate to him.

[90] *The fourth:* A Particular Examination should be made in order to eliminate faults and negligences that creep into our performance of the Exercises and Additions. This should be observed also during the following three Weeks.

Second Week

**CONTEMPLATION OF THE
KINGDOM OF JESUS CHRIST**

**through the likeness of an earthly king
calling his subjects to war**

The preparatory prayer should be made in the manner stated above.

The first prelude, the mental re-creation of the place, will be to see with our imagination the synagogues, the villages, and the towns that Christ passed through while preaching, and similarly other places.

The second prelude, which is that of petitioning for the suitable grace, will be here to ask God that we not be deaf to Christ's calling us, but quick to follow and obey Him.

[92] *First point:* I put before my eyes a human king chosen by God, to whom all Christian princes and peoples must offer reverence and submission.

[93] *Second point:* I imagine that I hear this king addressing all his subjects: "It is my intention to submit all regions of infidel peoples to my authority. Therefore, everyone who wishes to accompany me should be ready for no food, clothes, and other things besides those he sees me use. He should also persevere through the same daily labors, night watches, and other situations with me so that he will be a part of the victory and joy, since he stood with me in labor and difficulties."

[94] *Third point:* I consider what faithful subjects should answer to the most lovable and generous king, and how quickly they

29

offer themselves, ready to follow his entire will. I consider the contrary, if someone were to refuse to submit himself, how much he would deserve to be scorned by all men and to be judged as a coward.

[95] The second part of this Exercise consists in a comparison of the similarities between the aforementioned king and the Lord Jesus Christ, according to these three points.

First, we will apply the example like this: If the earthly king with his call to war deserves our attention and obedience, how much more Christ the Eternal King, conspicuous throughout the whole world, deserves it. He calls all individuals to Himself with these words: "It is my most rightful will to vindicate the dominion of all the world, to subdue all my enemies, and then enter into the glory of my Father. Therefore, anyone who wants to follow me must labor with me, for the reward will match the labor."

[96] Second, we will reason that no one of sane mind could be unwilling to offer and vow most passionately his total self to Christ's service.

[97] Third, we shall estimate that those who decided to offer themselves entirely to Him will not only submit themselves to the pain of labor but will also offer greater and more magnificent gifts after having rejected the rebellion of the flesh, the senses, love of self, and love of the world. Therefore, each person will somehow answer like this:

[98] "Here I am, O supreme King and Lord of all things, I, so unworthy, but still confiding in your grace and help, I offer myself entirely to You and submit all that is mine to Your will. In the presence of Your infinite Goodness, and under the sight of Your glorious Virgin Mother and of the whole heavenly court, I declare that this is my intention, my desire, and my firm decision: Provided it will be for Your greatest praise and for my best obedience to You, to follow You as nearly as possible and to imitate You in bearing injustices and adversities, with true poverty, of spirit and things as well, if [I say] it pleases Your holiest Majesty to elect and accept me for such a state of life."

[99] This Exercise should be made twice, in the morning as we get up and at the hour before lunch or dinner.

[100] During this second week, and the following ones, it will certainly be useful to read something from the Gospel or any other pious book, like *The Imitation of Christ,* and the lives of the saints, etc.

[101] FIRST MEDITATION OF THE FIRST DAY

**will be about the Incarnation of Jesus Christ,
and includes a preparatory prayer, three preludes,
and three points, with one colloquy.**

The preparatory prayer won't be any different from the previous ones.

[102] *The first prelude* is to recall the story of the subject to be contemplated. Here, how the three Divine Persons, looking at the entire surface of the earth, crammed with men falling into hell, decide in the eternity of Their divinity that the second Person would assume human nature for the salvation of humankind; and that, therefore, when the designated time would come, the archangel Gabriel would be sent to the Virgin Mary as a messenger, as it will be narrated below in the Mysteries of the Life of [Our Lord Jesus] Christ.

[103] *The second prelude* regards the mental re-creation of the place, which consists of an imaginary viewing, as if the entire extension of the whole earth, inhabited by so many different peoples, were offered to the eyes. Then the vision should focus on a specific part of the world, on the little house of the Blessed Virgin in Nazareth, in the province of Galilee.

[104] *The third prelude* contains the request for a grace: That I know intimately why the Son of God became man because of me, so that I would love Him more fervently and consequently follow Him more resolutely.

[105] It should be noticed here that the preparatory prayer as well as the three preludes should likewise be made throughout this whole week and the following, changing however the preludes according to the various topics.

[106] *The first point* is to observe all the persons considered here.

First, the human beings living on the face of the earth as diverse as they are in their manners, behaviors, and actions: Some are white, others black; a few enjoying peace, others troubled by war; this one crying, that one laughing; one healthy, another sick; many being born, and in turn many dying, and the almost innumerable other variations.

Then, to contemplate the three Divine Persons who from Their royal throne are looking at all kinds of people living on the earth as blind, and all dying and descending into hell.

Hereafter, we will consider the Virgin Mary with the angel greeting her, hence applying things to ourselves in order to procure some fruit from such consideration.

[107] *The second point* is, using our inner hearing, to listen to what is said by all persons: human beings on earth disputing, blaspheming, insulting one another; in heaven the three Divine Persons talking together about the redemption of humankind; in the little chamber, the Virgin and the angel treating the Mystery of the Incarnation. Having reflected upon all of that, and having applied it to myself, I make an effort to gather some fruit from each of these words.

[108] *The third point* will eventually be to also pay attention to the actions of the persons: how mortals attack, hit, and kill one another and run all down into hell; how the Holiest Trinity accomplishes the work of the Incarnation; how the angel for his part executes his mandate and how the Blessed Virgin, conducting herself most humbly, gives thanks to the Divine Majesty. As said before, we should reflect on and apply all of that to ourselves, in order to collect the fruit that presents itself.

[109] Finally, I will add a colloquy, choosing carefully the most proper words to address myself with due respect to the Divine Persons, to the Word Incarnate, and to His Mother. I would ask,

according to what I feel within myself, all that may help me to better imitate my Lord Jesus Christ, as if He had been incarnate just now. At the end, the Our Father will be recited.

[110]   **SECOND CONTEMPLATION**

about the Nativity

Preparatory prayer as above.

[111] *The first prelude* comes from the narration that has to be reviewed of the departure of the Blessed Virgin from the town of Nazareth: for example, how being already nine months pregnant, and sitting on a she-donkey (as we may piously meditate), with her companion Joseph, with a young maid servant and an ox, they left for Bethlehem to pay the tribute imposed by Caesar.

[112] *The second prelude* will be the consideration of the journey, estimating its length, direction, how smooth here and hard there. Thereafter, we may examine also the place of the Nativity, which was similar to a cave: how wide or narrow, flat or slanted, comfortable or not.

[113] *The third prelude* will not differ from the previous contemplation.

[114] *The first point* is to look at the persons: the Virgin Mother of God, and her spouse Joseph, with the maidservant, and the Lord Christ as a newborn infant. I may imagine myself as being there with them like a little poor servant, waiting on them according to their needs with the greatest reverence. Hence, I shall reflect upon what I could gain from the representation of all this.

[115] *The second point* is to apprehend in a fruitful manner the words they are saying.

[116] *The third point* is to examine all the events happening there. For example, the journey, the toil, and the reasons why the greatest God of all is born in absolute deprivation; He who, later in this life, will suffer perpetual poverty, pain, hunger, thirst, heat,

cold, insults, lashings, and finally the cross: all of that for me. Then I will strive to gain some spiritual benefit from each one of these considerations.

[117] Then all this will be concluded with a colloquy and finished with the Our Father.

[118]   **THIRD CONTEMPLATION**

is a repetition of the previous two.

As a third Exercise, or contemplation, the two previous contemplations will be repeated, with the preparatory prayer and the same three preludes; I will notice every time and treat with more attention those parts in which previously I have received some insight, either consolation or desolation. At the end, a colloquy is added, with the Lord's Prayer, as it was done before.

[119] It must be observed that the method and the order of repeating an Exercise are the same in this Week, and in the following ones, as they were in the First Week: The matter changes, but the form remains the same.

[120]   **FOURTH CONTEMPLATION**

**is another repetition of
the first and second contemplations,
similar to the one just before.**

[121]   **FIFTH CONTEMPLATION**

is to apply the senses to what was said before.

After the preparatory prayer, with the three preludes already mentioned, it is good to exercise the five senses of the imagination on the first and second contemplations in the following manner, according to the subject matter.

[122] *The first point* will be, with the imagination, to see all persons, and after having noticed the occurring circumstances regarding them, to draw out what is useful for us.

[123] *The second point* is to take out for our own use either what we hear them saying or what might be appropriate for them to say.

[124] *The third point* is to sense, through a kind of internal tasting and smelling, the great gentleness and sweetness of a soul imbued by divine gifts and virtues, according to the person we are considering, and adapting to ourselves whatever could be of any fruit.

[125] *The fourth point* is to feel, through an inner sense of touch, and to kiss the clothes, the places, the footprints, and everything connected with such persons; so that, from it, a larger increase of devotion or of any spiritual good will happen for us.

[126] A colloquy should end this contemplation, as with the previous ones; similarly add the Our Father.

[127] These following five points must be observed:
1. During this Week and the Weeks thereafter, I must never read or reflect about any Mystery other than the one considered during that hour or day, or one would somewhat disturb the other.

[128] 2. The first Exercise on the Incarnation of Christ is made at midnight; the next, at dawn; the third, about the hour of the Mass; the fourth, at Vespers; the fifth, a short while before supper. One hour should be spent with each one of them, and this has to be observed from now on.

[129] 3. If the one who exercises is old, or exhausted by the First Week, it would be better for him not to get up at midnight, and to make only three contemplations, at dawn, around the time of Mass, and before lunch, and add one repetition around Vespers and one application of the senses before supper.

[130] 4. During this Second Week, of the ten Additions given in the First Week, we must change the second, the sixth, the seventh, and partially the tenth.

The second Addition is changed in this way: As soon as I wake up, I must put into my mind the meditation I am going to make next, and provoke the desire to know more clearly the incarnate Eternal Word, in order to serve Him and to adhere to Him more willingly because I will have seen His incredible goodness toward me.

The sixth: I will frequently review in my memory the Life of Christ from the time of the Incarnation to the moment, or Mystery, about which I will be meditating during the present day or hour.

The seventh: I will enjoy light or darkness, clear or clouded sky, to the degree that helps to reach the desired goal.

The tenth: I shall conduct myself according to the type of the contemplated Mystery; some Mysteries may require penance, some may not. Therefore, the ten Additions must be used with circumspection.

[131] 5. Eventually, it must be noted that in all Exercises of the hours, other than midnight and dawn, an equivalent of the second and third Additions must be done: As soon as it comes to my mind that the hour of meditation is coming, before approaching the place where I am going to pray, from a distance I will look at where and in the presence of whom I will bring and show myself; and, after passing quickly through the matter of the Exercise, I will immediately start the contemplation.

[132]   **SECOND DAY**

**The subject of the first and second contemplation
will be the Presentation of Christ in the Temple
(see below) and the Flight to Egypt (also see below)
in the Mysteries of Christ's Life.
The two contemplations will be repeated twice,
and the application of the senses as above.**

[133] *Note*: It is expedient sometimes for the one making the Exercises, even though he may be gifted with a vigorous mind and a strong body, to alleviate in some measure the prescribed Exercises

of the Second and the two following Weeks, in order to be able to achieve more easily what he desires, with only one contemplation at dawn and another around the time of Mass, and with a repetition at Vespers and the application of the five senses of the imagination at suppertime.

[134]   **THIRD DAY**

The meditation is about the way the boy Jesus
was subject to His Parents in Nazareth;
then, how He was found by them in the Temple,
as below in the Mysteries of Christ's Life.
Two repetitions will be made,
with the application of the senses.

[135]   **PRELUDE**

to the consideration of the different states
or kinds of life

Christ's example was previously proposed as the kind of life consisting of the observance of God's commandments, which is called the first or common state. Now the same Lord, remembered as subject to His parents, seems to show the example of another or second state, which depends on obedience and brings evangelical perfection, as is clearly seen when He went to the Temple, having abandoned His adoptive father and natural mother, in order to be free for the service of the Eternal Father. Therefore, it will be appropriate here for us, too, while contemplating His life, to search and earnestly ask which proper kind of life He prefers for us to serve His Majesty.

Therefore, we may be introduced into that inquiry by the next Exercise, being attentive to Christ's mind as opposed to the enemy's opposite one. From this we will also learn which disposition we must have to achieve perfection in whatever state the Divine Goodness will have inspired us to elect.

[136]   **FOURTH DAY**
         MEDITATION OF THE TWO STANDARDS

            the one of Jesus Christ, our supreme sovereign;
            the other of Lucifer, the greatest enemy of humanity

The preparatory prayer is made as usual.

[137] *The first prelude* will be some historical consideration of Christ on one hand and of Lucifer on the other, both calling all people to themselves in order to enroll them under their standard.

[138] *The second prelude* is, as a mental re-creation of the place, to represent to ourselves a very large plain near Jerusalem, where stands the Lord Jesus Christ as the supreme leader of all good people. On the contrary, another plain in Babylonia, where Lucifer shows himself as the leader of all evildoers and adversaries.

[139] *The third prelude* will be for us to ask for the grace that the deceptions of the evil leader be disclosed to us, while invoking divine help to avoid them; and for the grace to recognize the true ways of Christ, the best captain, and to be capable of imitating Him by grace.

[140] *First point:* to imagine in front of my eyes, on the plain of Babylonia, the leader of the impious, on a throne of fire and smoke, horrible in his features, terrible in his aspect.

[141] *Second point:* to perceive how he sends throughout the whole world innumerable demons he has called, in order to do harm, sparing no city, no place, and no particular kind of person.

[142] *Third point:* to give attention to the kind of speech he makes to his ministers, whom he incites to drag men and throw them into nets and chains, first by attracting them through the cupidity for wealth (which is his usual method), so that then they can fall more easily into the greedy quest for mundane honor and finally into the pit of pride.

Therefore, there are three main degrees of temptations, grounded in riches, honors, and pride, which lead swiftly down into all other sorts of vices.

[143] Similarly, on the contrary, to consider our supreme and best leader and captain, Christ.

[144] *The first point* will be to admire Christ in a delightful place near Jerusalem, indeed established in a humble condition but of a very attractive beauty and of an extremely lovable look.

[145] *Second point:* to observe the manner in which He, Lord of all the universe, sends apostles, disciples, and ministers, whom He has chosen, throughout the world to share the sacred and saving doctrine with people of any kind, state, and condition.

[146] *Third point:* to listen to Christ's exhortation to His servants and friends all appointed to such work as He has instructed them: To devote themselves to help everyone, first by persuading them to have a spiritual attraction for poverty, and moreover (if the reason of divine obedience and a choice from above would lead to it) to embrace true and actual poverty. Finally, to entice them to desire insults and contempt, from which the virtue of humility is born.

And so three steps of perfection arise: poverty, rejection of self, and humility, which are directly contrary to riches, honor, and pride, and lead immediately to all virtues.

[147] Then, a colloquy will be made to the Blessed Virgin, imploring through her, her Son's grace that I be accepted and remain under His standard; first, only by spiritual poverty, or even by a total deprivation of things (if He deigns to call and accept me for it); then I would imitate Him more closely by being subject to rejection or humiliation, avoiding however bringing others into sin, so that despising myself would not be injurious to them and end in an offense to God. The first colloquy will be concluded with the Hail Mary.

A second colloquy will be addressed to Christ as a human being, that He would ask the Father the same grace for me, and, at the end, the prayer *Anima Christi* will follow.

A third colloquy will be addressed to the Father to look favorably on the request, ending with the Our Father.

[148] This exercise will be made once at midnight and then again at dawn. Two repetitions of the same will be made around the time of Mass in the morning and of Vespers, adding the three colloquies at the end. The following Exercise will be made before supper.

[149]   **MEDITATION**

**to be made the same fourth day,
on three different kinds of men,
in order for us to choose the best portion.**

The preparatory prayer: the same as previously.

[150] *The first prelude* is to propose, instead of a story, three distinct kinds of men: Each one of them has acquired for himself ten thousand ducats, with an intention other than divine worship and love; but now they wish to be at peace with God and be saved, by removing, in whatever way possible, that harmful attachment to things that is an impediment to salvation.

[151] *The second prelude* is a sort of imaginary re-creation of the place, where I see myself standing before God and all the saints with the desire, and persevering in it, of finding out the manner by which I could best please God Himself.

[152] *The third prelude* is a petition for what I want, which is the grace to choose what will be the most acceptable to God and most salubrious for me.

[153] *The first kind of man* wishes indeed to be free from attachment to the acquired thing, in order to be reconciled with God. But, during his entire lifetime, he does not take the necessary means or accept the necessary help.

[154] *The second kind of man* also desires to remove this disorderly attachment, but in the meantime he obstinately clings to the thing; he rather wants to draw God to his wish, instead of removing the impediment and aiming at Him by a more suitable way of life.

[155] Finally, *the third kind of man*, willing to reject that tainted attachment, is equally ready to get rid of or keep the thing, according to what he will have perceived through divine inspiration or the counsel of reason to be the most fitting divine service. Meanwhile, maintaining everything as it is, he only considers and looks for such a service, and accepts no other cause for giving up or retaining the acquired thing than the reason and desire of divine glory, so that this one be the greatest possible.

[156] The three colloquies will follow, as they were made before for the Standards.

[157] It should be noted here that when we feel an attachment opposed to perfect poverty (which is both spiritual poverty and the renunciation of things) and inclining us more to riches, it might greatly help in order to remove that attachment to do this: to pray to God to elect us for such a poverty, even though the flesh would resist. Meanwhile, we would keep the freedom of our desire, which would allow us to enter the way most conducive to divine service.

[158]   **FIFTH DAY**

What follows is the contemplation of the Lord
going from Nazareth to the Jordan River,
and of His Baptism, as below,
in the Mysteries of the Life of Christ.

[159] This will be made at midnight and early morning. There will be two repetitions around the time of Mass and of Vespers. Before supper, the application of the five senses will be made. Each of these five Exercises will be preceded by the preparatory prayer and the three preludes, as has been presented above with the Incarnation and the Nativity. The three colloquies will be added as they were for the three kinds of men or according to what was noted there.

[160] The Particular Examination will be made at lunchtime and dinnertime, here and thereafter, on the faults and negligences connected with the meditations of that day and the Additions.

SIXTH DAY

[161] Here is contemplated how Christ Jesus moved from the Jordan River to the desert and how He dwelt there. The same pattern of the Exercise of the fifth day will be faithfully adhered to.

SEVENTH DAY

How the blessed Andrew and the others have one after another followed Christ

EIGHTH DAY

How the Lord gave the Sermon on the Mount, teaching the eight modes of Beatitudes

NINTH DAY

How he showed Himself walking on the sea, to the disciples in the boat

TENTH DAY

How He taught in the Temple

ELEVENTH DAY

The resurrection of Lazarus

TWELFTH DAY

The events of Palm Sunday.

All the abovementioned Mysteries can be found further in the Mysteries of [the Life of Our Lord Jesus] Christ.

[162] Here three things must be noted.

1. During this Second Week, according to the time available and the usefulness for the person who is making the Exercises, it is possible to add some other meditations, for example, the Mysteries of the Visitation, of the shepherds, of the circumcision, and of the three kings, or, on the contrary, to omit some of the ones proposed. They, in fact, are outlined here only as an introduction to better prepare for the contemplation.

[163] 2. The discussion of the Elections has to be started with the contemplation of the departure of Christ from Nazareth to the Jordan River, and has to be included in the Exercises of the fifth day.

[164] 3. Before we approach the matter of Elections, in order to prepare our sensibility to grasp the true doctrine of Christ, it would be very helpful to consider, and repeat for the full day, the three following modes of humility, and also to make the colloquies frequently.

[165] *The first mode* of humility, which is necessary to salvation, is that I should profoundly submit to the observance of the divine law so that, even if I were offered the dominion of all the world, or my own life were in extreme danger, I would not deliberately transgress any commandment, divine or human, which obliges and binds us under mortal sin.

[166] *The second mode* is more perfect: that, with a strong spirit, I should remain equally inclined toward wealth, poverty, honor, contempt, a short or long life, whenever the opportunities of divine praise and of my salvation are equal. Thus I would never be persuaded, for whatever reason of human happiness, or even in a situation of my own death, to commit a fault, even though I would judge it only venial.

[167] *The third one* is the mode of the most absolute humility. After having already acquired the first two modes, even if nothing else is added and the glory of God would be equal, for a better imitation of Christ I would choose poverty, contempt, and a reputation for foolishness with Him poor, shamed, and laughed at, rather than riches, honor, and a reputation of wisdom.

[168] Thus, in order to reach this degree of humility, it would be greatly profitable to use the three previous colloquies of the Standards, to petition imploringly (if this pleases the Divine Benevolence) to be led to such an Election, whether my obedience to God and the increase of divine glory be greater or equal.

[169]   PREAMBLE TO
THE MAKING OF THE ELECTION

In order to choose properly, as far as it depends on us, we should consider with a pure and simple eye why we have been created, that is, for God's praise and our salvation. Therefore, only those things should be chosen that bring us to this end, because the means must be everywhere subordinated to the end and not the end to the means. Hence, they are wrong who decide first to take a wife, or to accept an ecclesiastical office or benefit, and then, afterward, to serve God in that state: They are reversing the order of the end and the means, not going straight to God but trying instead to draw Him by a crooked path to their perverse wishes. But we must act in a contrary manner, proposing first as our end divine worship and, after that, selecting marriage or priesthood or all other things as they must be ordained to the already established end. On that account, nothing should move us to use or not to use any means without first having obtained the certainty that it is as much for divine glory as for our salvation.

[170] **INTRODUCTION**

**to the knowledge of the things that
could be the object of an Election,
containing four points and one short note**

First point: All things that fall under an Election must necessarily be good in themselves, or certainly not bad, and also in harmony with the established practices of the orthodox Mother Church.

[171] *Second point:* There are two kinds of things that are appropriate for an Election. In fact, the Election of certain things cannot be changed, for instance, the priestly order and marriage; for some others it can be changed, like ecclesiastical or secular benefices, which we can accept and give up for a reason.

[172] *Third point:* About things for which an unchangeable Election has already been made, there is nothing else to choose. However, it should be remarked that if someone has imprudently and with distorted attachments elected something that cannot be retracted, then what remains to do is, as soon as he starts to repent of that fact, to compensate for the harm of the Election with an honest life and diligent deeds. In no way is it allowed to rescind the Election, which cannot be seen as a divine vocation, because it was obliquely and unwisely made. In this matter, many err, taking such a bad and sloppy Election as a divine vocation, which is always pure and clear, unmixed with carnal disposition or perverse inclination.

[173] *Fourth point:* If someone has elected in the proper manner and order, without any carnal or worldly attachment, something that can be changed, there is no reason to violate such an Election, but rather he must tend toward making more and more progress in it.

[174] *Note:* It should be noted that, if an Election of things that can be changed has not been made rightly and sincerely, it is proper to correct it, so that more abundant and God-pleasing fruit will be produced.

[175] **THE THREE MOST OPPORTUNE TIMES**

for making right Elections

The first time will be when the divine power so strongly moves the will that all doubt, and even the faculty of doubting, which would forbid one to follow that impulse, are taken away from the soul; as we read that this happened to the blessed Paul, Matthew, and some others when Christ called them.

[176] The second time is whenever the divine gracious purpose is clear and sufficiently known, as we have been taught by some previous experience of consolations and desolations, or of diverse spirits.

[177] The third time is when someone, in the tranquillity of his soul, after considering the end for which he has been made (that is, for God's glory and his own salvation), elects within the limits established by the Catholic Church a particular kind of life, as a means by which he intends to reach his own end more easily and securely.

Furthermore, that tranquillity is known to be present whenever the soul, undisturbed by different spirits, freely exercises its own natural powers.

[178] And thus, if an Election does not happen as described in the first or second time, there is recourse to a third one characterized by the following two modes.

THE FIRST MODE

for making a sound and good Election
consists of six points.

First point: To bring in front of me the thing on which to be deliberated, either an office or a benefice to accept or to reject; and so also for other things that pertain to a changeable Election.

[179] *Second point:* After having brought before my eyes why I was created, which is to praise God and that I be saved, I am not

to be inclined either toward accepting or rejecting the debated thing. Rather, I am to remain in the middle and in equilibrium, ready in my mind to bring immediately all of myself to the side that I will recognize as conducing more to the divine glory and my salvation.

[180] *Third point*: To implore God's clemency to deign to teach my mind and stimulate my will, so that I would use, for whatever I would tend to, nothing but the pious and faithful reasoning of my intellect, through which, having known and identified God's will, I should bring myself to the Election.

[181] *Fourth point:* To ponder how many advantages and gains to reach my own end would come from accepting such office or benefice; and also how many disadvantages and hazards will come from it. On the other hand, I should ponder how many advantages and gains, as well as hazards and damage, I may expect if I refuse it.

[182] *Fifth point:* Having done this, to reflect on both sides and, according to the judgment of reason itself and putting aside all wishes of the flesh, to conclude the Election.

[183] *Sixth point:* Once the Election is made, to go and pray without delay, and offer it to God so that, if it pleases Him, He would accept and confirm it fully.

[184]   **THE SECOND MODE**

**for choosing well,
divided into four Rules and one note**

First Rule: Since it is proper to make an Election through the attachment infused from heaven by God's love, it is convenient to the one who is choosing to begin to feel within himself that the affection (whatever it is, great or little) he has for the chosen thing comes from God's love and consideration of Him only.

[185] *Second Rule:* To consider, if one of my dearest friends, for whom I wish nothing but perfection, would be hesitating about

an Election of this kind, what would I advise him to choose? And after giving attention to this, I would make myself act according to the way I would recommend to somebody else.

[186] *Third Rule:* To reflect within myself also, if death suddenly came, about the way I would prefer to have followed in the present deliberation. Then I would easily understand that I should choose this way now.

[187] *Fourth Rule:* No less, to foresee, at the time I would stand for judgment before the tribunal, what kind of decision I would wish to have made. Having acknowledged this, I should make it now, in order to be more secure at that time.

[188] Finally, it must be noted that, after having accurately observed these four Rules for my salvation and peace of mind, according to the last point of the previous mode, I must determine the Election itself and offer it to God for confirmation.

[189]   **ABOUT CORRECTION**

**or reformation to be done
of anyone's state of life**

At first, it should be observed that if someone is bound in matrimony or in a position of ecclesiastical dignity (no matter how large or small the quantity of the temporal possessions is), and has no freedom or no disposition to deal with Elections about changeable things, it would be worthy to offer him, in place of them, a method or some formula with which he could correct his life and personal status.

In that case, whoever finds himself in that condition, in order to rightly express and follow the end of his creation and of his own life, must give attention to the above Exercises and Modes of Election, and with serious rumination conclude how large a household and family it would be proper for him to have; how it would be convenient to handle and manage them; with what words and examples he should instruct his people; how much, moreover, of his possessions he could use for himself or his family, and, on the other hand, how much it is fitting to disburse for the poor or devote to charitable works; desiring and searching for nothing but what favors God's honor and his salvation.

Everyone, in fact, must be convinced that he will advance in his spiritual endeavors as much as he will have separated and pulled himself away from self-love and attachment to his own advantage.

Third Week

---

[190] **FIRST CONTEMPLATION**

takes place at midnight.
It includes the preparatory prayer,
three preludes, six points, and a colloquy.

The preparatory prayer is the same as always.

[191] *The first prelude* is taken from the story: how Christ sent two disciples from Bethany to Jerusalem to prepare the Last Supper, where He Himself and the others also went afterward; how there, after having eaten the Paschal lamb and completed the Last Supper, He washed the feet of all, and gave them His most holy body and blood. Finally, He addressed them with a discourse, after Judas left to betray Him for money.

[192] *The second prelude* is the mental re-creation of the place, considering how the mentioned road is rough or smooth, short or long, with all other circumstances that could be there; then, observe the room of the Last Supper, wide or narrow, common or decorated, and similar things.

[193] *The third* is to pray for what is desired, i.e., sorrow, indignation, and confusion for the fact that the supreme Lord of all would expose Himself to such great torments because of my sins.

[194] *The first point* will be to look at the participants at the supper and to derive something useful for me.
The second point: to hear what they say and gather something fruitful from it.

The third point: to be attentive to what they do and to profit from all of that.

[195] *Fourth:* to perceive that from this moment Christ already wishes and starts to suffer according to the story; therefore, I, too, shall start to stir up within myself sorrow, sadness, and tears; and I would afflict myself similarly in the following points.

[196] *Fifth:* to meditate on how Christ's divinity is hiding itself, and does not destroy its adversaries, though it could do so, but lets its humanity suffer such cruel pains.

[197] *Sixth:* to reflect upon what I should do or suffer for His cause when He is accepting such things for my sins.

[198] The colloquy will be addressed to Christ and end with the Our Father.

[199] It must be noticed about colloquies (as we have partially explained before) that it is convenient to do and ask for something according to the current subject, that is, according to the consolation or trouble I sense within myself; according to my wish for one virtue or another; according to what I intend to decide about myself in this or that respect; according also to my desire to be sad or rejoice about what I contemplate. Finally, it will be asked what I most desire about a certain particular thing; and one colloquy could be made to Christ the Lord, or three, if devotion incites me to do so, to the Mother, the Son, and the Father, according to what has been said in the contemplation of the Second Week about the Three Kinds of Men, with the annotation that follows it.

[200] **SECOND CONTEMPLATION**

**at dawn, about the things done by Christ
after the Last Supper and in the Garden**

The preparatory prayer is always the usual one.

[201] *The first prelude* is about the story: How Jesus Christ, with His eleven apostles, descended from Mount Sion, where they had supper; and going through the Valley of Josaphat, left eight of them there and went with the other three somewhere in the Garden. Going farther Himself, He prayed until sweating blood, having already repeated three times the same prayer to His Father. Then, having awakened the disciples from sleep, threw His adversaries to the ground with a single word, when Judas betrayed Him with a kiss; He then replaced Malchus' ear, which Peter cut; finally He was taken like a criminal or a common thief, and through that valley was brought first to the house of Annas.

[202] *The second prelude* consists of reconstructing the place. To look at the path: steep, level, and rough; to do the same with the Garden, describing its size, shape, and appearance.

[203] *The third prelude*, according to our goal, is to ask for sorrow, tears, anguish, and other similar interior pains, so that I suffer with Christ suffering for me.

[204] Four things should also be noted.
First: After the preparatory prayer and the three preludes of this second Exercise, to proceed in the same manner and order through the points and the colloquy as it was done in the previous exercise about the Last Supper. Two repetitions on both contemplations should be added at the time of Mass and Vespers. Before supper, to apply the five senses, having made the preparatory prayer and the three preludes adjusted to the specific topic, as it has been sufficiently described in the Second Week.

[205] *Second:* According to age, physical constitution, and total disposition, five or fewer Exercises will be performed every day.

[206] *Third:* During this Third Week, the second and sixth Additions should be partially changed. About the second: As soon as I wake up, I will think of where I am going, tasting a little bit the contemplation to come; and when I get up and dress, I should exert myself vigorously to arouse sadness and sorrow for so many great pains of Christ.
About the sixth: I should reject rather than seek or accept joy-

ful thoughts, though as useful and holy elsewhere as the ones about the Resurrection of Christ and glory. Instead, I should, in meditating on His Passion, draw out anguish and pain of the frequent memory of the anguish and pain He Himself suffered, from the hour of His nativity to the end of His life.

[207] *Fourth:* The Particular Examination, about the making of the Exercises and the Additions, will be made as it was in the previous Week.

[208]   **SECOND DAY**

Another contemplation should follow during the night on what happened in Annas' House, as it is related in the Mysteries of the Life of [Our Lord Jesus] Christ; at dawn, on what followed in the house of Caiaphas; then the repetitions and the use of the senses as before.

THIRD DAY

At midnight we will contemplate how Christ was brought to Pilate, and what was done there, as it will be said below; at the beginning of the day, what happened, Christ having been sent to Herod. Then follow the usual repetitions and use of the senses.

FOURTH DAY

The night meditation will go through from the return from Herod to half the way of the Mysteries that followed at Pilate's place, and the second half will follow at the first light of the day. Repetitions and use of senses will be done as above.

FIFTH DAY

In the middle of the night, we will contemplate the progress of the Passion, from Pilate's sentence to the crucifixion; at dawn, thereafter, from the elevation of the cross to Christ's expiration; repetitions and use of senses as above.

SIXTH DAY

During the night, how the dead Lord is removed from the cross and transferred to the tomb; at dawn, from the time He was buried until the Blessed Virgin withdrew into some house.

SEVENTH DAY

During the night and the morning, we should go back to the whole of the Passion. Then, instead of the repetitions and the use of the senses, we will consider all day long, as often as possible, how the most sacred body of Jesus Christ remained separated from the soul; and where and how it was laid down in a sepulcher; and also the solitude of holy Mary His Mother, what desolation and how much affliction were hers; how bitter also the disciples' sorrow.

[209] It must be noticed that if someone would like to spend more time meditating on Christ's Passion, he should make each contemplation with fewer Mysteries; for example, the first would include only the Last Supper, the second the washing of the feet, the third the institution of the holy Eucharist, and the fourth the discourse that followed; and the same would be done for the rest.

After that, having gone through the entire Passion, it will be possible to repeat the first half during the following day and the remaining the day after; then, on the third day, all of it at once.

On the contrary, if someone prefers to shorten the time, he should contemplate the Lord's Supper by night, the Garden at dawn, the house of Annas around Mass, the house of Caiaphas around Vespers, Pilate's Praetorium before supper; and thus every day the five Exercises will be completed, omitting the repetitions and the use of the senses. However, having gone through the entire Passion, it would be worthwhile to go over the whole of it at once in one single day, either with everything brought together in one Exercise only, or divided among several, according to what he will estimate as more profitable for himself.

[210]   **SOME RULES**

for properly moderating the way of eating

First: We should abstain less from bread than from other food, for it does not promote gluttony or make us subject to temptation.

[211] *Second:* From drinking, we should abstain more than from eating bread. We should cautiously examine the quantity we need, so that we would always take it; the quantity that is harmful to us, so that we would remove it.

[212] *Third:* Abstinence applies mostly to tasty dishes and delicacies because they give a greater opportunity both for the appetite to sin and for the enemy to tempt. Therefore, they must be taken with moderation, in order to avoid excess. This is done in two ways: by getting used to eating more ordinary food, or by sparingly partaking luscious dishes.

[213] *Fourth:* The more someone abstains from food (avoiding however the serious danger of sickness), the faster he finds the right measure of food and drink for himself. Because, first, by better disposing himself in this manner, and tending more resolutely to perfection, he would feel now and then some rays of interior knowledge and some motions of consolation, both sent into him from heaven, and so he will be able to discern easily the most appropriate amount of food to eat. And also, if by so abstaining, he will have felt too weak to complete properly the Spiritual Exercises, he will easily notice what amount of food the necessity of nature requires.

[214] *Fifth:* It is profitable, while we are eating, to imagine that we see Jesus Christ our Lord eating with His disciples, observing His manner of eating, drinking, looking around, and speaking, and to resolve to imitate Him. Indeed, it happens that the more the intellect is taken by such a meditation rather than by the nourishment of the body, the more easily we will learn how to be moderate in our eating habits.

[215] *Sixth:* For the purpose of variety, other kinds of meditations can be adopted while eating, like the lives of the saints, or some pious doctrine, or some spiritual matter we have to deal with. Thus, the food itself and the enjoyment of eating are felt very little, because the mind is diverted.

[216] *Seventh:* It is particularly important to avoid that our spirit be totally preoccupied by the food to be eaten, and that we not eat with gluttony or haste. On the contrary, always mastering the appetite, we should moderate both the quantity of food and the manner of eating.

[217] *Eighth:* In order to eliminate immoderate eating and drinking, it is very advantageous, before lunch or supper, at an hour when hunger is not yet felt, to determine the exact amount of food we are going to eat, and never to exceed it later, either because of personal avidity or because of the enemy's instigation. But rather, in order to overcome both, we might even reduce that amount.

Fourth Week

[218]   **FIRST CONTEMPLATION**

How the Lord Jesus appeared
to His holy Mother after the Resurrection,
as we have in the Mysteries
of the Life of Jesus Christ below

The usual *preparatory prayer.*

[219] *The first prelude* is taken from the story: how the Lord, after He died on the cross, His body buried but always united with the Divinity, Himself in the soul continuously united with the Divinity, descended into hell and, having released from there the souls of the just, returned to the sepulcher, uniting again His body with His soul, and rising from the dead, He then appeared alive to His Blessed Virgin Mother, as piously we may conceive and believe.

[220] *Second prelude:* as a mental re-creation of the place, to observe the site of the sepulcher, and the domicile of the Blessed Virgin. We will carefully examine one by one the shape, the parts, and the rest of the setting, for example, her room and the oratory.

[221] *Third prelude* will contain the grace to ask that we might partake of the immense joy of Christ and His Mother.

[222] *The first, second, and third points* will be the same here as the ones disclosed above for the contemplation of the Last Supper, that is, to consider the persons, the words, and the actions.

[223] *Fourth point:* To notice how the divinity of Christ, hidden during the time of the Passion and death, manifests itself in the Resurrection, and then shines through so many miracles.

[224] *Fifth point:* Employing the similitude of consolation that can be offered by a best friend, to appraise how promptly and abundantly the Lord performed the office of consoling His own.

[225] After one or several colloquies, made according to the subject, the contemplation will end with the Our Father.

[226] Furthermore, it must be noted that, in the following contemplations or Exercises, all the mysteries of the Resurrection and Ascension, and those in between, will be reviewed one after another, always keeping the same methods and manner as in that Week where we contemplated the Mysteries of the Passion. According to the manner and example of this first meditation on the Lord's Resurrection, all the following ones must be shaped and regulated in their preludes (unless they have to be adjusted according to the subject), and also in the five points and each Addition. In respect to the repetitions and the application of the senses, as well as increasing or diminishing the number of Exercises according to the Mysteries, we could be directed by the same way we were taught in the previous Week for the meditation on Christ's Passion.

[227] *Second:* It must be noticed also that it is more suitable to this Fourth Week than to the preceding ones to make only four Exercises: the first in the morning after getting up; the second, around Mass time or just before lunch, in place of the first repetition; the third, at Vespers time, instead of the second repetition; the fourth, before supper, by using the senses to impress more strongly on the soul the three contemplations made during that day, having noticed and more deeply treated those parts or places where we felt more efficacious inner motions and greater spiritual taste.

[228] *Third:* Though a fixed number of points is prescribed to the one making the Exercises, three or five, for instance, he will be free to take more or fewer points for his contemplation according to what he will have experienced to be more appropriate for himself. For this, it will be very helpful for him, before starting the Exercise, to consider the points to be treated and how many.

[229] *Fourth:* It must be noticed that during this Fourth Week the second, sixth, seventh, and tenth Additions must be changed.

The second: As I wake up, I shall immediately put before my eyes the chosen contemplation, and I, too, shall strive to rejoice in the Lord's joy with His own.

The sixth: To bring to my memory what generates spiritual joy, such as the thought of glory.

The seventh: To take advantage of gifts of the light and the sky as they are given; for instance, in spring, the sight of green vegetation and flowers, or the pleasure of a sunny spot; in winter, the comfortable warmth of the sun or of a fire; and so with all the other delights suitable to the body and the mind, through which I could rejoice with my Creator and Redeemer.

The tenth: Instead of performing a penance, I should be content with practicing temperance and moderation concerning food, unless the Church has ordered fasting or abstinence for that time (for its precepts must always be obeyed, except for a just impediment).

[230]   **CONTEMPLATION**

for stimulating within us Spiritual Love

Before anything else, two things must be noticed.

First: Love itself depends more on deeds than on words.

[231] *Second:* Love consists in the mutual sharing of abilities, things, and deeds, for example, science, wealth, honor, and any other good.

We start with the usual prayer.

[232] *First prelude:* to see myself standing before the Lord, the angels, and all saints, all of whom are disposed in my favor.

[233] *Second prelude:* to pray earnestly for God's grace that, perceiving the magnitude of the benefits He has given to me, I may devote all of myself to His love, worship, and service.

[234] *First point:* To recall to memory the benefits of Creation and Redemption; to enumerate also the particular or private benefits, and within myself to ponder with love how much the most generous Lord has done and suffered for me; how much He has given me of His own treasures; and that, according to His divine decree and good pleasure, He wants to give Himself to me, as much as possible. After looking at that carefully, going back to myself, I should ask myself what part is mine and what is equitable and just to offer and present to His Divine Majesty. Without doubt, I must offer all that is mine and myself with great love, through words like these or similar ones:

Take, Lord, all my freedom. Accept all my memory, intellect, and will. All that I have or possess, You have given to me; all I give back to You, and give up then to be governed by Your will. Grant me only the grace to love You, and I am sufficiently rich so that I do not ask for anything else.

[235] *Second:* To observe God existing in every single one of His creatures: and indeed giving existence to all elements; to plants so that they have vegetative life; then, to animals so that they have sensation; finally, to human beings so that they would also have intelligence. As one of them, I, too, have received all those benefits—to exist, to live, to sense, and to understand; and that He willed to make me His temple, created in His image and likeness. From admiration of all that, I should return to myself and act as I did in the first point or in a better way, if one occurs to me; and this shall be done also in the following points.

[236] *Third:* To consider this same God and Lord, working and somehow laboring within His creatures for me, to the extent that He gives them being and preserves what they are, what they have, what they are capable of, and what they do. All these things, as before, should be considered in relation to myself.

[237] *Fourth:* To observe how all gifts and goods come from heaven, such as power, justice, goodness, science, and any other human perfection, bounded by some determined limits; they derive from that infinite treasure of all good like the light from the sun and

water from the spring. Then to add the above reflection to the consideration of myself.

A colloquy should be made also, ending with the Our Father.

[238]   **THREE METHODS OF PRAYING**

The First Method of Praying is derived from the consideration of the Commandments, of the seven mortal sins, of the three faculties of the soul, and of the five senses; thus, it does not have so much the form of prayer as the form of a spiritual Exercise, through which the soul is helped and the prayer made more acceptable to God.

[239] And thus, before praying with this Method, as an equivalent to the third Addition, I will sit or walk for a little bit (whichever seems best to pacify my soul), pondering where I should go and what I should do. This same Addition must be observed before every Method of Praying.

[240] *The preparatory prayer* should include the petition for this grace: to acknowledge in what I transgressed the precepts of the Decalogue, and to correct myself in the future, since I will have understood them more accurately, and (as it is right) observed them more carefully than usual for God's glory and my salvation.

[241] *First:* Therefore, I will examine each commandment, considering how I have observed or violated it, and I will ask for forgiveness of the transgressions that come back into my memory by reciting once the Our Father. Then, for each precept, it will suffice to spend as much time in examination as needed to recite the Lord's Prayer three times.

[242] However, it should be noticed that less time must be spent on a precept that we rarely break and more on a precept that we usually break more frequently, and it should be done likewise concerning mortal sins.

[243] After having completed the examination for each precept and having recognized my guilt and asked for the grace to ob-

serve the precepts more vigilantly in the future, I will direct my colloquy to God according to the circumstance.

[244] *Second:* We follow the same Method of Praying with mortal sins, after the Addition and the preparatory prayer, as we have done for the precepts. Nothing in either of these is different except the matter considered, since the precepts must be observed while the sins must be avoided. All the rest is the same, and then the colloquy is likewise made.

[245] It should be known that the comprehension of sins and vices is facilitated by the consideration of opposite acts and habits. Therefore, through divine grace and pious exercise, each individual must labor to acquire for himself the virtues that are opposite to the seven mortal sins.

[246] *Third:* The same process is followed for the three faculties of the soul, by making the Addition, the prayer, and the examination on each one, with a colloquy at the end.

[247] *Fourth:* About the five senses of the body, without any modification, except for the matter.

[248] It should be noticed here that if someone wishes to imitate Christ in the use of his senses, he must recommend himself for this to God in the preparatory prayer, and after the examination of each sense, finish with the Lord's Prayer; but if someone is inclined to imitate in the same way the Virgin Mary, he should recommend himself to her so that she would obtain this grace from the Son, and while reviewing each sense, likewise recite the Hail Mary.

[249]   SECOND METHOD OF PRAYING

**through pondering the meaning
of each word of a prayer**

[250] To start with the same Addition as above

[251] *The preparatory prayer* should be appropriate to the person toward whom it is directed.

[252] The Second Method of Praying is kneeling or sitting (according to the condition of the body and the devotion of the spirit), eyes either closed or focused on one spot and not moving around, we recite the Lord's Prayer from the beginning, and at the first term, which is *"Pater"* (Father), we stop to meditate on it as long as diverse significations, similitudes, spiritual flavors, and other devotional emotions come to us; and, in the same manner we will meditate about every single word of the same prayer, or of any other prayer.

[253] Three Rules about this should be observed.

First: We should spend one hour in such rumination of whatever prayer. After that the Hail Mary, the Creed, the *Anima Christi*, and the Hail Holy Queen will be recited according to the usual usage, mentally only or also orally.

[254] *Second:* While we are praying on one or two words with this Method, if the meditation and also the internal delight are abundant, we will postpone any concern of going further to another portion, even though the full hour is spent; however, at the end, we will rapidly recite the remaining part of the prayer.

[255] *Third:* When a full hour has been spent in meditating on one or several words, on the following day, after having rapidly recited what has already been prayed about, we will proceed with the consideration of the words following.

[256] After we have prayed with this Method on the entire Lord's Prayer, we will follow this with the Hail Mary, and thereafter another prayer, so that this exercise of praying may continue without interruption.

[257] Furthermore, our prayer being thus completed, we will address with few words the person to whom the prayer was related, asking for some virtue or grace of which we would feel the most need.

[258]   **THIRD METHOD OF PRAYING**

by combining words and times

The Addition does not differ from either of the two Methods above.

The preparatory prayer is made as it is in the Second Method.

This Third Method of Praying consists of putting some words of the Lord's Prayer or of another prayer between two breaths; and during that time, of considering either the meaning of the recited words, or the dignity of the person to whom the prayer is addressed or my own worthlessness, or finally the difference between both of them. It will be the same with the remaining words. The prayers listed above should be added, like the Hail Mary, the Creed, etc.

[259] Two Rules Concerning This

First: Having finished the Lord's Prayer according to this Method, we must use the Hail Mary on other days or hours and must treat it with the same rhythm of breathing, with the other prayers to be recited in the usual manner.

[260] *Second:* Whoever wants to practice this Method of Praying for a longer time could apply it to all the prayers mentioned above, or to parts of them, and should observe a similar rhythm of breaths and words.

[261] MYSTERIES OF THE
LIFE OF OUR LORD JESUS CHRIST

First, it must be noticed that only the words of the Mysteries that are within quotation marks are taken from the gospels themselves, and not the others. Also, in each Mystery, always or almost always, three points are proposed, so that the contemplation will be easier because it will be more clearly divided.

[262] About Christ's Incarnation Announced to the Blessed Virgin Mary (Lk 1)

1. How the angel Gabriel, greeting the Blessed Virgin, announced to her the conception of the Divine Word, "After entering, the angel said to her: Hail, full of grace, etc. Here it is that you will conceive in your womb, and give birth to a Son, etc."
2. The angel confirmed what he said before, bringing the example of the admirable conception of Saint John the Baptist: "And behold, your relative Elizabeth herself has conceived a son in her old age, etc."
3. The holy Virgin replied to the angel: "Here is the servant of the Lord; may it be done to me according to your word."

[263] About Mary Visiting Her Relative Elizabeth (Lk 1)

1. How Mary visited Elizabeth, and how Saint John, who existed in her womb, felt Mary's greeting and exulted: "As Elizabeth heard Mary's greeting, the infant in her womb rejoiced; and, filled by the Holy Spirit, Elizabeth cried out in a loud voice, and said, 'Blessed are you among women, and blessed the fruit of your womb!'"
2. The Blessed Virgin burst with joy in this canticle: "My soul magnifies the Lord, etc."
3. "And Mary stayed with her around three months, and went back to her own home."

[264] About the Birth of Christ (Lk 2)

1. The blessed Mary with Joseph her husband went from Nazareth to Bethlehem: "And Joseph went up to Galilee,

etc., to Bethlehem, etc., to register with his espoused wife Mary, who was pregnant."

2. "She gave birth to her firstborn Son, and wrapped Him in swaddling clothes and laid Him in the manger."
3. At that time, "All of a sudden a multitude of the celestial militia joined the angel, praising God and saying, "Glory to God in the highest, etc."

[265] The Shepherds (Lk 2)

1. The birth of Christ was revealed by the angel to the shepherds: "I announce to you a great joy, etc. Today a Savior is born for you, etc."
2. The shepherds went quickly to Bethlehem: "And they came in haste and found Mary, Joseph, and the Infant in a manger."
3. "And the shepherds returned, giving glory and praise to God, etc."

[266] The Circumcision (Lk 2)

1. The Child was circumcised.
2. "He was given the name of Jesus, as the angel had said, before He was conceived in the womb."
3. The Child was given back to his mother, who looked with compassion at the outpouring of blood from her Son.

[267] The Three Magi and Kings (Mt 2)

1. Three Magi and Kings came to adore the child Jesus, led by a star, as they said: "We have seen His star in the Orient, and have come to adore Him."
2. "Prostrating themselves, they adored Him, and opening their treasure they offered Him gifts of gold, incense, and myrrh."
3. "Having received a warning in their sleep not to go back to Herod, they returned to their homeland by another way."

[268] The Purification of the Blessed Virgin and the Presentation of the Child Jesus (Lk 2)

1. They brought the Child to the Temple to present Him to God, as a firstborn, offering for Him the customary gift, "a pair of turtledoves or a pair of baby doves."
2. Coming at the same hour to the Temple, Simeon "took Him in his arms and blessed God, and said —Now, Lord, let your servant go, etc."
3. Anna "arriving, too, proclaimed God and spoke about Him to all those who were expecting the redemption of Israel."

[269] The Flight to Egypt (Mt 2)

1. Herod, desiring to murder the little child Jesus, ordered the killing of the Innocents; Joseph, having been forewarned by the angel to flee to Egypt: "Get up, take the Child and His Mother, and flee to Egypt."
2. Joseph hastily left for Egypt: "Getting up by night, etc., he withdrew in Egypt."
3. "And he was there until the death of Herod."

[270] The Return from Egypt (Mt 2)

1. Joseph was advised by the angel to go back to the land of Israel: "Get up, and take the Child and His Mother and go to the land of Israel."
2. "Getting up, etc., he came to the land of Israel."
3. Because Archelaus, son of Herod, reigned in Judea, he retreated to Nazareth.

[271] The Life of the Lord from the Age of Twelve to Thirty (Lk 2)

1. How He was submissive and obedient to his parents.
2. "He grew in wisdom, age, and grace, etc."
3. He seems to have practiced carpentry, since Saint Mark says in Chapter 6: "Is this one not a carpenter?"

[272] Going Up to the Temple at the Age of Twelve (Lk 2)

1. When He was twelve, Jesus went from Nazareth to Jerusalem.
2. He remained there, without His parents knowing it.
3. After three days, they found Him in the Temple, sitting among the doctors; and, when they asked Him to explain the cause of the delay, He answered: "Don't you know that I must attend to my Father's affairs?"

[273] His Baptism (Mt 3)

1. Saying good-bye to His Mother, He went from Nazareth to the Jordan River, where John was then baptizing.
2. He was baptized by John, who first excused himself for his unworthiness, but was urged by these words: "No matter. We must fulfill all justice this way."
3. The Holy Spirit came down on Him, and a voice from heaven testified in this way: "This is my beloved Son, in whom I am pleased."

[274] The Temptation of Christ (Lk 4 & Mt 4)

1. After baptism, Christ withdrew into the desert and fasted there for forty days and nights.
2. He was tempted three times by the enemy: "Approaching, the tempter said to Him, "If you are the Son of God, tell these stones to become bread. Jump down. I will give You all these things, if You bow down and adore me."
3. "The angels approached Him and served Him."

[275] The Call of the Apostles

1. Saints Peter and Andrew seem to have been called three times: first, just to know Christ (Jn 1); then, to follow Him temporarily, with the intention of returning to their fishing (Lk 5); finally, to follow Him forever (Mt 4, Mk 1).
2. He called the sons of Zebedee (Mt 4), Philip (Jn 1), and Matthew (Mt 9).

3. The others were called, even though no clear mention is made in the gospel concerning the fact and the order of their calling.

Three things must be considered here:

1. How the apostles were of humble condition
2. What a great dignity they were called to, and how delightfully
3. How, through the gifts of grace, they were placed above all the Fathers of the Old Testament and the saints of the New Testament

[276] The First Miracle of Christ Made during a Wedding (Jn 2)

1. Christ was invited with His disciples to a wedding.
2. His Mother informed Him that the wine had run out: "They do not have wine." And she said to the servants: "Whatever He will say to you, do it."
3. The Lord changed water into wine: "And He manifested his glory, and His disciples believed in Him."

[277] The Merchants Fleeing Out of the Temple for the First Time (Jn 2)

1. He expelled from the Temple sellers and buyers with a whip made of cords.
2. "He threw away the scale of the moneychangers, and overthrew the tables."
3. To those selling the turtledoves, He kindly said: "Take these things away and don't make my Father's house a marketplace."

[278] The Preaching of Christ on the Mountain (Mt 5)

1. To His beloved disciples Christ presented eight Beatitudes: Blessed are the poor of spirit; the meek; those who weep; those who are hungry and thirsty for justice; the compassionate; the pure of heart; the peacemakers; those who suffer persecution.

2. He exhorted them to use rightly gifts and talents they have received: "May your light shine before men so that they will see your good works and give glory to your Father who is in heaven."

3. He showed that He does not abolish the law, but accomplishes it, by explaining the precepts of not killing, not stealing, not committing fornication, not swearing, and also of loving enemies: "But, I tell you: Love your enemies, do good to those who hate you."

[279] The Calming of the Storm at Sea (Mt 8)

1. While Christ was sleeping, a violent storm broke forth on the sea.

2. The terrified disciples woke Him up, and He reproached them for shallowness of faith: "Why are you afraid, men of little faith?"

3. He commanded the winds and the sea to quiet down, and immediately there was tranquillity; stunned by that, people said: "Who is this man, whom winds and sea obey?"

[280] The Walking on the Water (Mt 14)

1. While He was still on the mountain, after He ordered the disciples to leave by boat, Christ "having sent away the crowd, went to the mountain, and prayed by Himself."

2. During the night, as the boat was being tossed, He Himself came walking on the waters; frightened, the disciples thought it was a ghost.

3. After He said to them: "It is I, be not afraid," Saint Peter asked for the capacity to go near to Him, and while walking on the waters, because fear began to overcome him, he started to sink; and the Lord, reproaching him of little faith, got into the boat and the wind stopped.

[281] Sending the Apostles to Preach (Mt 10)

1. To the disciples He had called, Jesus gave the power of expelling demons from people and of curing all kinds of diseases.

2. He taught them prudence and patience: "I send you like lambs among wolves. Be therefore cautious like snakes and simple as doves."

3. He showed them the way they were to go: "Freely you have received, freely give; don't possess either gold or silver." And also He expressed the matter to be preached: "Go and preach, saying: The kingdom of heaven is near."

[282] Magdalene's Conversion (Lk 7)

1. When Christ was lying at the table in the Pharisee's home, a woman came in who had been a sinner in town (either she was Mary of Magdala, the sister of Martha, or someone else), carrying an alabaster jar full of perfume.

2. Staying behind Him, she started to wet His feet with her tears and to dry them with her hair, to kiss and to anoint them.

3. Christ defended her who was incriminated by the Pharisee, and said to him: "Her many sins are forgiven because she has loved very much." And then to the woman herself: "Your faith has saved you, go in peace."

[283] The Feeding of Five Thousand People (Mt 14)

1. The disciples asked Jesus to dismiss the crowd that was there.

2. He Himself ordered them to bring the loaves they had and, after a blessing, He broke them and gave them to be distributed by the disciples, after the crowds of people had been asked to sit down.

3. They ate and were satisfied, and there were twelve baskets of leftovers.

[284] The Transfiguration of Christ (Mt 17)

1. After taking with Him the three dearest disciples, Peter, John, and James, Jesus "was transfigured before them: His face shining like the sun and His garments became as white as snow."

2. He was talking with Moses and Elijah.

3. While Peter was asking that three tents be erected, a voice from heaven resounded: "This is my beloved Son, etc., listen to Him." Because of that, the disciples were frightened and fell to the ground in prostration; touching them, Christ said: "Get up and be not afraid, etc. Don't talk about the vision to anyone until the Son of Man is risen from the dead."

[285] The Resurrection of Lazarus (Jn 11)

1. Informed about Lazarus' sickness, Christ stayed where He was for two days, so that the miracle would be more evident.
2. Before resurrecting the dead, He stimulated the faith of both sisters: "I am the Resurrection and the Life; he who believes in me, even though he had died, shall live."
3. First He cried with them and prayed, and He resurrected him by way of a command: "Lazarus, come out."

[286] The Meal in Bethany (Mt 26)

1. Christ was eating at the house of Simon the leper, and so was Lazarus.
2. Mary poured out some ointment on His head.
3. Judas murmured against it: "Why such a waste?" Then Christ defended the Magdalene: "Why are you bothering this woman? In fact she has done something good for me."

[287] Palms Day (Mt 21)

1. The Lord ordered that a she-donkey and its colt be brought there: "Untie and bring them to me; and if anyone says anything to you, say that the Lord needs them, and right away he will release them."
2. He sat on the she-donkey covered with the apostles' garments.
3. Receiving Him, as He was coming toward them, people laid down branches and clothes on the road and sang: "Hosanna to the Son of David, blessed is He who comes in the name of the Lord. Hosanna in the highest."

[288] The Preaching in the Temple (Lk 19)

1. He taught daily in the Temple.
2. His preaching done, He returned to Bethany, nobody welcomed Him in Jerusalem.

[289] The Last Supper (Mt 26 & Jn 13)

1. He ate the paschal lamb with the disciples, and foretold His imminent death: "Amen, I tell you that one of you is about to betray me."
2. He washed their feet, including even Judas', starting with Peter, who, looking at Christ's majesty and at his own unworthiness, objected: "You, Lord, You wash my feet?" He did not know that he was being given an example of humility by the Lord, who then declared: "I have indeed given you an example, so that what I have done, you also will do."
3. He instituted the holy sacrament of the Eucharist, as a sign of the supreme love, using these words: "Take and eat, etc." The meal over, Judas went out to sell Him.

[290] Mysteries Accomplished after the Supper, in the Garden (Mt 26, Mk 14)

1. After the supper was finished and the hymn sung, Christ left for the Mount of Olives with His eleven disciples, who were full of fear; and He ordered eight of them to remain in Gethsemane: "Sit here, while I go over there and pray."
2. Taking three with Himself, Peter, James, and John, He prayed three times, saying: "My Father, if it is possible, may this chalice pass by me; however, not as I will it but as You do." And being in agony, He prayed more earnestly.
3. And He submitted Himself to suffer such a fear that He said: "My soul is sad to the point of death" and sweated a large amount of blood, as Luke testifies: "His sweat became like drops of blood flowing to the ground." Hence, one can suppose that His garments were already soaked with blood.

[291] The Arrest of Christ and the Transfer to Annas' House (Mt 26; Lk 22; Mk 14; Jn 18)

1. The Lord allowed Judas to betray Him with a kiss, and to be Himself arrested as a thief: "You came out with swords and sticks to arrest me, as if I were a thief. Every day I was among you, teaching in the Temple, and you did not take me." And when He asked: "Whom are you looking for?" all His enemies fell on the ground.

2. He said to Peter, who was hitting a servant of the high priest: "Put your sword back into its holder," and He cured the servant.

3. After being caught and abandoned by His disciples, He was taken to Annas' house, where He was denied once by Peter, who had followed Him at a little distance. There He was slapped by a servant, who reproached: "Is this the way You answer to the high priest?"

[292] About What Happened Next in Caiaphas' House (Mt 26)

1. Christ, bound, was brought from Annas' house, where Peter again denied Him twice, and as the Lord looked at him, he "went out and cried bitterly."

2. He remained bound all that night.

3. The guards around Him ridiculed and maltreated Him, and after covering His face and hitting Him with their fists, they asked: "Prophesy to us, Christ, who is the one who hits You?" and they were blaspheming in other ways.

[293] The Charge against Christ before Pilate (Mt 27; Lk 23; Mk 15; Jn 18)

1. Then Christ was brought to Pilate, and before him He was falsely accused by the Jews: "We found Him subverting our people and prohibiting them from paying tribute to Caesar."

2. After a first and second examination Pilate reported: "I don't find any case in this."

3. The Jews claimed that they preferred the release of Barabbas, a brigand, rather than Christ Jesus: "Not this one, but Barabbas."

[294] Christ Is Sent to Herod (Lk 23)

1. Pilate sent Christ to Herod, because he thought that He was from Galilee.
2. To Herod, who interrogated Him with curiosity, He did not give any answer, though He was vehemently accused by the Jews.
3. He was despised by Herod and his people and clothed with a white garment.

[295] From Herod back to Pilate (Mt 27; Lk 23; Mk 15; Jn 19)

1. Herod sent Christ back to Pilate, and the same day, having before been enemies, they are reconciled with each other.
2. Pilate ordered that Jesus be scourged; the soldiers crowned Him with thorns and clothed Him with a purple garment, and then laughed at Him, saying: "Hail, King of the Jews!" and hit His face.
3. "Jesus then came out wearing the crown of thorns and the purple garment," and Pilate said to them: "Here is the man." But the high priests shouted together: "Crucify Him, crucify Him."

[296] The Condemnation and Crucifixion of Jesus Christ (Jn 19)

1. Sitting in court, Pilate judged Christ, and handed Him over to be crucified, after the Jews denied Him as their King, saying: "We have no king but Caesar!"
2. Christ carried His cross until, His strength abandoning Him, Simon of Cyrene was compelled to carry it after Him.
3. He was crucified between two brigands; the sign said: "Jesus the Nazarene, King of the Jews."

[297] The Mysteries Done on the Cross (Mt 27; Lk 23; Jn 19)

1. He underwent blasphemies on the cross: "Ah! You who destroy the Temple of God, etc. Come down from the cross!" And His garments were divided.
2. On the cross, the Lord spoke seven words; He prayed for the ones crucifying Him; He forgave the thief; He committed to each other His Mother and John; He shouted: "I'm thirsty" when they gave Him vinegar; then He said that the Father abandoned Him, and later on: "It's done"; and finally: "Father, into Your hands I recommend my spirit."
3. When He expired, the sun was obscured, rocks were broken, graves opened, the curtain of the Temple is torn from the top to the bottom, and His side, perforated by the lance, put forth water and blood.

[298] The Mystery of the Burial (Same Chapters)

1. Once dead, the Lord was removed from the cross by Joseph and Nicodemus before the eyes of His very afflicted Mother.
2. His anointed body was brought into a sepulcher, which is then closed.
3. There some guards were put in place.

[299] The Resurrection of Christ and the First Apparition

1. After He was risen, the Lord appeared to His Mother, since Scriptures say that He appeared to many. Even though they do not mention her by name, they nevertheless leave it to us as certain, inasmuch as we have intelligence; if not, we would justly hear this: "Are you, too, without any understanding?"

[300] The Second Apparition (Mk 16)

1. Early in the morning Mary of Magdala, [Mary, mother] of James, and Salome came to the grave, saying to each other: "Who will remove for us the stone from the entrance of the sepulcher?"

2. They saw the stone rolled aside and heard the word of the angel: "You are looking for Jesus of Nazareth crucified. He is risen, He is not here."

3. He appeared to Mary of Magdala, who had stayed nearby the sepulcher after the others had gone.

[301] The Third Apparition (Mt, Last Chapter)

1. The women returned from the sepulcher with fear and also great joy, to tell the disciples what they had understood of the Resurrection of the Lord.

2. Christ, appearing to them on the way, said: "Hail!"; and they, approaching and kneeling at His feet, adored Him.

3. The Lord said to them: "Do not fear. Go and announce to my brothers to go to Galilee: There they will see me."

[302] The Fourth Apparition (Lk, Last Chapter)

1. Having heard of the Resurrection of Christ from the women, Peter ran to the sepulcher.

2. Having gone inside, he saw only the burial cloths with which the body had been wrapped up.

3. While Peter was thinking about these things, Christ showed Himself to him; thus, the apostles said: "The Lord is truly risen, and He appeared to Simon."

[303] The Fifth Apparition (Lk, Still Last Chapter)

1. Thereafter He appeared to two disciples who were going to Emmaus and talking about Him.

2. He reproved them for their incredulity and explained to them the mysteries of the Passion and Resurrection: "O fools and slow of heart to believe all that the prophets had said. Was is not necessary that Christ suffer and so enter into His glory?"

3. Having been asked, He stayed with them, and after breaking the bread for them, He disappeared. They returned immediately to Jerusalem to announce to the apostles how they had seen Him and recognized Him at the breaking of the bread.

[304] The Sixth Apparition (Jn 20)

1. All the disciples, Thomas excepted, were gathered together at home for fear of the Jews.
2. Though the doors were closed, Christ entered, "stood in the midst of them, and said to them: Peace be with you."
3. He gave them the Holy Spirit and said: "Receive the Holy Spirit; whose sins you will remit, they are remitted, etc."

[305] The Seventh Apparition (Jn 20)

1. Because he was not present at the previous apparition, Thomas stated: "If I don't see, etc., I won't believe."
2. Eight days later, the doors being closed, Christ showed Himself and said to Thomas: "Put your finger here, and see, etc., and be not incredulous but faithful."
3. Thomas exclaimed: "My Lord and my God." Christ added to that: "Blessed are those who have not seen, and have believed."

[306] The Eighth Apparition (Jn, Last Chapter)

1. Christ manifested Himself again to seven of the disciples who were fishing; they had not caught anything all night long, and "because of the multitude of fish they could not pull up" the net that they had spread at His command.
2. At this miracle, John, recognizing Him, told Peter: "It is the Lord." Peter immediately cast himself into the sea and approached Christ.
3. He gave them bread and fish to eat. Then He asked Peter three times if he loved Him; and He commended His sheep to Peter: "Feed my sheep."

[307] The Ninth Apparition (Mk, Last Chapter)

1. By command of the Lord, the disciples went to Mount Tabor.
2. Appearing to them, He said: "All power has been given to me in heaven and on earth."
3. And sending them to preach through the whole world, He thus commissioned them: "Go therefore and teach all

peoples, baptizing them in the name of the Father, and the Son, and the Holy Spirit."

[308] The Tenth Apparition (1 Cor 15)

"Afterward, He was seen by more than five hundred brothers together."

[309] The Eleventh Apparition (1 Cor 15)

Then He appeared to James.

[310] The Twelfth Apparition

It is read in some hagiographies that Christ appeared also to Joseph of Arimathea. It is a probable fact and can be piously meditated.

[311] The Thirteenth Apparition (1 Cor 15)

He appeared also, after the Ascension, to Saint Paul, who himself said: "Last of all He appeared to me as one born out of due time." He appeared in soul also to the Fathers in Limbo, and then they were taken out of there.

Finally, having taken back His body, He appeared in different places to the disciples and conversed frequently with them.

[312] The Ascension of Christ (Acts 1)

1. Thereafter, for forty days, many times Christ showed Himself alive to His disciples, and "through many arguments, etc., speaking to them about the kingdom of God," He sent them to Jerusalem to wait there for the Holy Spirit promised to them.
2. He led them out to the Mount of Olives, "and before their eyes He was lifted up, and a cloud took Him away from their sight."
3. Two men dressed in white, whom we believe were angels, told them while they were looking at the sky: "Men of Galilee, what are you looking at in the sky? This Jesus, who has been taken up in the sky away from you, will come back as you saw Him go up in the sky."

Rules

SOME RULES

**in order to discern the movements of the soul,
which the different spirits stir up,
so that only the good ones be accepted
and the bad rejected.
It must be noticed that these Rules are mostly
appropriate for the Exercises of the First Week.**

[314] *Rule One:* Before those who easily sin mortally, and add sin to sins, our enemy usually presents seductive pleasures of the flesh and of the senses in order to keep them full of sins, and always to augment the mass. On the contrary, the good spirit assiduously stings their conscience and keeps them from sinning by means of an ethical and rational judgment.

[315] *Rule Two:* In the other men, who conscientiously take care to cleanse themselves from vices and sins and every day progress more and more in devotion to the divine service, the evil spirit instills troubles, scruples, sadness, false reasons, and other perturbations of this kind with which he impedes that progress. On the contrary, it is proper and usual for the good spirit to increase courage and strength in the ones who act rightly, to console, to stimulate tears of devotion, to enlighten the mind and to give tranquillity, removing all obstacles so that these people would more easily and more eagerly always progress farther through good deeds.

[316] *Rule Three:* We recognize that there is properly spiritual consolation when the soul takes fire in the love of its Creator by some inner motion and then cannot love any creature but because of Him. Also when tears are shed, provoking that love, either because they come from sorrow with regard to sins, or from the meditation of Christ's Passion, or from whatever other cause that is rightly disposed for the worship and honor of God. Finally, any increase of faith, hope, and charity can also be called consolation; equally all joyfulness, which usually incites the soul to meditation on heavenly things, to zeal for salvation, to be at rest and peace with God.

[317] *Rule Four:* On the contrary, any obscuring of the soul, any disturbance, any instigation to inferior or earthly things, must be called spiritual desolation; likewise, any disquietude and agitation, or temptation leading to mistrust of salvation and to the expelling of hope and charity; and thus the soul feels itself becoming sad, tepid, and apathetic, and almost despairing of the clemency of God Himself, its Creator. In fact, as desolation is opposed to consolation, so, also, all thoughts proceeding from each of them are directly opposed to one another.

[318] *Rule Five:* In time of desolation, nothing should be questioned or altered concerning the resolution of the mind or the status in life: But we must persevere in what had been previously established, for example, during the previous day or the hour of consolation. When someone enjoys the consolation we talked about, he is led not by his own inspiration but by that of the good spirit; in the same way, when desolation takes him in the opposite direction, he is driven by the evil spirit, by whose instigation nothing is ever done rightly.

[319] *Rule Six:* Although the man affected by desolation must not change at all his prior decisions, it is profitable, nevertheless, for him to provide and intensify that which opposes the impulse of desolation, like persisting in prayer, meditation, and the examination of self, and adding some kind of penance.

[320] *Rule Seven:* As long as we are pressed by desolation, we must think that for the moment we are left to ourselves by our Lord in order to be tested, so that we can resist the insults of our enemy with our natural forces. We can do that without doubt because of

the assistance of divine help, even though at that moment it is not at all felt because the Lord has removed the previous fervor of charity, nonetheless leaving the grace that can be sufficient to act rightly and to obtain salvation.

[321] *Rule Eight:* The effort to remain patient greatly helps the man troubled by temptation, because it properly opposes the vexations of that kind and directly resists them. Hope must also be summoned as well as the thought that consolation will come in a short time: especially if the attack of desolation is broken by the saintly efforts indicated in Rule Six.

[322] *Rule Nine:* There are three main causes of desolation. The first: We are rightly deprived of divine consolation because of our tepidity and sloth in our spiritual efforts and exercises. The second: in order for us to be tested on who we are, and how we dedicate ourselves to God's service and honor when the stipend of consolations and spiritual gifts is not there. The third: in order for us to be absolutely certain that it is not within our power to acquire or to keep the fervor of devotion, the ardor of love, the abundance of tears, or any other inner consolation; that all of that is the free gift of God, and if we claim it as our own, we will be falling into the offense of arrogance and vainglory, which is a serious risk for salvation.

[323] *Rule Ten:* The man who enjoys consolation should foresee how he will behave thereafter when desolation occurs, so that already he would presently store energy and strength of spirit in order to repress its impetus.

[324] *Rule Eleven:* When consolation abounds, he should abase and humble himself as much as he can, considering within himself how much he will appear weak and cowardly when the desolation attacks if he is not quickly assisted by the power of divine grace and consolation. On the contrary, the one who is troubled by desolation must estimate that he can do a lot with God's grace and will easily overcome all his adversaries, provided that he puts his hope in God's power and strengthens his spirit.

[325] *Rule Twelve:* Our enemy reproduces the feminine nature and conduct regarding the feebleness of strength and obstinacy of mind. For, when a woman is quarreling with a man, if she sees him opposing her with a resolute and firm countenance, then she gives up immediately and turns away; if, on the contrary, she notices that he is timid and ready to flee, then she reaches an extreme audacity and attacks him ferociously. In the same way, usually the devil totally loses courage and power every time he sees a spiritual athlete resist temptations with a fearless heart and a head held high; if, on the contrary, the man trembles at the first attacks to be endured and seems to lose courage, then there is not a more savage, more enraged, and more pertinacious beast on the earth against this man for achieving, with our ruin, the desire of its evil and obstinate mind than that man's enemy.

[326] *Rule Thirteen:* Also, our enemy follows the conduct of a very bad lover, who, wanting to seduce the young daughter of honest parents or the wife of an honorable man, does everything possible so that his words and plans be concealed; and the worst thing he will fear and endure with displeasure will be if the young daughter will unveil those things to her father or the wife to her husband, because he knows that in this case it is the end of his wishes and efforts. Similarly, the devil does everything possible so that the soul, which he wants to deceive and ruin, keeps secret his deceitful suggestions. Indeed, he is extremely displeased and severely tortured if his machinations are unveiled to someone who hears confession or to a spiritual person, because in these cases he understands that he is radically cut off.

[327] *Rule Fourteen:* It is also usual for the adversary to imitate some military commander who, intending to capture and plunder a besieged fortress, explores first the nature and the fortifications of the place and then attacks the weakest side. He does the same indeed: He turns around the soul and skillfully examines whether it is fortified by or deprived of the protection of any moral or theological virtue; he rushes most of all with all his stratagems into that part which he has foreseen to be less fortified and guarded than the others, and he hopes to destroy us.

[328]   **OTHER RULES**

for a more complete discernment of spirits,
and mostly appropriate to the Second Week

[329] *First:* It is proper to God and to the good angel to fill up the soul, which they move, with true spiritual gladness after taking away all sadness and trouble brought by the demon; because, on the contrary, the demon is used to war against such gladness found in the soul with some sophistic arguments that present themselves with the semblance of truth.

[330] *Two:* It belongs only to God to console the soul without preceding cause for the consolation, because it is proper to the Creator to enter into His creature, and to convert, attract, and transform the whole of it into His love. We say that there is no preceding cause when nothing is offered to our senses, intellect, or will that can by itself cause this consolation.

[331] *Three:* Every time there is a preceding cause for consolation, its author may be either the bad or the good angel; but they tend to contrary goals: The good angel's goal is that the soul grow in knowing and doing the good, and the bad angel's that the soul do evil and perish.

[332] *Four:* It is the custom of the evil spirit to transform himself into an angel of light: Knowing the pious wishes of the soul, at first he follows them and soon draws the soul to his perverse desires. Indeed, at the beginning he pretends to follow and support the good and holy thoughts of the man; then, little by little he entraps that allured man in the hidden snares of his fallacies.

[333] *Five:* All our thoughts must be screened carefully and diligently: their beginning, middle, and end. If all three are right, it is proof that the good angel suggested them. But if, in the mind's discourse, something is offered or follows that is evil in itself, or drives away from the good, or impels toward what is less good than what the soul had previously decided to seek to follow, or fatigues, troubles, and disturbs the soul itself by removing calmness, peace, and tranquillity that were present before, it will be an

evident sign that the author of such thoughts is the evil spirit, who always is the adversary of our benefit and salvation.

[334] *Six:* Every time it happens that, in any suggestion, the enemy is detected through his serpentine tail, that is, his evil end, which he always strives to insinuate into us, then it is very useful to reconsider all the mind's discourse and recognize what kind of good thought he took as a pretext at the beginning, and how he attempted to gradually remove the previous spiritual sweetness, the serenity of the mind, and pour his poison into it; so that having known his deceits through such experience, we will more easily be on guard against them in the future.

[335] *Seven:* Both spirits insinuate themselves in a different manner into the soul of those who progress in the good of salvation. The good spirit does it gently, peacefully, and delightfully, like a drop of water falling on a sponge; the bad one does it harshly, troublingly, and violently, with a bang like heavy rain hitting on a stone. Exactly the contrary usually happens to those who are going from bad to worse day after day. The reason for this diversity is the extent to which the disposition of the soul is similar or dissimilar to either angel. If, indeed, either spirit finds the soul dissimilar to itself, then it joins with that soul with a loud noise and violence, which can be easily perceived; but if the soul is similar, it comes in quietly, as if to its own home through the open door.

[336] *Eight:* Every time a consolation without preceding cause comes to us, although no deceit can be behind it because it comes from divine Providence, as said earlier, we must, however, attentively and carefully distinguish the present moment of consolation itself from the time that follows, in which the soul is still burning and feeling the remnants of the divine favor just received. Because it frequently happens in the time that follows that, either by our personal habits, discourse, and judgment or by the incitement of the good or evil spirit, we feel or resolve some things that, because they do not emanate directly from God Himself, need a careful examination before they receive assent or are carried out.

[337]   **SOME RULES**

that must be observed
for the distribution of alms

[338] *First Rule:* If someone would like to give to people related by blood or friendship, for whom a stronger attachment is felt, four Rules must be observed, which we partly mentioned for the Elections. So, the first Rule is that my attachment for such persons should come directly from God's love; I must really feel this love in myself as the root and cause of any of my attachments for all relatives and friends; and I must act in such a way that, in this present business, this specific reason stands out as the main one.

[339] *Second Rule:* I should consider which way of distributing alms I would recommend to someone else who would consult me about such business, and for whom I wish the same status or degree of perfection as for myself. Then I make use of this way as well.

[340] *Third Rule:* I should think of what I would most like to have done in this matter if I were close to the end of my life. Therefore, I would decide to act in this way presently.

[341] *Fourth Rule:* I should similarly imagine what I would prefer, on the Day of Judgment, to have done about this matter. This is what I will certainly choose now.

[342] *Fifth Rule:* Every time I feel my attachment inclining more toward persons related to me by a human bond, I will consider carefully the four Rules mentioned above and examine my attachment according to those Rules, without thinking either of the alms or of the way of distributing them, until I have removed from my mind anything that is not right.

[343] *Sixth Rule:* Even though the goods dedicated to divine worship and ecclesiastic use can be taken without fault, in order to be distributed, by the one called to such ministry; however, because many usually fall into scruples of exaggeration when they are determining the just portion for their own expenses, it is important to order properly their own lifestyle according to the same Rules.

[344] *Seventh Rule:* For the reasons above and many others concerning the management of those things that pertain to our person, condition, house, or family, it is the best and safest for each one in charge of the distribution to live as much as possible more modestly, and conform himself most closely to the example of our Lord Jesus Christ, the highest Pontifex. As a matter of fact, during the Third Council of Carthage, where Saint Augustine was present, it was decreed that the bishop's household should be simple and poor. It is convenient to provide this in whatever state or style of life, considering at the same time the persons themselves and their status: Just as Saint Joachim and Saint Anne give an example concerning marriage, by dividing their means into three parts each year; one given to the poor, one dedicated to the ministry of the Temple and divine worship, and the third one kept for their own necessities.

[345]   **SOME USEFUL NOTES**

**for discerning scruples
put into the soul by the demon**

[346] *First:* People speak of a scruple when we conclude, through the action and judgment of our own free will, that something is a sin when it is not. An example is when somebody realizes that he has walked over a cross made by few straws on the ground and attributes this to himself as a sin. This should not be, in a proper sense, called a scruple but rather an erroneous judgment.

[347] *Second:* We can properly say that there is a scruple when, every time after walking over such a cross, or after some thought, word, or action, the suspicion comes to us from outside that we have committed a sin. And, although on the other hand it comes to our mind that we have not sinned at all, we nevertheless feel some uncertainty and trouble of the mind, obviously thrust into us by the demon.

[348] *Third:* The first type of scruple, improperly named so, should be absolutely abhorred as full of error. The second kind, for some time (especially when the undertaking of a better life is recent) is of no small advantage to the soul devoted to spiritual things; because it purifies the soul in a wonderful way and takes it away from every appearance of sin, according to Saint Gregory's words: "It belongs to good minds to perceive a fault where there is no fault."

[349] *Fourth:* The enemy is used to observe skillfully what kind of conscience each soul might have: more gross or more delicate. If he finds it delicate, he exerts himself to make it more delicate and bring it to some extreme degree of anxiety, so that he would finally drive it, excessively disturbed, out of spiritual progress. For example, if he knows a soul that does not consent to any sin, mortal or venial, and cannot even accept the shadow (so to speak) of a voluntary sin; then, because he cannot present to that soul a real consideration of sin, he does as much as possible to persuade it to believe that there is a sin (for this soul) where in reality there is none, for instance, about some word or some sudden trivial thoughts. On the contrary, when the soul or the conscience is gross, he is eager to render it more gross, so that after taking venial sins lightly, it would care little about mortal sins, and even less and less as the days go by.

[350] *Fifth:* In order that the soul make progress in the spiritual journey, it must tend to the direction opposite the one the enemy tries to pull it into. If the enemy tries to make the conscience more lax, then the soul should make it more strict, or, on the contrary, make it more lax if the demon would make it too strict. And thus, by avoiding the dangers of both extremes, the soul itself remains continually in a kind of quiet middle and secure state.

[351] *Sixth:* Every time we want to say or do something that is not discordant with the Church's practice or with our superiors' mind, and that tends to God's glory, if a suggestion comes to us from outside, dissuading us from saying or doing what we had intended by bringing in some false reason of vainglory or any other evil, then we must lift up our mind to God. And if it appears that this saying or doing concerns God's glory, or if it is certainly not con-

trary to it, we must go directly against such a thought, and reply to the enemy who is disturbing us, with Saint Bernard, "It is not for you that I have started this, it is not for you that I will end it."

[352]   **SOME RULES TO BE OBSERVED**

in order to truly feel with the orthodox Church

[353] *First:* Having put away all our own judgment, we must always keep our mind prepared and quick to obey the true Spouse of Christ and our Holy Mother, which is the orthodox, Catholic, and hierarchical Church.

[354] *Second:* It is convenient to praise the confession of sins, usually made to a priest, and the receiving of the sacred Eucharist at a minimum of once a year, though it would be more praiseworthy to receive this sacrament every eight days, or at least once a month, while observing the appropriate prerequisites.

[355] *Third:* To recommend to Christ's faithful to hear frequently and devotedly the holy sacrifice of the Mass; likewise to recommend ecclesiastical hymns, psalms, and long prayers, to be recited in or out of the churches; also to approve established times for the Divine Office and all kinds of prayers, including the ones we call canonical hours.

[356] *Fourth:* To praise very much the religious state and to prefer celibacy or virginity to marriage.

[357] *Fifth:* To approve the religious' vows to keep perpetual chastity, poverty, and obedience, together with the other deeds of perfection and supererogation. And here it should be noticed that, because the reason of the vow concerns what leads to the perfection of Christian life, no vow should ever be made concerning all other things that rather divert us from the same perfection, like business and marriage.

[358] *Sixth:* To praise relics, veneration, and invocation of saints; also stations, pious pilgrimages, indulgences, jubilees, and candles

to be lit in churches, and all such other little means of helping our piety and devotion.

[359] *Seventh:* To extol the practice of abstinence and fasting during Lent, Ember days, Vigils, Fridays, Saturdays, and other times by devotion; equally to extol the spontaneous self-inflicted pains that we call penance, not only the internal ones but also external ones.

[360] *Eighth:* To praise, furthermore, the building of churches, their ornaments, and the images that are rightly worthy of veneration for what they represent.

[361] *Ninth:* To support by all means all the precepts of the Church, and never to oppose them in any manner; but, on the contrary, to defend them promptly against those who attack them, with arguments that we look for everywhere.

[362] *Tenth:* To diligently approve decrees, orders, traditions, rites, and conduct of fathers or superiors. Though such integrity of conduct is not found everywhere, as it should be, if someone speaks against them in a public speech or in conversation with people, he causes injury and scandals rather than bringing any remedy or being useful; nothing else would follow but exasperation, and the opposition of the people against their princes and pastors. We must therefore abstain from these kinds of invectives. As it is damaging to rail at superiors in their absence and revile them in front of people, so it is worthy to warn privately those who can correct this evil if they want to.

[363] *Eleventh:* To highly esteem the sacred doctrine, the one called Positive as much as the one called Scholastic. For, as the goal of holy Doctors of old, Jerome, Augustine, Gregory, and others alike, was to move the minds to cherish the love and worship of God; so it was proper of blessed Thomas, Bonaventure, the Master of Sentences, and other more recent theologians, to transmit and define more exactly the dogmas necessary for salvation according to what fit their times and thereafter for refuting the errors of heresies. Because these Doctors who came later not only are gifted with the understanding of Sacred Scriptures and the assistance of ancient authors' writings but also, with the influx of divine light,

fruitfully use the ordinances of the councils and the decrees and various constitutions of the Church for helping our salvation.

[364] *Twelfth:* It is blamable, and must be avoided, to compare people still living (however praiseworthy they might be) with saints and blessed ones, by saying: "This person is more learned than Augustine; that one is another Saint Francis; he equals Paul in holiness, or is not inferior in some other virtue, etc."

[365] *Thirteenth:* In order that we be totally unanimous and in accordance with the Catholic Church itself, if the Church defines as black something that appears white to our eyes, we must in like manner declare it black. For, indeed, we must undoubtedly believe that the spirit of Jesus Christ our Lord, and the spirit of the orthodox Church, His Spouse, is the same one by which we are guided and led to salvation; and that it is the same God who formerly gave the precepts of the Decalogue who right now instructs and governs the hierarchical Church.

[366] *Fourteenth:* It must be observed that, even though it would certainly be true that nobody would obtain salvation unless predestined, we nevertheless must be very cautious when we speak about it, lest by chance we would give too much room to God's grace or predestination and seem to want to exclude the strength of free will and the merits of good deeds; or, on the contrary, by giving more than what is just to the latter, we take away from the former.

[367] *Fifteenth:* For the same reason, we should not talk frequently about predestination. If it happens sometimes, it is convenient to refrain from giving an occasion of error to listeners by saying, "If my salvation or damnation is already decided, whether I do good or evil, nothing can be changed"; for this reason, many neglect good deeds and other means of salvation.

[368] *Sixteenth:* Also it happens frequently, when faith is preached and praised without moderation, and without addition of any distinction and explanation, that people take the opportunity to be lazy about good deeds, which come before faith, or after it, when faith materializes because of its link with charity.

[369] Also we must not preach and insist on God's grace to the point of emphasizing it so much that a deadly error might creep into the listeners' minds and negate the faculty of our free will. It is proper, therefore, to talk extensively about God's grace itself when God so inspires; but so that it would increase His greater glory, and this has to be done in a manner fitting our present very dangerous times; so that the efficacy of our free will and our good deeds not be nullified.

[370] *Eighteenth:* Though it is extremely praiseworthy and useful to serve God by pure love, nonetheless the fear of Divine Majesty must be strongly recommended. This fear is not only the one called filial, which is pious and extremely holy, but also the other one, called servile. For this last one is very useful to us, and often necessary for making the effort to rise promptly from mortal sin when we have fallen into it; when we are devoid of and foreign to that servile fear, the filial one, which is deeply acceptable to God and is more easily attainable; and that filial fear gives us union of love with God Himself and keeps us in it.

COMMENTARY

Annotations

The purpose of the Annotations is to help retreat master and retreatant, for the Exercises are an undertaking between God and the retreatant, *served* by the retreat master. The goal of the Exercises is to search and find God's will as it applies to the retreatant's life. Practice alone leads the retreatant to understand the process, but it is helpful if some behaviors are immediately corrected or introduced. So, when we start, I invite retreatants to read all the Annotations a few times. Then I comment on them, both to satisfy a normal curiosity and to deal with retreatants as adults who have the right to know about what they are undertaking (n. 5, 10, 14, 15).

Some retreatants are so serious about anything in the Exercises that I ask them to read texts as if the texts were being told to them (thus their memory retains only what touches them personally). Experts assert that the text of the Exercises *has* to be "said," because the book is a manual solely *for* the retreat master, who must relay its content to the retreatant with the necessary adjustments (this may explain the words of n. 20: "It will be convenient to use written records of the essential in order to keep it better in memory"). The retreat master must have made the Exercises previous to assisting others to make them.

[1] The comparison with corporal activities alerts us that the Exercises are not a theory learned intellectually (n. 2), but a practice requiring work, and a journey. An Exercise is proposed; the retreatant practices it and reports later to the retreat master. Both decode what happened and define the next step, which will test

the assumptions obtained by decoding. This work is not always easy and pleasant, but will, with its ups and downs, give good results (n. 6).

The Spiritual Exercises are not just internal actions; "spiritual" does not mean outside of daily life. Prayer is emphasized, but only to change our behaviors in this world where we meet God (n. 23), as the Examinations and many Rules show (n. 23–43, 210–217, 337–344). Ignatius already asserts here the goal of the Exercises (and n. 22): to become free from "inordinate attachments," discover God's will, and manage one's life accordingly in order to reach salvation (n. 169–189). He implies a warning to the retreat master, which is that if the retreatant does not become sufficiently free from attachments, it is not realistic to hope for a satisfying discovery of God's will, a new orientation, or a clear Correction of Life (done at the time of Election, n. 168–189).

So the Exercises are not an end in themselves but *a technique for making a discovery* ("preparing and disposing" echoes "Prepare the way of the Lord," Mt 3:3). They don't always succeed; that is why some retreat masters don't give them to everyone who asks but try to get to know each candidate a bit beforehand.

[2] Since the Exercises are not an intellectual matter, the retreat master does not give wordy lectures to the retreatant about methods or texts to use (when we prepare our prayer, we read footnotes, commentary, etc.). On the contrary, the retreat master shares a minimum of insights, not because of lack of trust in the retreatant's intelligence, but in order to keep the retreatant's intellect sufficiently quiet in prayer. Ignatius, like most spiritual masters, favors another kind of knowledge, served and not ruled by the intellect (n. 53). It is a knowledge more intuitive than rational, on the order of "savoring"—the word *gustus* ("taste, flavor") is found twice in the Annotation—and it can never be separated from its impact on the retreatant's emotions. In the Bible, the place of such knowledge is usually called the "heart." We have here a warning against any rationalization, which is treated in n. 6.

Also, this refusal to overwhelm with lectures, which would reinforce the retreat master's influence, gives priority to the freedom of both God and the retreatant. This liberates retreatants from scruples like, "I should act according to the retreat master's words," and it guarantees personal discoveries more convincing than ones received secondhand. Ignatius believes that retreatants can manage, by themselves or through divine inspiration, any proposed text or method, and he wants to lessen as much as possible the retreat master's impact on their spiritual journey, out of respect for the unique relationship between God and the individual. This respect explains all the advice about adjusting everything to the retreatant's own nature.

What does "the basis of the historical truth" mean? The gospel, being the subject of prayer in the Exercises, might call on retreat masters to assure the necessary information for Christian faith: that God became historically a human being, Jesus (n. 102).

[3] Through the topic of reverence, Ignatius warns retreat master and retreatant about problems created by the emphasis on emotional knowledge (n. 2). Our intellect can revere God as known rationally as unconditional Love, for instance. Our emotional approach is less predictable, for when we are touched internally and react, we don't control well our subconscious projections onto God, born in the inner wounds of our childhood. For example, in our gut feelings we might be furious against God, because we project onto this authority figure our anger against our parents, who did not give us the love we wanted. Retreat master and retreatant must not be surprised by this and must learn how to deal with it.

[4] After the First Week, the Exercises follow Jesus' life. Thus the retreatant shares the disciples' experience. The pattern here is the thirty-day retreat, which ends, as scheduled, wherever retreatants may have arrived; some don't reach the Ascension. Ignatius' concern about adjusting the process to the individual retreatant urges the retreat master to be flexible within the general structure; such freedom aims at respecting the retreatant's individuality. This creates some problems when the retreat is for a group of retreatants (e.g., scheduling the same break days for all retreatants). The Three Methods of Praying are included in the process, probably because

Ignatius does not want to let the retreatant leave the retreat without these useful tools of prayer life.

[5] This answers a possible question from the retreatant, "What do I have to do first?" It is a call not to stay with too specific expectations and limit our hope while starting the Exercises, for God's "power now at work in us can do immeasurably more than we ask or imagine," and "God is greater than our hearts" (Eph 3:20; 1 Jn 3:20). It is also a call to offer ourselves totally at the beginning, no less than at the end (n. 234; this is often named the circularity of the Exercises). This was Samuel's behavior when he said, "Speak, LORD, for your servant is listening" (1 Sm 3:10). This invitation is necessary, because some Annotations imply the possibility of some difficult times for the retreatant (n. 6, 7, 9, 10). Openness and offering of the self presuppose a retreatant who is trying to trust God and not be scared by the adventure, to be free and let God be free as well.

The Annotation also suggests that, at least at the level of the will, the retreatant must refuse any conscious opposition to God's work, desires, and revelations. God is named Creator here, with no mention of Jesus; we might think that, because we are just starting the Exercises, we have here the necessary minimum about God: someone who made us, and who therefore already has some bond with the retreatant. During the process of the retreat, God will become more than that. Praying with Mary's extravaganza in Bethany may help (Jn 12:1–11).

Let us notice that the Latin text of V is not clear about who "might decide" *(statuat)* about the retreatant's person and possessions. Since the Exercises are being made to help retreatants to reach a decision through their Election, we chose to attribute the verb to the retreatant and not to God. Texts A and P seem, on the contrary, to portray God as the One who employs, uses, and disposes of the retreatant, through the verbs *"utatur"* (A) or *"disponat"* (P).

[6] Information depends on consolations and desolations that are part of emotional knowledge (n. 3). Ignatius worries if the retreatant does not feel any of these. Both retreat master and retreatant must discover why (Is there some denial, resistance, fear,

or is the retreatant not ready for the Exercises, etc.?). They have to look at what is going on in the retreatant's life, and also verify if the method given by the retreat master is observed (n. 319), for it is the retreat master's job to guide the proceeding. However, the Annotation means that it is normal during the retreat for the retreatant to experience diverse motions, both upward and downward, which are usually necessary for any discoveries; the worst state is probably to be lukewarm (Rv 3:15). These movements, pleasant or not, are the soil for discernment (n. 89, 176, 183); nothing is wasted! It is advisable to tell the retreatant at the beginning about all of this and to guarantee more explanations later. It also appears here that retreat master and retreatant have both submitted to the method of the Exercises, which is a specific pedagogical way to pray with the gospel that Ignatius discovered during the first years of his conversion.

[7] This Annotation seems obvious, but I have heard that some retreat masters behave like authority figures. They order, judge, moralize, and force decisions or changes, forgetting that they are only the indirect witnesses of what occurs between God and the retreatant.

Like n. 6, the Annotation says that the Exercises might be tough going for retreatants, and that it is unwise to add to it any harshness from the retreat master, who must behave like Jesus' God. This is essential, for the dynamics of the Exercises sometimes transform the retreat master into a subconscious symbol of God for the retreatant (n. 22). Also, though a retreat master might find it easy to be gentle with a desolate retreatant, he or she might not be so gentle toward the retreatant's temptations, such as erotic fantasies, despair, exploding anger, etc. Ignatius knows that when one tries to face God, it can become a time of terrible temptations, for he himself was tempted by suicide in Manresa. Thus this Annotation describes a test for the retreat master's balance and wisdom, for his or her freedom, hope, and faith. The retreat master is gentle, kind, and encouraging (n. 5), both unveiling the enemy's deceits and functioning as a consolation (n. 315–316).

The word "soon" (not found in text A or P) applied to the consolation to come expresses Ignatius' certainty, hope, and faith, and invites the retreat master to have the same. Again, it is advisable to tell the retreatant that temptations may come during the process and to point out that they will be a source of useful information (n. 17).

[8] Unsurprisingly, Ignatius now points out the use of the Rules for Discernment. However, he says "can be used" and not "must be used." The following Annotations might explain this, for all the Rules are not made for all retreatants. Also, this gives the retreat master the possibility of using other means found elsewhere; for instance, in other currents of spirituality.

[9] For Ignatius, some Rules of Discernment are for everyone and some are not. Is this spiritual discrimination? I'll go back to this when I comment on the Rules (n. 313–314). But the Annotation clearly says that even people not knowledgeable about spiritual matters can make the Exercises. Ignatius simply recommends *postponing* teaching them the Rules of the Second Week, probably until they have matured. Thus the retreat master must give this retreatant what he or she can fruitfully absorb; no more, no less. This again stems from respect for the retreatant. In fact, in many Ignatian religious congregations novices make the Exercises soon after entering; often, many of them are not very experienced in spiritual matters.

[10] Some commentators have tried to reconcile the four Weeks with the classical division of spiritual growth into the purgative, illuminative, and unitive ways*; the task has never been easy, for Ignatius never said where the unitive way fit into the Exercises; morever, he expressed his discoveries in the language of his time, which is not always clear to the modern reader.

Thus many readers have misunderstood Ignatius. For instance, Ignatius learned an essentialist theology and yet knew, like all mystics, an experience that was "existentialist," emphasizing freedom and choice; even though, as a humanist, he has a cosmic vision, we cannot expect him to be like a contemporary environ-

---

* The most effective attempt is found in *La dialectique des Exercices spirituels de Saint Ignace de Loyola*, by Gaston Fessard, Paris: Aubier, 1956.

mentalist; although he is focusing on individual freedom, he lives in a social and religious world extremely hierarchical and not democratic.

However, for us, when the process starts, it is important and sufficient for both retreat master and retreatant to know that temptations might come "under the appearance of good," and to learn what to do then. A minimum of explanation is given in n. 14–15.

[11] This is the usual motto of spiritual masters, "Focus on the present moment." It is also given because neither retreat master nor retreatant know what is going to happen later.

[12–13] Both Annotations concern how to manage time in prayer (see *Structure of a Retreat* in Appendix [p. 228]). The retreatant must stay at peace if the prayer period lasts a little longer than decided: The decision was to give God sixty minutes; if this is done honestly, the contract has been fulfilled, and such fidelity must give peace. This is important for prayer periods with no strong consolations; touched internally or not, the retreatant gives God the promised time; and if nothing spectacular happens, the retreatant loves God gratis.

I say to retreatants, "We lose track of time when feelings are powerful; but normally we are conscious of it. If prayer is very appealing, let us stop at the decided time so that we avoid spiritual greed, which aims at the gifts and forgets the Giver. If it is not easy to pray, let us stay one or two more minutes; it is too short a time to feed any pride in spiritual athletics, but sufficient to face and overcome the frustration of our selfish spiritual sensuality." I quote to the retreatant Saint Bernard's phrase to the devil, as Ignatius does: "It is not for you that I have started this, it is not for you that I will end it" (n. 351).

[14] The Tenth Annotation mentioned the temptation under the appearance of good and the use of the Rules of Discernment for the Second Week. Here, Ignatius cautions the retreat master in the event that the retreatant thinks it advisable to make any promise or vow (n. 332–336). In a stronger expression than in texts A and P, our text recommends opposition to such a thought occurring during great consolation and fervor (chiefly if a retreatant appears to be unstable).

For Ignatius, to invite people to consider religious life is an option that the retreat master must not reject. However, during the Exercises a very careful and wise caution is required when emotions are great (by looking at the individual person's situation, at the advantages and disadvantages of such a promise, we prepare the fourth point of the Election, where the soul is supposed to be quiet, not overly consoled, n. 181). This kind of temptation is so risky that Ignatius goes back to it in Annotation 15.

[15] The Fourteenth Annotation forbids the retreatant to make any promise in time of great consolation. The Fifteenth Annotation forbids the retreat master in strong terms to push the retreatant to follow any particular direction. This would be "under the appearance of good" a temptation for the retreat master, who would thus interfere with the work of God and with the retreatant's free will. The retreat master is neither God nor the retreatant, and so, because no one can slide in as a mediator between God and another, the retreat master must be very discreet and keep an equilibrium like the one suggested to the retreatant who is making a decision (n. 179). Both retreatant and retreat master must try to remain free; "indifferent" is the term used by the spiritual writers. Both the Fourteenth and the Fifteenth Annotations imply the retreat master-retreatant relationship during the Exercises is so special that actions usually acceptable (e.g., inviting people to consider religious life) are totally forbidden during this time.

[16] This is the first time that the notion often translated by the word "attachment" appears. It is a key word in the Exercises. It designates a bond we may have with a person or a thing so emotionally strong that it influences our behaviors (to my knowledge, it is only in the Rules about alms, n. 337–344, that we find the concept of attachment to a human being). If such a bond aims at "something less than proper," it works against God. In texts A and P, such attachment usually goes with the adjective "inordinate"; in our text it can be "inordinate" but also "harmful," "an impediment to salvation," "distorted," "carnal or worldly" (n. 21, 150, 154, 172, 173); however, it can also come from God (n. 184).

The problem evoked here is essential, for its solution is one of the reasons for the Exercises (n. 1, 21); God cannot reveal to the retreatant the road to take if the retreatant is already attached to something in a disorderly way, for the die is cast. As soon as the retreat starts and the Annotations are given to the retreatant, he or she is invited to make efforts against any known inordinate attachment, in order to achieve distance and become freer and more open to what God will say—to attain a certain equilibrium that was recommended to the retreat master in the Fifteenth Annotation (n. 21, 23, 173, 150, 153, 154, 155, 157, 179, 184).

To make efforts in the opposite direction constitutes a generalization here of one note about scruples (n. 350). Those efforts, made by the retreatant "in order to offer himself to God," imply trust in God. Such trust is not always present at the beginning of the process, nor is having the divine worship and honor as the ultimate reason for a decision (n. 23, 168, 79); this Annotation more directly prepares the retreatant for the Principle or Foundation (n. 23).

[17] This Annotation deserves the words "most useful"; its first sentence, too, which asserts that the retreat master must not will (*nolens*) to know the retreatant's thoughts and sins. But the retreat master must know what "the different spirits" suggest to the retreatant, in order to be helpful.

The mention of "a greater or a lesser good" here, and of temptations in n. 9–10, have taught me to comment thus: After having explained the Annotation, I point out that Ignatius never encouraged retreatants to go to confession to the retreat master, assuming he is a priest (the Annotations don't say that the retreat master has to be a priest). I affirm to the retreatant that I have no right to know his or her sins, and I add, "But it does help if you can talk about your temptations. Often they reveal more about us than our sins. For instance, when we don't act on our thoughts but let our mind fantasize unbridled. If you talk about your sins, know that I'll listen to you, not as a moralist, a judge, or an authority who can tie or untie, but with one single question in mind: What does that mean in your journey with God? For my first duty is to help you to discern." There is no room for an unhealthy curiosity on the part of retreat masters, although they must do their job, which includes asking questions about the Exercises (n. 6).

[18] Ignatius explains the adjustments mentioned in n. 4 and n. 9, which allow practically anybody to make the Exercises. He asks the retreat master to adjust them to the retreatant's idiosyncrasies. The minimum is: The First Week, the Examinations, the Modes of Prayer, some teaching about Christian doctrine, and an invitation to go regularly to confession and to receive Communion more frequently than was usual for that century.

Ignatius does not explain the words "mediocre progress and fruits" or the opposite. I have said (n. 9) that I would clarify this apparent spiritual discrimination when I comment on the Rules of discernment (n. 313–314); but Ignatius imagines a retreat master able to evaluate the retreatant's capacities at least before the Second Week. We can remember that some of the first Jesuits who became "brothers" only, and not priests, were very simple people. Finally, the remark about the limitations of time could suggest that Ignatius aims at effectiveness by favoring "better" retreatants. However, I think it expresses, rather, a mixture of realism and seriousness in the business, based on respect for the uniqueness of each retreatant. For me, this says to the retreat master, "Respect and don't force those whose capacities or desires are limited, because it won't work; but give them all they can handle (and this is already a lot). Propose the maximum to those who want it and can use it with great benefit. This shows your respect for all."

[19] This passage explains how the Exercises can be made in daily life. It illustrates Ignatius' saying "To find God in all things" and is a great adjustment for many laypeople. Not everyone can afford to make a retreat in a secluded way (n. 20), because of the expense and time commitment involved.

The Nineteenth Annotation offers the solution. Ignatius sets as conditions that the retreatant have the time to make two examinations of himself and pray formally one hour a day and, surprisingly, that the retreatant be "gifted and cultured." I explain this point thus: A person who is making the Exercises in daily life cannot be weak-minded, for it is necessary to overcome with determination the distractions created by daily concerns (family, work, etc.). Ignatius knew this (and so do I) from all the times he had given very busy people, many of them laypeople, this sort of retreat. Ignatius states clearly the number of days spent with the First Week but gives no information about the length of the other Exercises.

For me, this lack of information from a very meticulous man says that he does not want to predetermine the pace that daily life will give the retreat (this is another form of respecting the retreatant). Through daily events and with the retreatant, God will be the One deciding the tempo and the steps of the dance. I give the retreatant the time necessary to pass through all the Exercises; it has usually been around six to seven months, with some pauses occasionally, consisting of short stays in a retreat house for evaluations, clarifications, timeouts in moments of crisis, etc.

[20] This describes the usual way of making the Exercises, of which the prototype is a thirty-day retreat (n. 4): in solitude in a secluded place with no distractions caused by things or people. Ignatius explains the advantages, maybe in comparison with the method of the Nineteenth Annotation (where no advantage is listed). Does this show his preference? No doubt, freedom, solitude, conditions more conducive to concentration of mind, and access to daily Office and Eucharist, put the retreatant in a sort of "laboratory." So the encounter with God frequently takes on more force and clarity than in daily life.

However, I see a unique and priceless advantage of a retreat according to n. 19, unknown in a thirty-day retreat; in this latter, our daily life enters into our spiritual journey through memory *only*; thus the legitimate and frequent question of some retreatants at the end of the retreat is, "How am I going to integrate into my normal life what I discovered here?" In contrast, the Exercises in daily life intertwine permanently prayer and day-to-day situations, and so the Good News more easily becomes the daily news and vice versa. Making the Exercises in daily life also removes the risks of delusion we experience when we are too much out of the world. Moreover, we often forget that Ignatius envisions retreatants making a retreat at home; I know that this solution has given retreatants the grace of making a "sacred ground" within their own home, and of understanding that God can be found not only in every*thing* but also every*where*.

Ignatius does not say anything about meetings between retreat master and retreatant, except to urge retreatants to write down the essential of the Exercises, probably while listening to the retreat master. This suggests that either the retreat master visits the retreatant at home or wherever the retreat takes place, or that the retreatant is the one going to where the retreat master is. There is nothing about this question in n. 19: So, for the Exercises in daily life, I meet retreatants wherever it is convenient for them. What could be more symbolic of God met in ordinary life than to discern with the retreatant in a train station, a mall, or a McDonald's? (It is interesting that Ignatius speaks of "business less directly relevant to God's worship" in text V, as opposed to "business not rightly relevant" in A and P, even though, in n. 357, he sees "business and marriage" rather as diverting us from the perfection of Christian life, to which religious vows lead us.) We usually meet for around one hour (in a thirty-day retreat, the daily appointment has never been longer than thirty minutes; I was surprised once to hear a retreat master say, "*I* need longer than one hour, because of what *I* have to say.").

GOAL AND PRESUPPOSITION OF THE EXERCISES

[21] The title does not mention God but implies that something in us must become free (n. 47 speaks of a prison). An analogy can be made to a desire that cannot fully exist because of obstacles (see Desire in the Appendix [p. 224]). The Exercises have been called a "school of freedom"; they are not an ethical undertaking, but they deal with the condition for any ethical life, freedom (for service, as we'll see later). We must say *individual* freedom, for Ignatius is one of the pioneers who opened the way for such a discovery. The tendency in his time earlier was to think in terms of a hierarchical social group; for instance, his contemporaries subscribed to *Cujus regio, hujus religio*, meaning that people of a land were of the same faith of their leader. But the term "liberation" is even more accurate than "freedom," because we cannot be perfectly free.

I explain to retreatants, "We become fre*er*, for the knowledge we acquire allows us to manage our life without being too enslaved by our more or less conscious attachments and dependencies, as we were before. It does not mean that we *look* better. Our new freedom might even make us look less good than we did before, for example, if we have always said yes to people in order to please them, and if we become free enough to say no to them when necessary." The Principle or Foundation (n. 23) will start to expose the retreatant to this work of the liberation of inordinate or harmful attachments found here (n. 1, 16).

[22] The first condition for the Exercises to work successfully is that the best possible communication and understanding exist between retreat master and retreatant. The one who has to "kindly correct" the other is not clear in Latin; it probably means the retreat master (n. 7). But the retreatant may be misunderstood, too, and may have to correct the retreat master! After all, it is the retreatant who hears God speaking to him or her, and the retreat master must strive to understand the retreatant in order to understand God as well. So the text invites both retreat master and retreatant to make efforts to understand each other.

At the conscious level, this advice is obvious, but it is not so at another level. The dynamics of the Exercises often cause the retreatant to project onto the retreat master the image of an authority figure, and thus of God—the ultimate authority figure—acquired more or less consciously during childhood. The retreat master must be able to discern and cope with that situation. I explain that dynamic to the retreatant, repeat what I said about the Seventeenth Annotation, and add, "For instance, you might feel angry with me; just let me know, and we'll discern what might be behind that feeling. You may also feel afraid to speak about something with me; try to figure out why and to discern if you can talk about it."

This is yet another reason for the retreat master to have a respectful attitude toward the retreatant. But if it is evident that communication and mutual trust are impossible (e.g., because of clashes between two very opposed natures or theologies), it would be better for both not to continue working together. The question to discern then is if the retreatant cannot make the Exercises or must make them with another retreat master.

N. 22 opens the Exercises by stating that "first of all" the individual freedom, or liberation, of the retreatant is accessible through a mutually respectful relationship between him or her and the retreat master, and that the retreat master's role is possible only if this condition is realized. This strong statement gives the lie to those who say that the Exercises favor individualistic behavior, for it asserts that relationship is essential for the revelation of everything that is supposed to happen, even between God and the individual (and this relationship is symbolized by the necessary and unavoidable dialogue between retreatants and retreat masters).

That emphasis on relationship is present throughout the Exercises: With God as Creator, *through* created "things" in the Principle or Foundation (n. 23); with a forgiving God *through* angels, cosmos, people, and Christ as a crucified friend in the First Week (n. 53, 54, 60, 71); with God *through* fellowship with Jesus and His disciples in the other Weeks (n. 95, 146, 167, 197, 221); with God as Lover, *through* everything and everybody, *through* the Church (n. 230–237, 352–370); and even, somehow, *through* consolation if we remember that Ignatius speaks of the risen Jesus comforting His own, "employing the similitude of consolation that can be offered by a best friend" (n. 224).

We know that for Ignatius, the origin of relationship as defining our identity is not just in our Creation by God, but in the Trinity; in that Divine Union, relationships define the different Persons as Origin, Begotten One, and Interplay of Love, and define us as children of the same God through the Word made flesh and the Spirit's presence in us. Accordingly, the *first* Exercise of the *first* day of the Second Week *starts* with the decision of the three Persons about Incarnation (n. 102). This gives retreatant and retreat master a criterion of discernment: Although prayer and solitude, discernment and decision, perception of self and other things or people, cannot be other than self-centered, something is probably wrong in the retreatant's spiritual journey and discoveries if he or she forgets the world.

Principle or Foundation

[n. 23]

SITUATION AND PURPOSE OF THE TEXT

This capital text is mentioned only once in the Exercises: The Nineteenth Annotation refers to it as starting the Exercises (one sentence of Ignatius in a draft for a Directory does not give us useful information about that). Nowhere is it asserted as part of a Week (nor is the "Contemplation for stimulating within us spiritual love" at the end; the Jesuits say it more briefly: Contemplation *ad Amorem*). Thus it is often given to retreatants over the course of a few days before they begin a thirty-day retreat. I see it as a presupposition: Before entering the Exercises, retreatants get their bearings as sailors do, in order to see where they are spiritually in this world of God (n. 15, 21); they do the same with the Contemplation *ad Amorem* at the end (n. 230), and verify if they have harvested one of the fruits of the Exercises, "to find God in all things."

The first word of the text is "man" and not God; but this meshes with the humanist Ignatius and immediately sets the tone of the Exercises: We human beings are the subjects of an adventure with God in the cosmos. The text seems to be about our creation; it is, to the degree that everything depends on our origin, the fact that we are created, and, for Ignatius, in the certainty that "all things have been created because of man" (cf Gn 1:28–29). But the first phrase *literally* aims at what we must achieve on earth: To praise, revere, and serve God, and be saved.

N. 169 and 179 keep only "praise," emphasizing the priority given to praise in the beginning of the Principle or Foundation and of the Exercises. This implies that we see reasons for praise not only in the fact that we exist, but everywhere (*The Contemplation ad Amorem* lists some, n. 230–237); and so it makes us verify how we look at ourselves, our environment, at God, and at our *history*. If we can see God's gifts there, we are grateful and easily praise (this is clear in the Contemplation *ad Amorem*), and it is worthwhile to embark on such a journey; if not, we might be tempted to quit before starting it.

And so I invite retreatants to list God's gifts that they received through other people and things in the events of their life, whether pleasant or not. Such a "holy history of my life" shows a God so bountiful that the word "God" can be changed to "Love." A Love we came from and go back to, from our conception and birth till our death; a Love permanently all around us and creating us. Such discoveries, made by pondering the Principle or Foundation, provoke *gratitude and praise* in the retreatant.

Ignatius then asserts that everything in this world is given us to reach our end (this gives a beautiful dimension to our environment), but that we must use only things that do so. Thus he takes into account the specifics of individuals, times, and places: "this" thing helps me but not you, now but not tomorrow, here but not elsewhere. A discernment and a choice are implied here, although the words "to choose" appear in the last phrase only, and this is solely an individual matter. A specific human being has to build himself or herself through his or her choices.

After those assertions, Ignatius gives us the *principle* of behaving: As long as our discernment is not complete, "we must harbor no difference among all created things" and remain interiorly *free*. Things are created for us, we are not created for them, and we lose ourselves if and when we let anything or anybody rule us. Rooted in the world, we must keep a certain distance in the face of a choice (1 Cor 7:29–31). Commentators on the Exercises see here the famous notion of "indifference" (the word itself is never used by Ignatius). Understood rightly, this notion shows that our choice does not deal with two opposed terms, "health" or "sickness," for instance, but with three. "God" is the third term for believers. That which *helps* us to reach [1] or *prevents* us from reaching [2] our *end* according to God [3].

To stay free before two alternatives does not mean "I don't care," but "I so much desire the end God wants me to discover that it does not matter for me which way I must take to get there." Illustrating this, I say to the retreatant, "Picture this: to be sick but in love or to be healthy without love." *Preference* is the root of indifference (it is clear in the last sentence of n. 179). Thus, before our discernment is over and tells us which road to follow (the Election is still far off), it is advisable for us to be open to all possible alternatives, i.e., to be free.

DISCOVERIES

The explanations given above create no problem for our intellect, but this is not always the case in terms of our "gut feelings." The text confronts our conscious or subconscious perceptions of ourselves, the world, and God, and they do not always lead to freedom, gratitude, and praise. The wounds and gratifications we have experienced in our lives since childhood have created in us a particular image of ourselves, our environment, and God that may make it difficult or impossible for us to be free, to thank and praise. A conflict is within us. For example: If we still feel within ourselves that we were unloved children, we will find it difficult to thank and praise God, for we can't easily be free when life does not quench our subconscious thirst for love; if in the past we were badly ill or very successful, we might not easily be able to say today "it does not matter" in regard to sickness or health, honor or contempt, and give thanks and praise in all circumstances. Ignatius rightly uses the word "desire," for in spite of the agreement of our *intellect* with the Principle or Foundation, we may not *at gut level* have integrated well enough our relationship with ourselves, others, and God, and may not *desire* freedom, gratitude, and praise (n. 3; see *Desire* in Appendix [p. 224]).

Thus the Principle or Foundation sets the stage for the journey of the Exercises. The actors are now there: God and the retreatant with conscious or subconscious attachments. It is a first step on the road to liberation, liberation from the impact of the dangerous attachments created by our more or less conscious perception of ourselves, others, and God on our behaviors (n. 21). It is a *foundation* of what is to come in the Exercises, for it reveals where the retreatant *really* is right now. Pleasant or not, this truth is good, for it will set the retreatant free and give him or her a rock to build on (Jn 8:32; Mt 7:24–27). A mistake for retreat master or retreatant would be to expect one hundred percent freedom at this stage of the Exercises. The greatest freedom I saw was in retreatants starting a thirty-day retreat; but they were far from home, daily work and problems, and it did not last too long. In shorter retreats or in the Exercises in daily life, it is different.

So I warn the retreatant, "If you feel one hundred percent free, enjoy such a grace. But don't be too affected if you realize that you are only sixty percent or zero percent free, because of inordinate attachments in your life. To feel oppositions in ourselves is a necessary step toward liberation, and the Exercises are intended precisely to increase and deepen our freedom" (n. 5, 21, 155, 179). In fact, the discovery of a lack of freedom prepares retreatants to enter the First Week.

SUGGESTIONS

The word "suggestion" is accurate, for it implies that retreatants (with the Spirit) verify if what is given to them by the retreat master is appropriate for them; my suggestions to retreatants are based on what I call my "assumptions," for I am never sure about what I think I have "heard" through their report, or what stage of the Exercises we are at. So here I ask retreatants to pray with the Principle or Foundation; I translate "to be finally saved" by "to be finally forever with God, who is Love." I explain, "It is often difficult to pray with Ignatius' texts, which are dense syntheses of elements of faith through a theology that is not always up-to-date. But we must continue to try them." For the texts of Scripture, I suggest, "Select the ones giving you consolation; pray with them as long as they touch your heart strongly enough" (see *Structure of a Retreat* in Appendix, and commentary about Rules of discernment [p. 80]).

If retreatants find praying with Ignatius' texts tiring, I invite them to make "sandwiches" with "slices" of Ignatius' text, then "slices" of Scripture, then back to Ignatius. The Bible refreshes us sufficiently to return to Ignatius. And also, given that the goal of the Exercises is to meet God, why would we wait to deal with God's Word Itself?

I then invite retreatants to list the graces received (in the past year for short retreats, in their whole life for long ones). Rereading our life is to do what Israel did to commemorate the Covenant (Jos 24). First, looking at their past, up to their creation as God's People (Genesis and Exodus), they recognized God's fidelity; then, comforted by such a history, they looked at the future with hope, certain that God would be faithful again; but this challenged them to choose God "here and now." Listing the graces he or she has personally received invites the retreatant to share Israel's certainty and hope (at least for the coming retreat), and to be present to God right now.

Ignatius mentions "things" only as aids to help us reach our goal; this is unsurprising as he lived in a time when the technical mastery of nature by humankind was first being emphasized. Accordingly, he does not talk about the value of things: The question is what we *do* with them. I invite retreatants to add people to the list of blessings; for, serving us or needing us, they are sacraments of Love, of God loving us or calling us to love (and people, like things, can inhibit our freedom if we are unhealthily dependent on them).

I also suggest that retreatants stay for a while with the memory of blessings that console them. Thus life appears to the retreatant as a permanent gift of God, who desires us from the beginning till the end, even before our conception (Jer 1:5). Even if our parents didn't desire our conception, at least God desired us!

For the first phrase of the Principle or Foundation and the list of graces, I recommend Ephesians 1:1–14, Psalm 139; 1 Corinthians 1:4–9; 3:21–23, and to make a personal Psalm 136 help to give thanks and praise; for the "holy history of my life," and God's everlasting love fashioning us each day through events, Jeremiah 1, 18, and 31; Isaiah 43:1–5 are precious texts. Also, quoting Luther, "We are loved not because we are beautiful, but we are beautiful because we are loved," I mention the Song of Songs where bride and bridegroom are in ecstasy in front of each other's beauty; so might the retreatant be before God, so *is* God before the retreatant.

Concerning freedom, I give Romans 8:28–39, 1 Kings 3:1–15 (or Gn 13, where Abraham's "indifference" is immediately rewarded by God). I always give several texts from Scripture, so the retreatant can select the ones that bring him or her consolation (also because I don't know where he or she is right now). The Spirit tells the retreatant's heart which word of God fits him or her for today.

Jesus is not mentioned in the Principle or Foundation. Ignatius was giving the Exercises to Christians in a Christian society, where Jesus would always be implicitly present, so His lack of explicit presence was probably not a problem for anyone in Ignatius' own time. But how can we explain this absence? Maybe Ignatius, who wants the retreatants to share the disciples' experience, puts them before the Incarnation, as members of the People of the Covenant before Jesus. God is there, but not yet seen in Christ.

It is only in the Second Week that Jesus becomes the center of contemplation. Perhaps also Ignatius had realized that some retreatants were not, in their "will," dealing with Jesus' God, but with other gods unveiled by the Principle or Foundation (n. 3). If so, the Principle or Foundation works as a mechanism to facilitate a first awareness and purification of the retreatant's faith. This corroborates what I said earlier: The god of our gut feelings is often far from the evangelical God. So Ignatius would try to save Jesus' God from being confused with the god we carry within us. Accordingly, when we meet Christ's God in the First Week, we face a God we cannot be afraid of, angry at, cautious with, etc.: a God who is other than any of our subconscious idols.

Some people are also surprised that "to serve" is in third position rather than first or second. Retreatants soon discover that a service not rooted in gratitude is probably grounded in slavery of one kind or another.

Retreat master and retreatants must remember that any text requires some interpretation. For instance: The word "man" means "human being"; therefore, women can apply the texts to themselves. Or the notion of "reverence" reminds us that God must be treated as God; however, here "reverence" also refers to the obedient love of a vassal for his lord, with a connotation not of humiliation but of honor (the Spanish word means "loving humility"). Finally, it is desirable for the retreat master to have an acquaintance with the theology of Ignatius' time and the beginnings of the Reformation, so that he or she can explain matters to the retreatant that might otherwise create unnecessary problems.

First Week

[n. 45–90]

INTRODUCTION

FROM THE PRINCIPLE OR FOUNDATION
TO THE FIRST WEEK

The Principle or Foundation speaks of a God already-for-us, a Love making a beautiful Creation—which includes us—but not yet a *saving* Love. The next step is to realize that we need to be saved. For our wrong choices and our misuse of God's gifts often hindered us from achieving the end we were created for. We do not yet conduct ourselves with a determination free from harmful attachments. What was implied in the Principle or Foundation emerges: We are sinners. To truthfully locate ourselves in relation to ourselves, others, and God elicits this acknowledgment. Retreatants are often the first ones to mention their sinfulness (n. 17); this signals the retreat master that the First Week can be started (when retreats work well, retreatants are often "ahead" of the next step in the process, showing that the logic of the Exercises functions by itself). So, finishing the Principle or Foundation, the retreatant says, "This is great, but *I* am far from great!" Thus the retreatant announces his or her readiness for the First Week, in which Ignatius will teach the retreatant to pray about sin correctly.

THE FUNDAMENTAL GOAL OF THE WEEK
AND ITS CONSEQUENCES

The colloquy is the time when our will and our heart express us in a very personal way to God; here, we find Ignatius' hope for

116

the retreatant. In n. 71 and 61, we read, "The greatest thanks shall be given" and "a colloquy praising the infinite mercy of God, giving Him thanks." So the purpose of the Week is to allow the retreatant to experience *gratitude* to God, repeating the logic of the Principle or Foundation. But this occurs now before a merciful and forgiving Love, with the features of Jesus dying on the cross for us (n. 53). A prayer about sin not rooted in gratitude to God cannot guarantee healthy fruit.

I said that the desire *to serve* comes from gratitude: The colloquy proves that, for there the retreatant says in front of the Crucified One, "What worthy of being mentioned have I done thus far for Christ? What will I do eventually, or what must I do?" (n. 53, which echoes Acts 2:37). The desire to act that is born here will bloom in the Second Week through the imitation of Jesus and the Election and is already a positive use of freedom, a "yes" and not a "no" to God. But we cannot act intelligently and according to God's desire without *knowledge*. So in the colloquy of n. 63, we ask for the grace of knowing the negative paths free humans follow, in ourselves and in the world. A prayer about sin that does not look for knowledge won't bring effective changes.

In sum, this is what occurs during the First Week: Full of gratitude, the retreatant wants to use his or her freedom to serve the God who saves in Jesus and asks for the grace of knowing what sin is all about, in order to avoid saying "no" to God and to be able to say "yes" adequately.

EXAMINATIONS
[n. 24–44]

(We speak of Examinations here, their place in Ignatius' book. But it would be better to consult this section after *reading what concerns the First Week. Thus they won't be overemphasized, for the focus must stay first on retreatants' experiences during the Exercises themselves.)*

This part shows Ignatius' concern to teach methods that he thinks helpful for spiritual growth (even for someone "limited in his capacities," n. 1, 18, 19). Socrates said, "Know yourself." Every wisdom tradition has taught people to examine themselves in order to correct wrong thinking and acting. This section of the Exercises has often been misunderstood: It is not pure ascetical theology, because its root is a mystical experience of Jesus' God through the Exercises, which endlessly emphasize God's grace.

All serious mystical attempts have always generated *some* asceticism, for if asceticism does not always lead to love, love *does* always lead to sacrifices for the beloved. These pages summarize the teaching of the Church of that time about this subject, trying to keep a balance between the twin risks of laxity and scrupulosity. Sometimes it is helpful to remind retreatants of the obvious, like some of the precepts expressed in n. 41.

The examination of n. 43 is famous, but unfortunately has often been reduced to two of the five points (to see the sins committed and ask for forgiveness). The first two points assert clearly that we start by giving "thanks to God our Lord for all the benefits received" (echo of the Principle or Foundation), and by asking for the grace of light and strength. So, in my view, the goal of examination is not just to look at our sins, but also to find where we are on the map of our spiritual journey. Just as sailors look at the stars to keep on course when sailing, we use examination to keep on the course we want to follow (or to go back to it, in the First Week).

Thus examination must be used to verify in any Week if we have answered a specific temporary call from God. For example, if right now the Lord invites me to be more abandoned, I examine when I was or was not so during the day. Examination was for Ignatius a daily (and somehow permanent) discernment process concerning God's calls and our answers, not only during a retreat, but throughout a lifetime.

We then read some remarks about the sacrament of Reconciliation. It is often good to invite retreatants to postpone this sacrament for a while, because their increasing knowledge can give a deeper dimension to their confession. Once, a retreatant said to me at the end of his retreat, "I am glad we delayed my confession; in fact, I won't make it with all the details I had in mind; I have realized that I wanted to impress the priest" (the matter was about his sexual life).

Concerning general confession, I have seen retreatants impelled to make one because their First Week had revealed a depth of their sins they had never before seen, as Ignatius says (n. 44). Or in other cases, retreatants desired to offer up to God the chains of evil they had started, of which they knew only the starting point, with the belief that the One who is Alpha and Omega could apply His grace to the whole.

My usual counsel is, "Make the kind of confession you feel at peace with; a general confession of all your sins, a confession about a specific sin all along your life, your usual confession, or no confession at all." As a retreat master, I have usually invited retreatants to go to a priest other than myself for confession; this is Ignatius' advice in his draft for a Directory (n. 4). As a matter of fact, the goal is different: In confession we look for absolution, with a retreat master we want to make discernment possible and effective (n. 17).

FIRST EXERCISE
[n. 45–54]

The Preparation

Ignatius piles up instructions for the retreat master who must remind (or teach) the retreatant how to pray; those instructions do not reappear in the following pages because they are no longer necessary. This Exercise is called "meditation" because of the use of intellect, memory, and will (n. 45, 50; see *Faculties of the Soul* in the Appendix [p. 225]). It starts with three steps that must be learned. With the preparatory prayer, we enter into God's presence, leaving behind our usual behaviors and companions for a special activity and Being: God's Person, glory, and service are the center of our attention, as the Principle or Foundation stated (n. 46). The first prelude is designed to give our imagination something to occupy it, so that it won't distract us (n. 47); later, it will be the main tool for prayer (n. 66–70, 114). It is a sort of mental construction of the "place" suggested by the text used during the prayer period (see *Contemplation* in Appendix [p. 221]).

It might seem strange to ask for a specific grace before praying with the suggested text ("what I desire," n. 48; see *Desire* in Appendix [p. 224]). This focuses our will on the topic of prayer, as we did with our imagination in the first prelude. It purifies our intention: Consciously, we want to be in tune with that topic (subconsciously, however, is another matter). In an act of freedom and trust, we freely ask God for what we desire, believing that the request is not made in vain. This step reminds us that any gift is God's grace; so, it is already in itself the affirmation that we depend on God.

These three steps, which depend on us and are made in a few minutes, are "preparing and disposing the soul" to God's grace in the heart; they are preparing the paths for God's action, as all the Exercises are supposed to do (n. 1). The rest is up to God; for instance, the retreatant might be so taken over by one of these preparations that it pervades the whole prayer period. That is acceptable, for it is God's decision. This may be why n. 71 does not even put the colloquy at the end of the prayer period.

THE THREE SINS [n. 50–53]

We are invited to pray about three sins that are extremes (extremes tend to reveal truths more clearly than usual situations) and show that sin affects all creatures, including angels (the same technique of using extremes is employed in n. 65–71, 136–146, 149–155, 165–167, 186–187).

At Ignatius' time, the angels' sin was believed as a fact. In it, we consider creatures outside of history committing with perfect awareness and freedom a perfect sin leading to the perfect break from God, which is hell. Adam and Eve are closer to us; their sin was seen as a historical event in Ignatius' epoch (for us their story is about the existential facts of the human condition, resembling myths in many other cultures). In a kind of innocence, Adam and Eve freely committed the first sin of our history, which started all the miseries of humankind up to the present. Next, we face a human sin that is "perfect" because its consequence is the ultimate one, hell; with this sin we are anywhere in human history. Angels, Adam and Eve, that human being, all have misused God's gifts. Can we discern a common thread in these three sins?

Praying about those radical "no's" to God makes us size up the marvelous gift of human freedom. The angels refused "through their *free* will to revere and obey their Creator" (this sounds like the Principle or Foundation; n. 50). Getting closer to our own situation with each of the three sins, we understand more and more the power of our own freedom. Later, I'll show that the first two sins must not be ignored in favor of the third, which is tempting because the third is the closest to our own condition; even now we can say that all the "no's" have the same structure.

Finally, in the colloquy, we ask ourselves about what we did and will do with our freedom. While reflecting about perfect freedom and our own, we see that we have said our "no's," actively or passively; but we have also discovered that, if we can say "no" to God, we can also say "yes" to God. For me, the common thread here is the vast capacity of our freedom. I find the proof of that at the end of the Exercises in the Contemplation *ad Amorem*: The *first* thing offered by the retreatant in the prayer, "Take, Lord…" is freedom (n. 234).

Psychologists see our first attempts toward freedom in our first "no's." Transgression seems to be our way of testing our freedom and others' love for us. And when we see ourselves spared (compared to some people, n. 50–52), forgiven, when love is given back to us in spite of what we did, we can say, "I am really loved!" Then, facing the "infinite goodness of God," we ask, "What will I do eventually or what must I do" in return? (n. 52, 53).

And so the realization of God's total love for us, complete respect for our freedom, and unconditional mercy for us through Jesus' death, creates in us gratitude, praise, and reverence, and hence the desire to serve. Our parents might have been the first ones revealing such a love to us. Our reactions result from meditation by our intellect, an attempt of objective analysis, rather than an emotional exploitation of the subject.

N. 54 implies God is our friend in Jesus Crucified; servants, in Ignatius' time, were members of a household for their lifetime and served their masters with a mixture of respect, gratitude, and love. With this in mind for the colloquy (n. 53), I say to retreatants, "How would we feel at the bedside of a dying friend who saved our life in an accident?"

FOLLOWING EXERCISES [n. 55–72]

SECOND EXERCISE

Gratitude impels us to sin no longer, and so to learn how to do that. The Second and Third Exercises clarify what generous retreatants must do: Examine the mechanism of their sins in their use of God's gifts in order to avoid them from now on. The better we know our slaveries, the more efficient is our fight against sin. Ignatius sounds very thorough (in the Examinations, too), but it is a question of consideration for others. He keeps the word *pudorem* (*vergoña* in Spanish, "shame," n. 48); it is the sense of decency we feel when we say to ourselves in the face of a temptation, "This would damage my beloved, me, and our relationship; I cannot do it. The thought of doing it makes me feel already ashamed!"

Thus the Second and Third Exercises favor an ascetic view of our behaviors, but first based on God's love for us and our love for God in return (n. 24–44). The Second Exercise invites us to look at our sins, their ugliness and consequences, and their opposition to God's being. But the fifth point leads to the colloquy: Given all the proofs of having been accepted and spared, protected and served, the retreatant gives thanks and wants to change. This is again gratitude and its fruit.

Concerning Ignatius' ugly picture of ourselves as sinners (n. 58), "our soul chained in this corruptible body as if in prison" (n. 47), I had to remind some retreatants that Ignatius knew firsthand hospitals and prisons of his time, because he never stopped ministering to people in those places that were of greater dereliction than today.

THIRD EXERCISE

Ignatius explains what he hopes for retreatants: "knowledge," not only of our sins, but of the "depravity of the world" (n. 63); this last point makes us aware that we are in solidarity with what we would call "collective sin." This grace is so large that we must "dwell longer and more diligently" on what we have noticed as affecting us the most (n. 62) and make a triple colloquy wherein we use intercessors to obtain from God the desired grace. For

Ignatius the best intercessors are Jesus and Mary. Such advocates show the importance of the requested grace (with perfect knowledge, would we sin? Look at the angels!). This colloquy *always* comes back for crucial Exercises (n. 64, 147, 148, 156, 159, 164, 168, 199). It's the gospel: Mary interceded with Jesus at Cana, and Jesus with God for Lazarus (Jn 2:1–12; 11:41).

FOURTH EXERCISE

This exercise starts a technique often used in the Exercises, repetition. It is "a kind of rumination over the same subjects" meditated on before, about "points and places" noticed as giving "consolation, desolation, or any spiritual impression" (n. 62, 64, 118); "insight, consolation, or desolation" show that we must "dwell longer and more diligently" on them, treat them "with more attention." This technique gives time for God's Word to sink into us and to produce all its fruit for the present time (see *Structure of a Retreat* in Appendix [p. 228]).

FIFTH EXERCISE

The Week ends with another extreme, the one created by the logic of a radical "no" to God: the total rupture from God in a situation of no-Love-at-all. The medieval description of hell shows the consequences of sin. This prayer drives the quest for knowledge to an extreme, too, as if this would work if the last Exercises did not; we ask for "an intimate apprehension of the pains" of those in hell, "so that, if by chance [we] should start to forget divine love, [we] would at least be kept from sinning by the fear of that punishment" (n. 65). This was a classical teaching. But Ignatius prefers that the retreatant feel gratitude, as the colloquy proves (n. 71).

Indeed, we must be grateful because we have been spared; but also, for a reason bigger than the protection of creatures, angels, saints, elements, etc. (n. 60). For God has not just been "sustaining [our] life until this day" (n. 61), but, in Christ, "has *walked with* [us] to this day with the greatest compassion and mercy" (n. 71; Mi 6:8).

This end of the Week announces the contemplation of God's companionship, in blood and flesh through Jesus, Emmanuel, God-with-us. Already, at the moment when retreatants see the extreme consequences of their sins, they are invited by Ignatius to be totally Christ-centered in the last colloquy of the Week (n. 71).

This exercise is not a meditation (with the three faculties of the soul, n. 65). It is made by applying the five senses of the imagination to the topic of prayer, although it is done here with things of "another" world. Contemplation usually consists in imagining the things and persons of the story we pray about. To apply the five senses means that we try to see, but also to hear, smell, taste, and touch what is in the scene. I explain in the Appendix such systematization (see *Contemplation* [p. 221], *Structure of a Retreat* [p. 228], and n. 227).

SUGGESTIONS

GENERAL REMARKS

Following the Principle or Foundation, as soon as we start the First Week, as retreat master, I mention gratitude as its fruit. I want to give the retreatant a criterion of discernment: Praying about sin is distorted if it does not produce gratitude; the retreatant is probably focusing on himself or herself, on his or her sins with laxity or a guilt complex. If a lax retreatant tells me, "I don't see big sins in my life," I say, "Is your love always perfect?" The lie of laxity is then impossible, because we often hurt ourselves and others. This explains my presentation of sin: It is when we damage the beauty of ourselves or others; sin disfigures the beauty implied in the Principle or Foundation, and this appeared in the disfigured crucified Jesus.

At the opposite extreme, a guilt complex is also a lie (n. 349–350). Despair, or utter lack of hope, is wrong because we are no longer under the Law but before the One who accomplished what the Law could not achieve (Gal, Rom). Salvation has been accomplished; it is not something we have to *find*, but something to which we return (Paul uses the past tense of verbs when speaking about salvation). We are sinners, but *saved sinners*, and it is a mistake to deal with only one of these two words. Also, we return not to something, but to Someone, God as Savior, when we end our prayer with Jesus on the cross. Neither laxity nor a guilt complex can resist God's immense Love manifested there.

My remarks explain why I prefer to suggest, as a first prelude, that the retreatant picture not "our soul chained in this corruptible body as if in prison" (n. 47), but rather Jesus on the cross as the colloquy does (n. 53). After all, when we sin, we stop treating other people, Jesus and his God, and even ourselves, as friends whom we love (n. 54).

THE THREE SINS

As I interpret this, Ignatius wants us to be more aware of the evil we often choose to do with our freedom, so we can understand that we can do something else—follow and imitate Jesus when we contemplate Him in the Weeks to come. Therefore it is useful to meditate about the sin of the angels, and of Adam and Eve. I remind retreatants that those who climb mountains, those who attempt suicide, and professional killers all freely take extreme risks; I mention that, as new Adams and Eves, when we sin, we start chains of evil that create calamities around us (and where are the *ends* of those chains?).

For this meditation, I suggest Ezekiel 28 or Genesis 3. For the third sin, I give 2 Samuel 11:1—12:7, the story of David and Bathsheba; there, a human being like us starts a chain of evil with covetousness and ends it with a murder. I think that we must select and stay in prayer with the sin affecting us the most, but I invite the retreatant to pray at least once with each one of the three.

SECOND AND THIRD EXERCISES

Retreatants review the sins of their past and add the word "Savior" to the "holy history" of their life. The picture is now *complete* because it is "the holy *and* sinful history" of the retreatant's life. The holy history of our life provokes our gratitude and praise for

God, *and* the sinful history of our life, forgiven by God in Jesus, does the same. In fact, it is our holy *redeemed* history. Our *whole* truth is there.

It's not very fruitful merely to list our sins (except perhaps for confession), so I invite the retreatant to look at *patterns* (e.g., I usually sin when I am dealing with money, truth, etc.), *process, or mechanism* (e.g., how does it start, how is it fueled, etc.). The task is to try to know more about ourselves and "the depravity of the world": Knowing ourselves makes us understand the world and vice versa (n. 63). The Rules of discernment for the First Week and Notes about scruples improve such knowledge, so I invite retreatants to read them frequently, to "translate" them into their own words, and to apply them to themselves (n. 313–327, 345–351).

I also highlight the fact that "small" sins may reveal our true selves more than big ones, for they are more habitual and thus more revealing. Also, they don't give way to the subtly proud, romantic, theatrical claim, "I am the greatest sinner in the world!" (Retreatants are not often major criminals.) The second prelude invites the retreatant to ask for the grace of "shame and confusion" (n. 48); I suggest that retreatants ask also for "the knowledge of my sins," for no change is possible without this, and the necessity of knowing our sins impregnates all Exercises of the First Week.

Retreat masters face a challenge here, because they become one of the sacraments of Jesus' God, the God of unconditional acceptance, understanding, and mercy (I had to say to a thirty-day retreatant, "You want to know where you are with God? Look at the way you deal with the retreat master." See my commentary on n. 15, 22). Retreat masters must not moralize, judge, or condemn, but rather ought to be "gentle and kind, encouraging the [retreatant]," and helping him or her to discern so that "the stratagems of our enemy [may be] uncovered" (n. 7).

I always invite retreatants to try the triple colloquy, because it is a fantastic grace no longer to be blind about ourselves; in John's Gospel sin *is* blindness. Also, for some retreatants the triple colloquy becomes an excellent tool they use for prayer after the retreat. A few retreatants I have known called on some more personal advocates, their own beloved dead for instance, imitating the churches that call on all the saints in a litany during presbyterial ordination. This colloquy also offers the prayer *Anima Christi* ("Soul of Christ," attributed to Ignatius, see Appendix [p. 221]) which corresponds to the crucified Jesus of n. 53. This prayer also has another value. I mentioned that being indifferent is difficult because of our wounds. Some of our sins have their origin in these injuries, which have created in us some weaknesses that the Enemy likes to play with (n. 327). These wounds create risk, but they can also become channels of grace, for it is through them that we most experience God's mercy and salvation. Accordingly, the retreatant is invited to hide his or her own wounds in Christ's everlasting stigmata, where they can be healed as all the wounds of humankind have been.

I must mention that Ignatius' comparisons of ourselves to others (n. 58), for instance to sinners who may have been damned, has not always worked well with retreatants making the Exercises with me (n. 48, 50, 52, 59); however, the statement of some mystics, "We are nothing by ourselves but everything in God," has sometimes helped retreatants.

FIFTH EXERCISE

Some retreat masters dismiss this Exercise, thinking that Ignatius' hell is just a typical unhealthy medieval depiction. However, I never hesitate to invite retreatants to pray with it, for hell exists. As I tell them, "I saw hell. Once I saw it in a prison, a huge four-tier cage made with four hundred small cages; there, many of Ignatius' words were literally illustrated. During World War II, it was the bombings of my city; in the war between France and Algeria, it was the fighting I knew as a French soldier; in the United States, it was a suburb impregnated by fear and violence, drugs and killing, misery and dirt."

We have plenty of proofs in history and around us that when love is banished, hell is created. New Adams and Eves, have we not seen a lot of hells result from chains of evil we started? We are, individually, a part of the universality of sin because we share solidarity with all sinners (this comes back in the Two Standards, n. 136–147). Ignatius' supposedly "medieval" depiction is still experienced in our American streets and in other parts of the world;

to dismiss this reality with the pretext that his fresco is from another century would be dishonest. A retreatant told me that "this valley of miseries [filled with] irrational animals" (n. 47) could be found in Bosnia-Herzegovina or Rwanda.

Also, through this Exercise some retreatants faced a hell connected with the wounds of their childhood: the anguish of being radically separated, or rejected ("exiled" in n. 47). But they could deal with their pain in the retreat because they experienced Someone walking with them, the Jesus who goes into all hells (the retreat master may be this caring presence). Using the five senses to evoke hell can make the experience very powerful. I recommend the Exercise also because some people find in the use of their senses a tool for prayer that suits their particular spiritual nature very well (see *Contemplation* in Appendix [p. 221]).

This extreme of praying about hell *ends* the Week, because if the extreme of all we stand to lose in hell is prayed well, the extreme of God's mercy in Jesus appears *here and now* for the retreatant's faith. Knowing himself or herself to be still alive on earth, the retreatant experiences the grace of having been protected and spared (sometimes I suggest praying with Daniel 3:24–90; 6:17–25). But also the retreatant has been sustained, helped, served, accepted, and forgiven by God (possibly even sacramentally). At least something of that is shown through the retreat master. Sometimes, here, a comparison of our own plight with that of others helps; a retreatant said to me in 1994, "I know I am not in the hell of Sarajevo." Now, the retreatant knows what the faith of the Church (seen in the retreat master) asserts: "We have a Savior, Jesus."

Having met the compassionate and merciful God of Jesus, having a better knowledge of sin and of the parameters of his or her freedom, the grateful retreatant is ready for a new life, life according to God-Love, which is the following of Jesus that starts with the Second Week. In fact, since the first colloquy, we have spent less time praying *about* sin than praying *before* Jesus crucified, the image of our forgiving God. Thus I suggest praying chiefly with Luke's Gospel of mercy (7:36–50; 13:10–17; 15:11–32; 19:1–10; also Jn 4:1–42). There is a Jesus revealing first not sin, but God as perfect Love.

HOW THE FIRST WEEK ENDS

Thus the First Week does not imprison us in the memory of our sins or provoke a guilt complex; nor does it encourage a subtle spiritual game that fosters pride in our prowess as sinners or allows us to wallow in a perverse eroticism. The Principle or Foundation implied that we are fundamentally beautiful (since we were created by God) and loved (everything is given to us). Indeed, the First Week shows us that Jesus, as the expression of God's Love, wants only to give us back our original beauty. This understanding, and only this understanding, helps us to look at our sins in a healthy, productive way.

Retreatants making the Exercises for the first time very often see their conscious or unconscious false gods disappear before the *real* God, in Jesus on the cross, in whom all false gods died (n. 53). Hopefully, this loving God in Jesus is perceived also in the retreat master's behavior. A retreatant who had been badly hurt as a child said to me, "So, Jesus' God is not like my dad!"

This discovery triggers in some retreatants what is already in us, the image and likeness of such God-Love. Their experience of being loved and forgiven in such an unexplainable way awakens in them gratitude, and also their own divine capacity to love. They have undergone a liberation from their wrong attachments, they no longer want to sin and say "no" as they selfishly did before; now they are available for others. This openness to other people generally occurs in all retreatants, and it is already love.

Some retreatants are ready to do even more, to serve (and to enter the Second Week faster than others; for them the First Week can be short). Beyond their sins, which they no longer excuse or deny or reduce merely to nonethical behavior, they have reintegrated their deepest beauty, their capacity to be Christlike and "set [themselves] in order according to God" (n. 63). But they don't know yet exactly how to say "yes." So they now want to follow the One who was the perfect yes, and let His example rub off on them through the companionship they find with Him in contemplation (2 Cor 1:19). And because they now realize that they have been saved by God through Jesus (and, by extension, through His human "sacraments"), they want to be a part of His work as the unique Savior of humankind. This is the purpose and the content of all the following Exercises, where Jesus is Christ-for-me and I am also in-solidarity-with-Christ-for-others till the end of time.

We could compare the First Week to the time spent by some of Jesus' future disciples with John the Baptist (Jn 1:35). However, the God of the First Week is not as frightening as the one implied in the Baptizer's words (Mt 3:1-12).

ADDITIONS
[n. 73–90]

These notes, which refine some of the Annotations, are adjusted to each Week and are important enough to require an examination about their practice (n. 90). Ignatius wants the retreatant to focus on the topic of prayer and to avoid any distraction all day long (n. 73–74, 78–81). The retreatant must use the body with flexibility and discernment; it means to find and maintain the posture that is most conducive to prayer (n. 76). A quick evaluation of what happened closes the prayer period (n. 77).

N. 82–89 are a short classical treaty about penance that omits the usual word "mortification," instead calling for moderation, adaptability, and discretion in public (this reminds us of Mt 6:16–18). Ignatius knew personally the risks of physical penance when he was in Manresa. External penance is not a goal in itself, but facilitates the most important goal, internal penance; the outward penance is the *servant* of the desired inward one, "such as the feeling of sorrow or of consolation." This is clear in the advice to "play" with penances as we do with bodily postures (n. 76, 89, 133, 213).

Ignatius treats external penance meticulously, maybe because it is easier to deal with its problems than it is with the ones that accompany internal penance, as the Notes about scruples show (n. 345–351). I say to retreatants, while talking about n. 87, "Penance eventually becomes a daily practice [like Adam and Eve in n. 51], but it must always be *ridiculous* so that we avoid pride (e.g., no woman will boast of 'forgetting' to put on lipstick), and *symbolic*, for it signifies our disapproval of our sins and our yearning for God's grace (e.g., no man would see one less teaspoon of sugar in his coffee as a very efficient penance)." I also give a traditional piece of advice: "Please, don't practice any physical penance during the retreat without talking with me first."

EVALUATIONS

The examination of n. 90 evaluates how the retreatant has made the Exercises of the day (n. 77). Another kind of evaluation must be done, through decoding consolations and desolations ("peaks" and "pits," they have also been called). This evaluation is not about our wrongdoings, but about what the Lord has said (n. 62, 199, 227). The retreatant must answer the question, "What does the Lord or the Enemy say to me through these peaks and pits?" This is done with the Rules of discernment. I invite retreatants to make this evaluation at the end of a retreat. In a thirty-day retreat or the Exercises in daily life, it is also done at the end of the First and the Second Week, in order to avoid dealing with too many notes at the end of the retreat, which is a burden for the memory. Here are two methods:

1) On a sheet of paper the retreatant makes a table with one column for consolations and another for desolations. Then the retreatant divides both columns horizontally by the times when these feelings occur and briefly puts down what created them (text, event, thoughts, etc.). Then the retreatant makes a synthesis of the content of each column at the bottom: Through the texts, events, thoughts that caused consolations appear the Lord's calls, and through those that provoked desolations, the temptations of the Father of Lies are revealed. The result is a self-portrait of which it is good to summarize both sides (often of the same coin) in order to remember them easily. Finally, it is useful to find a few means that are going to be used as daily physical reminders. But this method is too static, and that is why it can be fruitfully completed by method number 2.

2) The retreatant makes a chart. The vertical axis is divided into degrees of consolation or desolation above or below a level 0. The horizontal axis is divided into columns, one for each prayer period. In each column, the retreatant puts a mark at the level fitting the intensity of the experience made. Joining the different points with a line creates a graph that reveals something less static than the self-portrait. In front of a line going downward, the retreatant's question is, "What happened that caused this falling down?" and in front of a line going up, "What helped me to recover?" The answers are very valuable, for they help retreatants to anticipate what is going to affect them, negatively or positively, during (and after) the retreat.

Of course, to keep a minimal journal after each prayer period (each day for the Exercises in daily life) is necessary. It is sufficient to put down *what* affected us and *how* (much), with some explanations about *"why"* when possible. This journal helps the retreatant's memory when it is time to report to the retreat master or to make an evaluation. Through evaluations the retreatant learns more and more to let God define him or her, and to succumb to the opposite tendency less and less. Since this grace of knowing comes from God, its effectiveness is guaranteed (and this might become the basis of the Election).

Second Week

INTRODUCTION

This Week, the longest one, often has a slow pace and calls us to be patient. It covers Jesus' life until His Passion. The First Week made us know our ways of saying "no" to God; the Second Week unveils our ways of saying "yes" in solidarity with all who did so in history. This is rooted in the desire to imitate Jesus; retreatants learn how to serve by seeing how He loved ("till the end" in the Third Week).

The technique of prayer in this Week and the following ones is *contemplation* (see Appendix [p. 221]). It re-creates companionship with Jesus through the imagination; we hear His teaching words, we see His deeds, and we are captivated by His charming presence, "so handsome to behold" is He (1 Sam 16:12). In Jesus, God was seen, heard, and touched (1 Jn 1:1–4). This contemplation of the Mysteries of Jesus' life is interrupted for two days, when the Two Standards, the Three Kinds of Men, and the Three Modes of Humility are considered (n. 136, 149, 164).

It seems that gratitude now disappears: However, it has been sufficiently brought forth by the First Week, and its consequences will continue to unfold until the end of the Exercises. Having found again their Christlike beauty, which is their capacity to love, the grateful retreatants want to serve and to follow the Perfect Servant.

The Week starts like an opera, with an overture giving all the themes of the days to come. This overture is the contemplation of the kingdom of Jesus Christ. There we find what summarizes the disciples' experience: His call, His companionship, and their answer. Retreatants make this experience their own (the Election will show the specific disciple he or she is called to be).

THE KINGDOM OF JESUS CHRIST
[n. 91–100]

This Exercise is *not* part of the Second Week. The *"first* day" starts with the Incarnation (n. 101). Also, n. 99 says that retreatants will contemplate the kingdom of Jesus Christ only twice during the day, with a more relaxed schedule compared to the usual daily one. Maybe Ignatius envisions a break between the First Week and the Second Week, and sees the contemplation made during that time (in his draft of a Directory, n. 14, Ignatius suggests giving some rest to retreatants after their general confession at the end of the First Week).

TWO PARABLES

The preludes already offer some themes of discipleship. We imagine Jesus' ministry and journey, seeing the places He "passed through while preaching" (n. 91); we ask for the grace of sharing His action by hearing and following His call. Some retreatants dislike the word "war," found in the title (in text V only); I remind them that Ignatius' military career was very short, but that he kept the mind of a faithful vassal to his lord. More important, I invite them not to forget that serving with Jesus is to enter a battle, present throughout the Exercises. The disciples did not know that when they were chosen. But we do!

Some retreat masters dismiss the earthly king's story; they see it as merely a useful means at that time for imagining Jesus' call, because everyone still remembered the crusades for liberating the Holy Land or Spain. This is partly true, but the gospels also use the picture of a king, even for Jesus (Mt 22:42; 25:34; Lk 19:12).

Also, in Ignatius' century, if bishops were the ecclesiastic power, kings were the secular one. So, with some scholars, I think that Ignatius wants the retreatant to face a secular leader with a secular cause. A man of the Renaissance, he thinks that Humanism in itself carries respectable values. This asks us if we would volunteer for a cause without direct reference to God (after all, love is not Christians' private property). If we need faith to be honest in our family or at work, to care for justice and the poor, then what does that mean; and how do we deal with other believers or nonbelievers? Do we imply that a secular cause cannot deserve by itself interest and dedication even when human dignity is at stake there?

A cause takes on greater value when it is seen by Christians as concerning God's glory; and the Passion will give it a deeper dimension. This is obvious for Ignatius: As soon as he speaks about Christ, he says "*how much more* Christ deserves" attention and obedience, an offering of self "most passionately" given, and "greater and more magnificent gifts" (n. 95–97). And the generous answer to Jesus is justified by more explanations than the answer to the earthly king.

THE ANSWER TO JESUS
[n. 96–98]

For Ignatius this response is made with intelligence and heart. Texts A and P distinguish "judgment and reason" and "the greatest affection." Text V is not so clear-cut, but the words "we will reason that no one of sane mind" and "I offer myself entirely to You" imply both intellect and heart. Maybe Ignatius downplays the emotional side of the retreatant's answer because he is writing an *official* text; after all, he was imprisoned and suspected in Alcala and Salamanca of being close to the *"Alumbrados"* or *"Illuminati"* (1526–1527). Inflated emotions obscure judgment and have produced religious gurus who misled many people. Intelligence saves us from treating God like an aphrodisiac.

Wisdom also teaches us that the desire to serve as Jesus did is right thinking. Struggling for Love (and thus for compassion, justice, forgiveness, and peace) can be justified rationally as the greatest task for humankind, no less than fighting for improvements in medicine, the environment, roads (all of which can be the fruit of love). Therefore, if retreatants hesitate: "Foreseeing the possible pains to come, am I going to say 'Here I am?'" Ignatius answers: "It is the right thing to do!" (Also, faith reminds us that Christ eventually won.) Answering the call is for Ignatius a blend of reason and feeling, which probably explains why he changed the sharp distinction of texts A and P. Here, to answer Jesus' call is like a vassal freely responding to his lord, a soldier to his chief, a servant to his master, with the mixture of affection, attachment, and sense of honor typical of that century (n. 54, 74, 94). Thus, in spite of the "more" found in n. 97, the offering of self is not spiritual athletics, because it is rooted in intelligent awareness and it will be purified (by the Third Week, and also by life!).

The affectionate preference for Jesus and His companionship appears here, and will remain throughout the Exercises, as the root of indifference (e.g., n. 147, 167). We move from the cause to the person as soon as we face Him, calling us "to Himself" (n. 95): "I offer *myself* entirely to *You*" (*me tibi*). In the same way, n. 96 in our text already said, "to offer and vow most passionately his total self to Christ's service" as opposed to "to labor" in texts A and P. After all, from the First Week the retreatant knows that Jesus is the friend who died for him or her. But while the retreatant feels the gratitude that creates the desire to share Jesus' radical lifestyle and mission of service, he or she nevertheless continues to discern with intelligence and reason.

SUGGESTIONS

I explain Ignatius' use of the word "war" to retreatants who object to it. Instead of a king, I invite retreatants to imagine a contemporary secular leader with a secular cause, because most of us feel an affinity with role models who somehow express our vision; but I do so in order to favor openness to other believers or nonbelievers in our non-Christian world (indeed, the retreatant's own spouse might be a nonbeliever). I hope, too, that this will help retreatants, in crises of faith, to remain attached to the ideals of service and love. Finally, I believe with Ignatius that Jesus' call will seem even more compelling in a comparison with secular figures, because He is the perfect divine and humane face of Love.

For the contemplation of Jesus (n. 95–97), I comment on loving as the right thing to do. Concerning our affection for Him, I suggest texts of Scripture. Jeremiah 20:7 and John 21:15–19 match the state of the retreatant's heart after the First Week, which is ready to say gratefully, "Lord, you know I like you," and to accept the call. To help the retreatant to focus on Jesus, I give him or her other scriptural calls. In Mark 1:4–9, Jesus' own call, the retreatant hears God say, "You are my beloved." In John 1:35–51, Jesus is calling disciples in various ways that may speak to retreatants' own experience. Luke 5:1–11 shows Jesus already in us, serving people from "our boat," calling us, sinners that we are, to go deeper and follow Him. Matthew 9:9–13 can link the First and Second Week.

The stories here come later in the Exercises, but I give them as "slices" of Scripture that help us to deal with the dense text of the kingdom. Ignatius takes the logic of the Creed (Incarnation, Nativity, etc.); I prefer to follow the gospels, where the disciples met Jesus as a grown-up man. As a background to the calls portrayed in the gospels, I also give, as readings, some calls in the Old Testament (e.g., David's, prophets' calls).

I invite retreatants to use Ignatius' words or their own for the offering (n. 98), pinpointing a few things for them: The majestic setting (Is 6; the court for Ignatius) magnifies any secular cause molded by faith; any call concerns earth and heaven, just as the chains of evil do in the First Week; the retreatant's situation opposes the one of n. 50 and 74, except that it is always before the One who gave "many and great favors and gifts" (echo of the Principle or Foundation); to offer oneself is to join all Jesus' followers since the twelve apostles. I don't emphasize "bearing injustices and adversities, with true poverty…" because the disciples only understood that later (it also comes back later in the Exercises as well), and because we don't *hear* such things when we fall in love. I don't remember one single retreatant noticing this part of the text.

Thus I let retreatants savor the "honeymoon" that the beginning of this Week often is. But I emphasize the last sentence, especially the phrase "*if* it pleases Your holiest Majesty…" This maintains the freedom of both God and the retreatant, reminding us of the Principle or Foundation (clearly there in "provided it will be for Your greatest praise"). Finally, I urge the retreatant to read and reread the Rules of discernment, chiefly the ones for the Second Week (n. 313–336), and n. 349–351 about scruples.

DISCOVERIES

Contemplating Jesus challenges the retreatant: "Who is this Jew for you, intellectually?" It is an opportunity to choose Love because it is the right thing to do. But contemplations reveal that the intellect does not go far enough. "The heart has its reasons that Reason does not know," Pascal reminds us. So the retreatant hears other questions: "In my heart, who is Jesus of Nazareth for me? What relationship do we have with each other, what do I want with Him?"

Each retreatant faces the mystery of his or her personal attachment to the person of Jesus, and to His God through Him, and gets more and more in touch with that love within his or her own blood and flesh. That love, already triggered in the First Week, comes out more clearly in front of Love in Jesus' blood and flesh —same Love, same Spirit. One retreatant told me, "My story is His, and His story is mine." This will lead retreatants further than the First Week; they'll see that Jesus' battle is within themselves, between His love that is their love and their inordinate attachments (Rom 7:14–25).

Finally, the retreatant discovers that God dares to need us, sinners, and, by grace, chooses us (Jn 15:16). This is as if parents selected their youngest child to set the table with their best china, fully aware of the risks! Such favor increases our sense of dignity and responsibility, our gratitude and eagerness to serve. But, "*if* it pleases Your holiest Majesty…" can keep us humble. All our most generous desires are given up to God, who won't ask for more than we can do (1 Cor 10:13). This addresses the presumption of our childish instinct, which claims, "I can do it" and overburdens ourselves (this is often the temptation under the appearance of good of the Annotations and the Rules of discernment for the Second Week, n. 332–334).

There is no room for a Messiah complex, for it is God who saves through Jesus: We are simply invited to partake in the task, as members of an immense body called by "the Eternal King" (here, some comparisons of the First Week find their positive side, n. 58–60). I saw a few retreatants unable to pray about the secular king; in their faith, no leader could even come close to competing with Jesus, no love could be the equivalent of God as Love in Jesus (n. 184).

Some retreatants understood that contemplating the Kingdom of Christ made them relive the consecration of their baptism (its "cleansing" aspect being experienced in the First Week) and confirmation. This confirmed for me the change Ignatius made in our text. He no longer speaks, as he does in A and P, of two kinds of people, one of whom wants to do more for Jesus; thus he puts aside a tradition in which religious life was considered more perfect than the life of other Christians (n. 96–97).

THE LETTER OF THE TEXT

Some passages need reinterpretation today. For example, for Christ's words, "It is my most rightful will to vindicate the dominion of all the world, to subdue all my enemies" (n. 95), I suggest, "to establish Justice and Compassion, Reconciliation and Peace, Love everywhere, against all forces of evil"; for "the rebellion of the flesh, the senses, love of self and love of the world," I substitute "mundane and selfish lures" (n. 97). After all, Ignatius shows Jesus calling us to His love, which is opposed to the world (especially in John's texts, where the conflict between Jesus and the World is sharply emphasized).

Finally, I mention to retreatants books about the life of some witness of Jesus, because I know the emotional impact of such readings on Ignatius after his conversion. One of these, *The Imitation of Christ*, may not always suit our current sensibility, but the very name of the book summarizes the purpose of the Exercises (n. 100).

THE INCARNATION
[n. 101–109]

"THE" STORY

After the call, we contemplate Mary as the first person to assent to God coming into our world (n. 98); but the real first "yes" to God was said by the Word Itself on entering our history (Lk 1:26–38; Heb 10:5–7). We may also forget that Mary and Gabriel's dialogue concerned the whole of creation, history, and God. So, Ignatius gives us the limitless dimensions of the event of Nazareth. He invites us to enter not only into God's "Election," but also into God's compassion in the heart of the Trinity where salvation belongs to "the eternity *of their divinity*" (only in text V, n. 102).

The Being Itself of the One we call God is an everlasting "yes" to others, and their salvation (2 Cor 1:19). As God comes into the heart of humankind, Ignatius wants us to go into God's heart (this is the Origin of the reciprocal love of n. 231, 234). This is the Song of Songs. We may pause here and try to understand why Ignatius had a strong Trinitarian spirituality and why the Jesuits always saw the source of their entire apostolate in this contemplation.

SUGGESTIONS

I suggest that retreatants insert Luke's story into Ignatius' vision. Sometimes I also invite them to pray in front of a globe after having read the news of the world, and to locate the small dot marking Nazareth. This explains why I have *never* forbidden thirty-day retreatants to read the newspapers (they are intelligent enough to know how to do that in a retreat). Finally, I invite the retreatant to enter into God's heart, which is full of love for the world, and we start passing through Luke 1–2 and Matthew 1–2. Joseph also enters the retreat here.

DISCOVERIES

And so retreatants go from the Word's "yes," to the "yes" of Mary and Joseph, to their own. This movement is like the one in the First Week, but "how much more" overwhelmingly consoling, for it reestablishes the proper order (n. 95). Instead of the sinful series with the angels, our first "parents," Adam and Eve, another human, and ourselves, we have the grace-filled succession of God, Jesus, His parents, us. "Where sin abounded, grace abounded all the more," for Love has always been eternally first (Rom 5:15–21). From the Incarnation and through all incarnations of Love in those who offered themselves to Christ, retreatants become ready to offer themselves as well, in their own flesh and blood.

Some mystics would say that after the "empty me, fill me" of the First Week, the retreatants beg from the heart, "Fill me, so I'll be empty of myself" (I give the reading Phil 2:5–8). Offering their flesh, in marriage or work, in friendships or citizenship, they become a new incarnation, allowing God's Love to exist through them just now (the "just now" of the colloquy, n. 109). In touch with Love in themselves, they savor Paul's words, "The Word is nearby you, already in your heart" (Rom 10:8). Meister Eckhart had said that contemplation produces in us something like a new incarnation of God's Word to benefit all humankind. The retreatant inscribes himself or herself in the long succession of those who have embodied God's Word: Moses, the prophets, the writers of the Bible, so many others, and ultimately Mary.

To contemplate Mary does not require a special devotion, but simply an awareness of the ways God's Word has *always* entered our history. Thus this contemplation is not simply to evoke Nazareth centuries ago; it is to see this mystery in ourselves, as ours *today* (n. 107). The retreatant shares the compassion of the Trinity for the world, and says with Mary, "I am the servant of the Lord. Let it be done to me as you say."

THE LETTER OF THE TEXT

In n. 102, the word "story" appears for the first time in the Exercises. For us Christians, the real origin is not Creation; we date history before and after Christ, for the *real* history started when God became historical in Jesus, and in Him the companion in all of our personal histories. Strangely, this first Exercise of the day is entitled "meditation," although the points describe a contemplation. The word may just mean "prayer" or perhaps Ignatius wanted consistency in the daily structure of the Exercises (see *Structure of a Retreat* in Appendix [p. 228]).

Since I have already given the disciples' calls, I justify this return to Jesus' conception by reminding people of what we all do. When we start a new friendship, we soon ask the other, "Where do you come from, etc.?" The disciples certainly did so with Jesus, and He narrated His past, His childhood. The early Church took the same route. The evangelists began with Jesus' public life, then wrote about His childhood, and through John went back to His origin.

I often have to comment on "the entire surface of the earth, crammed with men falling into hell" (n. 102), because for some people this statement of Ignatius seems an exaggeration. I explain it thus: "Wherever Love disappears on earth, hell appears!" Retreatants concerned with environment are sensitive about the cosmic panorama of this contemplation; but the better the contemplation works for retreatants, the more universal is the love they experience.

N. 104 justifies letting the retreatant enjoy the "honeymoon" of the beginning of the Second Week. The retreatant wants to know, but must know "intimately," and the goal of that knowledge is "that I would love Him more fervently" (n. 104). Ignatius wants for the retreatant more than the intelligent choice of love: he also wants the grace of a total and free attachment to the person of Jesus Christ.

FROM THE INCARNATION TO THE TWO STANDARDS
[n. 110–134]

THE NATIVITY [n. 110–117]

I'll treat Ignatius' words "as we may piously meditate" and "I may imagine myself as being there with them...." in my commentary on the Mysteries of the Life of Our Lord Jesus Christ, and in the section Contemplation in the Appendix (p. 221) (n. 111, 114). Here, I will merely observe that to be present to the scene often produces a powerful experience. Many retreatants enjoyed holding the Infant, given to them by Mary and Joseph (indeed, Love is in our hands; but are we shepherds or Herod?). This contemplation sends some retreatants back to their childhood, with tenderness for their vulnerable "inner child." They see their responsibility to be for him or her the first sacrament of God's love, and give thanks for the people who were actually such sacraments for that child they were years ago, especially if they carry deep wounds from childhood (the massacre of infants of Mt 2 can serve to illuminate that past, as well as n. 106–108, and relevant current events).

Such memories make retreatants aware that the Nativity is not a "nice" story, and they feel an affinity for Ignatius when he speaks of the sufferings the Infant starts enduring; of course, since the contemplation of the Kingdom of Christ, retreatants know that Jesus' life was a war, and so will theirs be to the extent that they devote their lives to His companionship (n. 116). For some retreatants, this contemplation can provide a healing experience: For instance, while being present to Mary, Joseph, and the Infant, they see their past jealousy, because Mom and Dad cared for their baby brother or sister, fade away. It is at this stage of the Exercises that I see more clearly the differences between childish and childlike reactions.

FOLLOWING EXERCISES AND ADDITIONS
[n. 118–133]

Ignatius describes again the day; n. 118 and 125 once more emphasize noticing and staying with what touches the heart in order to discern what is going on (see *Structure of a Retreat* in Appendix [p. 228]). Additions are adjusted to the Week, with one main purpose: to lighten the weight of the Exercises, if the First Week has been exhausting, but also because the retreatant is dealing with Joyful Mysteries (n. 127–131); this last point also justifies the climate of freedom and the "circumspection" about penance found here. Some techniques from the First Week are still suggested, like the means for remaining in the present moment (n. 127, 11), but adjusted to prayer periods about Jesus' childhood.

PRELUDE TO THE CONSIDERATION OF THE
DIFFERENT STATES OR KINDS OF LIFE [n. 134–135]

It is right to find this prelude here. Retreatants are reaching the time when Jesus goes to John the Baptist (n. 158) and starts His public life. He has certainly understood the risks and the temptations of the undertaking, and has clarified the main points of His Good News. Now He feels impelled to dedicate Himself totally to God's affairs as an obedient son, to be "free for the service of the eternal Father." With the childlike obedience He showed His parents, He obeys God; not childishly, because He accepts the necessary detachments. This is frequently where the retreatants are in their journey at this stage of the Exercises. In texts A, P, and V, Ignatius keeps the two classical states of life, the "common" one (for laity) and the one that "brings evangelical perfection" (vowed religious life); the Election will decide which one God wants for the retreatant. However, our text V includes a restriction: The boy Jesus in the Temple only "*seems* to show the example of" the second kind. Maybe Ignatius has realized that his logic about Elections connects evangelical perfection not with a specific state, but with a personal answer in *any* kind of situation.

Ignatius shows his psychological wisdom when he puts this prelude here in the Exercises. It comes just when Jesus becomes religiously adult and will leave His parents: Spiritual maturity and leaving our security blanket (Mom and Dad) are necessary for serious decisions. And this is in the text just before the Two Standards, telling retreatants that to choose Christ is to enter a battle.

At this step of the Exercises, the retreatant has grown sufficiently in gratitude, freedom, and knowledge of self. The will to answer Christ's call is there, in spite of the foreseeable difficulties (always mentioned by Ignatius), because of the intense, loving desire to imitate and be with Jesus. Through contemplation, Jesus' own growth in wisdom, age, and grace has rubbed off on the retreatant; this has created a sufficient identification between the retreatant and Jesus to guide the retreatant when he or she decides a new direction for his or her life, as Jesus did when He decided to go to John the Baptist.

The retreatant is now ready for a total offering of self for the specific discipleship that is going to be revealed (through the decoding of emotions). But this very generosity is going to be the problem the retreatant has to look at intelligently.

THE TWO STANDARDS
[n. 136–148]

OVERVIEW

During the first steps of the Week, most retreatants forget Christ's warnings in His call (thus, my word "honeymoon"); they taste the disciples' joy in the beginnings of Jesus' ministry (Lk 10:19). But the gospels have a turning point (Jn 6; Jesus predicts His Passion in Mt, Mk, Lk). The Second Week also has the Two Standards, which describe Christian life as a battle (cf. Augustine's *City of God*).

This Exercise interrupts the contemplations about the Mysteries, bringing retreatants back from the gospels to this world today. The grace is still to know the strategies of the opponents and to discern, because the Election is coming and will specify how to follow Jesus (n. 139). Perhaps the word "meditation" is in the title because this Exercise starts the day, for the text seems like a contemplation (see *Structure of a Retreat* in Appendix [p. 228]). The Exercise must be linked to the Three Kinds of Men and the Three Modes of Humility, for all of these refine retreatants' discernment and lead to the maximum of freedom and love to which we are called. The recurring triple colloquy emphasizes all of that.

SUGGESTIONS

Ignatius' words are classical, but are often misunderstood or misused today (even the word "Standard," meaning "banner"). So I give retreatants Ignatius' text, with comments about what leads us "into all other sorts of vices." Concerning Lucifer's strategy, and the temptations of riches, honors, and pride, I speak of "wanting to possess, to be the center, to be almighty, even though others may pay the price and we may forfeit love in relationships" (n. 142). This reminds the retreatant of the angels, of Adam and

Eve (but here, for the only time in the Exercises, the Enemy appears).

For Jesus' message, I speak of "desiring not to possess, to be the last, to be just the one I am," for "poverty, rejection of self, and humility" (n. 146). Retreatants are not invited to petition for humility in the colloquy (n. 147); probably, Ignatius thinks that this grace will be the fruit of poverty and rejection. It is true that we are more easily ourselves when we don't let the goods we have accumulated or the world's applause define us. Jesus used strong language about the hazards of riches and worldly glory (e.g., Mt 6:19–21; 19:23–24; Lk 6:24; 12:16–21; Jn 5:44; 12:43). Finally, for retreatants, "to desire to be the last" makes it easier to deal with Ignatius' phrase "to desire insults and contempt"; because "to take the backseat," as someone said to me, makes us ready *in fact* for insults and contempt. We do not, however, lapse into sadomasochism, because looking for self-humiliation is not humility, which is to be simply and truly oneself.

I summarize Jesus' words with the biblical picture of the Servant (Is) who did not possess, was the last, and was not almighty.

As Scriptures, I give Jesus' temptations and the Beatitudes (Mt 4;5; Lk 4;6; n. 161). In order not to intellectualize or moralize the Beatitudes, I invite retreatants to contemplate Jesus. He *was in Himself* the Beatitudes. A colloquy is addressed "to Christ as a human being" (*ad Christum hominem*, n. 147): perhaps Ignatius wants to emphasize that looking at Jesus makes us realize that the struggle described by the Two Standards takes place here on earth. The expression is found only here.

DISCOVERIES

Ignatius' vision is impressive (living at the time of America's discovery, he dared, for instance, to send a Jesuit brother by land in order to find a route to China other than by boat). Retreatants see this world, in history and the daily news, as a universal battlefield, *and themselves as such* (as well as the stake of the battle). We and the world reflect each other, and we learn from this that we are both continually torn between worldly appetites and Jesus' Good News.

Saint Bernard prayed, "Lord, take care of me today, for there is no crime that I am not able to commit before tonight." In Lucifer's words, retreatants hear the song of their own idols besieging them through their inner wounds (n. 327); dealing with their Election, they recognize their own ways of possessing, and of trying to be the center and almighty. This good, if not welcome, knowledge is priceless. More important, retreatants realize that this "Christ… in a humble condition… of a very attractive beauty… of an extremely lovable look" is theirs (In texts A and P, only the "place" is beautiful; n. 144). Somehow they fall in love with their capacity to love, and are so attracted by this priceless pearl that they no longer want to toss it to dogs and swine (Mt 6:21; 7:6; 13:44–46).

One retreatant spoke to me of "integrity." Escaping evil by the only Way possible, they go to God within as the Queen of Sheba went to King Solomon with her questions or Queen Esther to her spouse with her request (I sometimes give as readings 1 Kgs 10 and Est 5). In their own individual way, more consciously than usual, they share Paul's experience of Christ living in them (Gal 2:20). They are so touched by the beauty of this Love within that they want to serve It (here we can speak of obedience because to serve is to obey this Love in their heart).

More accurately, we can say that, looked at by this Love in their inner depths, they are ready to go and serve It with what they have and are, knowing that they act for the sake of Love (Mk 10:17–31; Rom 2:17–24). Moreover, they want to follow Christ's standard as disciples. Finally, they see in the opposition of Lucifer's and Jesus' words that their temptations and calls are often two sides of the same coin, as our childish or childlike behaviors are.

Indeed, with stones or words we can build walls or bridges! One retreatant saw that she could express her aggressive impulses either in violence or in passionate service; another understood that to act like God was not to be despotic, but to serve as Jesus did (Phil 2:7; Lk 22:27 replying to Gn 3:5). Praying with the Two Standards often makes retreatants leave what I called the "honeymoon" phase, and enter an inner struggle deeper than in the First Week. I warn them of that possibility, and I give them Isaiah 43:1–5 and texts where Jesus calms the storm (Mt 8 and 14; n. 161).

THE TEXT ITSELF

Ignatius' imagery is old, probably connected with some visions of Revelation. The description of Lucifer fits what we see when evil reigns: Things are "horrible... terrible in [their] aspect" (n. 140). But the text contains two risks, symbolized by the personalization of evil in Lucifer. The Exercises are not made to treat this metaphysical question. I merely emphasize that Lucifer appears in the retreat after we have contemplated Jesus for several days: Evil is seen clearly only when we know what Love is all about, in and around us.

If Ignatius' picture bothers the retreatant, I just say what I heard years ago: "Don't we see something like a power of evil at work in the world?" The other risk is to demonize specific things or people and put all the blame on them in order to escape our responsibility for and participation in the destruction around us; Ignatius carefully says that Lucifer sends demons, while Christ sends human beings. In n. 147, I emphasize the words that complete the *if* of the offering of self in n. 98, so that our desire to follow Christ would not bring "others into sin" and "be injurious to them and end in an offense to God."

THE THREE KINDS OF MEN
[n. 149–157]

OVERVIEW

Here is one more meditation for recognizing the Enemy's tactics under the appearance of good (n. 14–15). In Ignatius' parable, the three kinds of men are in a situation jeopardizing their salvation. All want to remove their harmful attachment to wealth and find peace with God (n. 150): an excellent desire, but not achieved by two of the three types of men. Their behavior is described without judgment, for only God searches heart and loins (Rv 2:23). We are given this as a meditation in order to keep our intellect sound as we get closer to the Election.

SUGGESTIONS

My comment on the text is, "All these men have good thoughts; in the first group, they never act according to their thought, and events decide for them; in the second, they never make a clear decision or choice." Concerning the third group, I emphasize that we expect a total renunciation of the money, but this could be a temptation under the appearance of good (in fact, all these men want their own salvation *first*). For me, the men of the third kind are aware that *everything is ambivalent, even our generosity*, and so must the retreatant be at this stage of the Exercises (helped by the Rules of discernment for the Second Week and Notes about scruples, n. 332–334, 349–350). I point out that they reach the peak of freedom: They are indifferent about keeping *or* losing the money, and they try to be detached from it as long as God does not speak clearly. This is such a grace that the triple colloquy is back. If we have time, I invite retreatants to contemplate Jesus' freedom in action in Matthew 8–9.

DISCOVERIES

Many retreatants recognize themselves in the two first groups. If they are surprised by the decision of the third group, it is not for long, because the Exercises have led most of them to the same awareness. They know now that *everything* is ambivalent. But their inner struggle often grows deeper, because now they have to acknowledge that there is an element of pretense in their desire to serve with pure love. The First Week revealed a greed for "seductive pleasures of the flesh and of the senses," through sins of weakness (n. 314). The retreatant now discovers under an apparent good a greed for subtle control and power, glory and fame, a greed shared by Peter, John, and James (Mt 16:22–23; Mk 10:35–37; Lk 9:54). Retreatants usually meet their most cunning temptations grafted onto their inner wounds. It is better, then, with God's grace, to try to be detached from *any* solution, even the one that seems unimpeachable (this explains Ignatius' caution about penance in the Second Week, n. 130).

Thus we discover that we must stop defining ourselves and

leave God free to define us, as the men of the third group do. We must chiefly do this when we face an *already existing fact*: Ignatius' example shows an *already* existing dangerous situation facing which the third group waits for God to tell them what to do (however, I suspect that Ignatius keeps in mind what he wrote just before, "avoiding however bringing others into sin," n. 147). So, "the best might be the enemy of the good," as a proverb asserts (this wisdom, in front of possible excess, is also relevant to n. 189, about correcting one's life; to n. 343, concerning alms; to n. 350, about scruples; and to n. 366–370, concerning speaking about theological questions).

In these stages of the Exercises, retreat masters are also put to the test, for they might have a preconceived idea about what constitutes "the best" for the retreatant and hence not be indifferent themselves. This might be due to lack of respect for the retreatant because of the lust for power, unwise emotional care for him or her, lack of patience (somebody I knew needed six years to make an important decision), their own subconscious fears, etc. The best retreat master I have known showed me his evangelical wisdom and care: He dared to support a friend of mine, who thought that ending an ambivalent relationship with a clergyman would be worse than continuing it, although it did not exactly fit the norms of their church (but "any fault of others" was avoided); the future proved that both retreatant and retreat master were right.

THE TEXT ITSELF

I always tell retreatants that we find here one of the most significant differences between our text, V, and A or P. N. 155 says, "Meanwhile, *maintaining everything as it is* [emphasis mine], he only considers and looks for such a service, and accepts no other cause for giving up or retaining the acquired thing, than the reason and desire of divine glory ..." The words I emphasized were added by Ignatius to the text of V but omitted in A and P, and support what I have just explained above about an already existing ambivalent situation.

Getting close to the Election, the retreatant translates *in personal terms the general reflections* coming from the meditations since that of the Two Standards. N. 152 says clearly, "to find out the manner by which *I* could best please God…" But the words "best," "the most acceptable part," "most salubrious," and "perfect poverty" create a risk (n. 151, 152, 157). The retreatant (and the retreat master as well) may be deceived by the evil spirit disguised as an angel of light (hence the name Lucifer, which means "light bearer," in the meditation of the Two Standards).

During this time, the retreatant may be led to a wrong decision through apparent consolations (n. 331–332), for what might generally be best may not be good for him or her right now (see Paul's prudence about marriage in 1 Cor 7). That is why Ignatius always says *"if* God…" and insists on what will be "the most acceptable to God and most salubrious to me." He wants us to let *God* choose (n. 152, 157).

Here, we understand the depth of indifference: It is a *temporary* personal detachment from everything, in order for us to hear what *God* prefers most for us, and to choose, not our way, but the Way (Jn 14:6). The Principle or Foundation may give the impression that indifference and the decision making that follows are for our self-interest, our own salvation. Retreatants see that this detachment is not self-preservation; it is a means for acquiring an inner freedom that will serve God and others as Jesus did. "You have been called to live in freedom—but not a freedom that gives free rein to the flesh. Out of love, place yourselves at one another's service," said Paul (Gal 5:13).

Our salvation is to serve because to love saves. This has been so since the call of Jesus the True Servant, our answer to Him and our companionship with Him (n. 95). Finally, since the contemplation of the Incarnation, that freedom for service, even lived in a Nazareth, embraces the whole world. This gives us a criterion for weighing the value of any decision by looking at its openness to universality. Ignatius was always concerned with "the most universal good"; that is one of the reasons why he wanted Jesuits to answer to the pope and not to any local bishop.

THE NOTE OF N. 157

A retreatant helped me to understand this text (prepared by n. 16). She was able to offer herself to God for an assignment she disliked, and she found peace. Weeks after her retreat, she was injured so badly in a car accident that she could no longer do anything. She said to me, "I passed through the accident, the surgeries, and their harsh consequences with an astounding peace. That would never have happened if I had not been able to offer myself for that assignment I did not want and become free."

What we face, at this stage of the Exercises, is *the current visible challenge* to our inordinate attachments and resistance. If we overcome our slavery in the present situation by offering ourselves as Ignatius suggests, freedom and peace are given to us for a while, *even* for things other than what is in our mind at the moment. I myself have experienced that Ignatius' note is an excellent (if not pleasant or easy) means for becoming free. If I am able to ask for what I dislike the most because of fear or unwillingness, I make myself emotionally indifferent and ready for anything, even the worst. Someone said to me, "I was ready for a ten; so it was pretty easy to accept a six!"

We become free, but it does not mean that *what* we offer ourselves for will happen; the note ends with "we would keep the freedom of our desire…" so that we will not imagine nightmares. "We'll see," one retreat master used to say. So, after my explanations, I invite retreatants facing something very difficult to practice n. 157, and to pray with Jesus calming the storm. For the others, I quickly comment on the note as I did here, in order to give them a tool that may be very useful someday if not now.

I take this opportunity to tell retreatants that the usual example of Ignatius, poverty, is accurate, because the indifference and freedom reached here are signs of a total spiritual poverty in which we admit that *everything is given us*. Since the beginning of the Exercises, we have more and more perceived that everything is God's grace: to use well our faculties, to know the depth of sin and contrition, to be liberated from inordinate attachments and to attach ourselves to Jesus, to discover with Him which way is best for us to serve. So people who see the Exercises as a glorification of human will (Pelagianism) are quite wrong.

THE THREE MODES OF HUMILITY
[n. 165–168]

OVERVIEW

Now the retreatant faces the ultimate step toward freedom and love, and this ends the Second Week. Nothing states whether or not the text is a meditation, but n. 164 and the mention of the triple colloquy imply that it must certainly be prayed.

"In order to reach humility," Ignatius invites the retreatant to choose never to deliberately commit a mortal sin, whatever may be the cost (Mode 1). Mode 2 repeats the same invitation for any venial sin, accomplishing the indifference of the Principle or Foundation. Finally, Mode 3 calls the retreatant to embrace extreme humility: all things being equal, to choose to imitate Christ in His ordeals. We are far from the time in which Ignatius lived, and some things in this text need to be "translated." First, the word "humility": Fortunately, we have a text of Pierre Ortiz, who made a forty-day retreat with Ignatius himself, in which we read almost literally the words of n. 164, and, "Before entering into the elections… it is very profitable to consider and give attention to the Three Modes or Degrees of *Love* of God…"* The word "Love" has allowed me to comment on the Three Modes in a way easily understood by everybody today.

SUGGESTIONS

I read the text to the retreatant and explain why I use the word "Love." Then, with what I learned through a laywoman, I describe the first two Modes thus: "If and when I love someone, I don't want to kill Love in this relationship by any deliberate deadly deed—that is mortal sin. If and when I deeply love a person, I will never deliberately hurt that loved one and our relationship, even slightly—that is venial sin." For the third Mode I ask this question, "Suppose that your beloved is put into a prison, a concentration camp, or sent in exile, where do you want to be?" The answer was

---

* Saint Ignace de Loyola, *Exercises Spirituels*, Texte définitif (1548), Traduit et Commenté par Jean-Claude Guy (Paris: Editions du Seuil), p. 38.

always, "*With* him or her!" So, I can easily add, "Indeed, we choose to love our cherished one and our relationship with him or her, in any room of our home, in any sector or time of our life. Love even impels us to be as the precious one is; how could we enjoy being rich if he or she is poor?" And I remind people of the words of the marriage vows, "I marry you...for better for worse, for richer for poorer, in sickness and in health, until we are parted by death." So, for Ignatius, the words "that I be accepted" in the text of the Two Standards becomes "I would choose poverty...with Him poor" (n. 147, 167). The logic of the Three Modes accomplishes the one found in the Two Standards, and everybody can understand it.

DISCOVERIES

Starting the Second Week, retreatants realize that to choose to love as Jesus did is the right thing to do. This remains so (n. 180–181), but priority is now given to the attachment to Jesus' own person. "To *whom* should we go?" Peter asked accurately, before being asked "Do you love *me*?" (Jn 6:68; 21:16). We are no longer facing an attachment to a cause, but long to be "with Christ" like Paul at his most passionate. Since n. 85, we have been in this mode, which is emphasized by the use of "I" in the text of the Three Modes. This being "with Christ" will take a specific and personal shape for the retreatant in the maturing Election. The contemplation of Jesus, of His love for God and for all of us, has worked in retreatants by a type of osmosis, as it did for the disciples. In their companionship with Jesus, the person outpaced the message without diluting it.

Often retreatants discover in their heart their attachment to Jesus Himself, their ability to love as He did, far beyond what they had thought possible. Some are powerfully confirmed in their desire to live till the end the limitless love they have already experienced, as parents, for instance. This might explain Ignatius' correction in n. 168: In texts A and P, God chooses the retreatant for the Third Mode, in our text it is the retreatant who makes the choice (this explains our translation of the Fifth Annotation).

In front of such a loving and loved Jesus, retreatants can only say, "Stay with us..." (Lk 24:29). But they also say to Love, so admirable in His "attractive beauty...and lovable look" (n. 144), "I'll stay with You, whatever the cost." One retreatant answered Jesus' question, "Do you want to leave me?" with Isaiah's words, "When *we* pass through waters, I will be with You, etc." (Jn 6:67; Is 43:1–5). The struggle is not over, for the stake is clearer than ever (n. 165 recalls Christ's temptations). But the time has come to love Love without bargaining, till we desire never to leave Him—exactly as we never abandon a cherished one in any situation. To love Love. Period. This is taking risks: Stockbrokers take risks for money despite the odds. Would we do less for Love?

This peak of Love, which already includes the risks of rejection, poverty, loss of reputation, contempt, etc. (n. 167), *is the peak of freedom*. Whatever the situation or the reaction of others, our love stays unchanged because it is freely given for now, without any ifs, ands, or buts about it. One retreatant said, "My wife divorced me and does everything she can against me. But I stay free from all of that in my love for her." Another asserted, "I am ready to serve without expecting anything in return." To reach such peaks is a grace that requires the triple colloquy!

I have seen signs of such love and freedom. A Baptist minister revealed to me the truth of Jesus' sentence, "My yoke is easy and my burden light" (Mt 11:29); the minister said, "Each time the burden is not light, it is because I am lacking in love and in freedom." Another sign is this: Of all the people who have made a thirty-day retreat with me, years later more than ninety percent are directly serving the poor who "cannot repay [us]," even though this call did not come in the retreat for most of them (Lk 14:14). When Love is free, Love likes to work for free. So did and does the Perfect Love of the Trinity for us, so does Love in and through us when we choose to follow the Poor One, Jesus (n. 58, 114). After his conversion, Ignatius was always serving the poor in hospitals, prisons, etc.; even in Rome, when he was the superior of the Society of Jesus. But finally, the third sign is that the freedom I talked about exists for both us and God: The retreatant is free and leaves God free, for the phrase "*if* this pleases the divine Benevolence" is usually real for the retreatant now (n. 168 sounds like n. 157, and keeps retreatants away from masochism, because it is God's pleasure only that is desired).

BACK TO THE TEXT ITSELF

My comments show the retreatant that the word "humility" belongs here. When we have reached the kind of love of the Third Mode, we are finally ready to take or to be put in the last place in humility, not because of negative motivations, but because everything is possible with God's grace.

As I said above, I invite retreatants to go back and forth from the text of the Two Standards to those of the Three Kinds of Men and the Modes of Humility; "playing" with these Exercises is in line with the freedom we see in the Additions for the Second Week (n. 127–131). Retreatants also pray with the Mysteries found in n. 158–161, but I have no text of Scripture to suggest for the Three Modes of Humility, for a few reasons. First, it is impossible to find one matching the Exercise in Jesus' public life; second, the preparation and the completion of the Election are more and more the personal Scripture of the retreatant; and finally, the Third Mode of Humility is the last text of the Second Week, because it brings us to the gate of the Third Week, and Jesus' Passion. Often the retreatant is ready to follow Jesus there, where He is king but not in the manner of an earthly king.

ELECTION OR CORRECTION OF LIFE
[n. 169–189]

OVERVIEW

Contemplating Jesus—His call, deeds, and message—is not an abstract mental game; it becomes a personal story for retreatants when the time comes for them to make an Election or correct their life. This is done concurrently with the last contemplations of the Second Week. Ignatius repeats what he said in the Principle or Foundation: We must not confuse means and end, this end being God's praise and our salvation (n. 23, 154). Then he explains that we must make an Election only concerning things "good in themselves, or certainly not bad" (n. 170), and that some Elections are irrevocable and some are not. Finally, he describes three "most opportune times" for an Election. We must be ready for any of them and use the third one if the other occasions don't arise (and we get two methods for this third time). Ignatius' word, "time," reminds us that any decision requires time.

SUGGESTIONS

I read Ignatius' text with retreatants. Concerning n. 175, I advise them not to *expect* such inspiration, for they could wait a long time. I am not sure if I have *ever* seen this experience after decades of giving retreats. The kind of sudden revelation that occurred to Paul and Matthew might suggest that this experience is unusual (is it the consolation without preceding cause of n. 330?); but I have often seen a slow but powerful certainty rising up in retreatants' hearts with no room for doubts. I emphasize n. 176, because decoding the movements of diverse spirits through discernment must be done throughout the retreat, and because the alternance consolation-desolation often shows quite clearly the choice to make. But I *always* recommend that the first method of the third time be used (n. 177–183), because I think it wise to use reason with God's grace, even when we think we have been inspired (Ignatius himself emphasizes in n. 180 of our text, as well as in texts A and P, the use of our "mind" and "reasoning of [our] intellect" when he speaks of imploring God's clemency to help us).

I also tell retreatants not to be surprised by the feelings experienced. They are often reduced to a very strange peace that we cannot name either consolation or desolation: a peace so hardly felt that I call it "neutrality" (for me, it is the "tranquillity" of n. 177). Commenting on Ignatius' words, I explain that it is often a good sign that the deepest emotions have quieted down, making objectivity possible in the deliberation to come. I think of Meister Eckhart's remark, "As long as we get sensible consolations, our love is not yet purified."

"To bring in front of me the thing on which to be deliberated" (n. 178) suggests to me that the question faced by the retreatant must be clear and distinct; if not, things are probably not yet ripe for an Election. I invite retreatants to take literally n. 179–180, which send them back to the freedom of the Principle or Foundation and of the third group of men (n. 155); the equilibrium implied by "to remain in the middle and in equilibrium" explains the neutral feeling I mentioned earlier (n. 179). Then they list their pros and cons, reasons for or against the two alternatives they face (n. 181).

I add these remarks: "The reasons must be really your own, and not just things you have read or heard unless they have *become* your own [All the statements of one retreatant started with the words 'I should,' as if they were extracted from a law book]. Don't dismiss reasons that might seem silly [A friend of mine saw the religious habit as a reason to be a Trappist monk]. Don't forget to look at the dangers of each option. Try to rank your reasons by importance, because, when you look at the whole, you might see one reason so big that it will eclipse all the others [e.g., 'I don't have the physical health for this job.' One retreatant ranked each reason on a scale of 0 to 10, and added the figures for each option at the end. The result was interesting]. Concerning the 'hazards,' you might do what one retreatant did: He was finally able to make his decision by choosing the alternative wherein he would sin less." I recommend spending around forty-five minutes on the pros and cons, and to go back to them once; this has always been sufficient for retreatants who were ready for the Election, and it avoids complicating rationalizations.

I always suggest brevity in writing down the reasons (once, starting with a long form helped a retreatant; coming back to me with a shorter version of her pros and cons about religious life or marriage, she saw the phrase "I want children" without "from...." The name of the man she thought she loved had been omitted). Most of the retreatants I worked with perceived that their Election was made when their intellect could propose no more new pros or cons, and when they found themselves in a state of motionless stillness.

Finally, I emphasize the offering of the decision to God in order to see if this choice of beginning a new life is confirmed. I explain to retreatants that if consolation does not come, at least as peace, it means that somehow, somewhere, some "wishes of the flesh" (n. 182) have crept into the process and damaged the retreatant's freedom and power of reasoning, and that it is better to start the Election all over again. In 1963, in the first retreat I gave, one retreatant systematized the offering in a way that is described in Ignatius' draft for a Directory (n. 21), although she did not know this. After the retreat, she still offered, alternatively, one week staying in religious life, one week leaving it. Consolation occurred always with the same solution, and desolation with the alternate solution. We realize that her final decision was made very peacefully when we know that she acted so for one full year!

Concerning the second method, I mention Ignatius' Rules with caution. To picture ourselves at our death or at judgment is difficult today, for it often creates a guilt complex, consisting of thoughts like "I should have done this or that" (n. 186–187). It is different when a retreatant actually faces death, as Ignatius did in Manresa (*Autobiography*, n. 32), and as one thirty-day retreatant, who had a deadly cancer, did. Also, it is not easy to be sure that our feeling "for the chosen thing comes from God's love and consideration of Him only" (n. 184), even though Ignatius carefully says that the retreatant must "*begin* to feel" so (I saw that happening in only *a few* people).

The only Rule I have taught and found fruitful is for retreatants to divide themselves into two people, one advising the other (n. 185); our text speaks about what counsel we would give to "one of [our] dearest friends," and not to someone we have never seen or known as in texts A and P. I suspect that Ignatius probably realized that our deep love for a friend is the best guarantee of the value of our advice, better than the supposed objectivity we would have with an unknown person. I invite the retreatant to add this means to the first method, if necessary; this Rule is very useful, once we are accustomed to it, when we have to make quick decisions. N. 188 repeats the offering of n. 183. My book *Discernment, The Art of Choosing Well* (Liguori, Mo.: Triumph, 1993), elaborates on this subject.

THE TEXT ITSELF AND THE PROBLEMS
I HAVE ENCOUNTERED

A first question is, "When do retreatants make their Election?" Ideally, around the end of the Second Week. But it may be later: One retreatant could not enter the Fourth Week until he faced a choice about which God had been silent during the first three Weeks. I invite retreatants to try to make their Election if it seems that they have become sufficiently indifferent and free for the readiness that ends n. 179. Often, it is the retreatant who feels that it is time to make a choice; this awareness, at its highest intensity, is the inspiration of n. 175. Also, if the movements of the spirits have been strong enough, the desire to make the Election comes by itself (n. 176). But this is not the most difficult problem.

These pages of Ignatius are priceless and effective (their systematic method seems unique in Christianity), but they belong to another century, one very different from our own. Still, even today everybody would agree with Ignatius about what concerns means and end; but what about things "good in themselves" (n. 170)? Did Ignatius ever encounter someone who had to choose between tyrannicide and slavery?

In any Christian denomination, with or without hierarchy, disagreements exist openly on serious matters today (e.g., the role of women and laity; styles of governing; sexuality; freedom of thought and speech). Ignatius says that those things must be "in harmony with the established practices of the orthodox (in texts A and P, "hierarchical") Mother Church" (n. 170); but these practices have often changed. The Church at one time refused to fully reintegrate renegades (but decided to do it around the time of Augustine); reconciled some public sinners at their deathbeds only (this practice also changed); condemned loans with interest (but eventually accepted them); denied religious funerals to people committing suicide (today this is usually not the case); was divided for centuries between scholars seeing the marriage vows as the root of the sacrament of marriage and others who insisted on adding sexual consummation; taught till this century that Creation was completed in six astronomic days and that Adam and Eve were historical beings; accepted democracy in Europe reluctantly, etc. Indeed, Ignatius wants, by recourse to the visible Body of Christ, to avoid illuminism or the disturbing and rebellious independence many Christians showed during the time of the Reformation. But, when we accept the history of the Church's "established practices," can we easily speak of Elections being changeable or not? On December 4, 1963, the Council of Vatican II accepted vernacular languages for the Eucharistic liturgy, which had been refused by the Council of Trent (Session XXII, 1562); so what was the meaning of "established practices" about liturgy on December 3, 1963?

It is also difficult to keep to the letter of some Ignatius' remarks if we accept the discoveries made in psychology. With the knowledge of his time, Ignatius points a direction. He sees an Election as changeable or not according to its *object*; but when he looks at the *person*, he strongly asserts that an Election made by a wrong method is "a bad and sloppy Election," which cannot be called a "divine vocation" (n. 172).

We would often say the same today for a decision revealed by a solid psychological evaluation as having been made with destructive unconscious motivations. But here we leave Ignatius. Ignatius says, "in no way is it allowed to rescind the Election," "there is nothing else to choose" (n. 172). Most of the time today, we refuse such absolute thinking, and the Church itself does, too. Churches have taken into account current psychological knowledge in their "established practices," as the courts do: In many churches, people are ordained only after being seen by a psychologist; ministers are forbidden to act as such, and monks are released from their solemn vows if they are too emotionally disturbed; nymphomania is recognized as nullifying a marriage. We are all more cautious about the motivations behind a choice; we have all known people who stayed with an ambiguous choice for their own reasons, and of whom it was difficult to say how much they were in or out of the commitment they had chosen. (A man in religious life said to me, "At my age, you don't leave.") And we are aware that "to compensate for the harm of the Election with an honest life and diligent deeds" may not be enough for avoiding future risks for anyone (n. 172).

Finally, do we judge people torn between an unbearable situation and an impossible decision? Do we refuse our help if they say that they can no longer carry out their "unchangeable" Election? There can also be extenuating circumstances due to conflicts between civil law and ecclesiastical codes.

For decades I have worked with retreatants making their Election among changes in "the established practices" of churches and society. Ignatius also knew changes in the world and the Church. Reformation shook Europe and provoked centuries of religious wars. Indeed, Ignatius was a very partisan Catholic. Today we are ecumenical, seeing each other as "churches" (Pope Paul VI actually used this word for non-Catholic Christians). Today, too, there is a greater general awareness not only of psychology but also of the diversity of cultures, value systems, behaviors, traditions, etc. Therefore people are less inclined to take at face value pronouncements by the authorities of a church and view respect as something they should *get from* their church's hierarchy as well as *give to* it.

Christians from several different denominations have made the Exercises with me, and my ecumenical tendency to respect them and their tradition has increased with time. Also, most retreatants I have worked with were searching for something, clear or not; being fairly mature, they knew and wanted to follow the deepest beliefs of their church, the visible Body of Christ for them, in spite of any suffering they may have endured in it. All had some emotional problems, but very few would have been seen as unbalanced. (On the other hand, I still thank God for an "odd" retreatant I almost never understood, except for a very brief moment when she spoke about past wounds I had previously suspected. Yet this woman taught me, more than anybody else, that I was the servant of something beyond my understanding.)

Facing a grave choice, retreatants have always accepted that I treated them as belonging to their present state of life until an actual decision was made to change their situation. Thus we have been "maintaining everything as it is" and trying to stay indifferent, even prepared for something not too pleasant (n. 155, 157, 169, 179). The Exercises have worked very well, and most of the time their churches have agreed with the retreatants' choice. All of this has confirmed my conviction, drawn from Ignatius' text, that I have to, above all, respect the decision of each particular person. If Paul is so careful to distinguish what is good for him from what is good for others, the Lord's advice and his own, why would not I be? (1 Cor 7:10–12; we remember Ignatius' caution in n. 135). In the fourth century, the first monks retreated from society *and* the Church into the desert in Egypt because they saw *both* as too corrupted; one wonders if a retreat master would have supported them.

DISCOVERIES

The retreatants no longer see God as telling them what to do, like an external authority figure. Their choice is identical to God's choice and God's choice to theirs; it is a choice desired by God, by the Spirit in them, and by their own filial depth, in a communion similar to that of the three Persons of the Trinity. Moreover, they feel extremely free. One retreatant could articulate his experience this way: "God has walked with me, giving me light and strength, perseverance and hope, and ultimately courage. God cleansed my ways and showed me the Way, which captivated me like Jeremiah [20:7]. Eventually, God confirmed *my* choice, for *I* am the one who has searched, found, and decided what *I* am going to do. God never stole my responsibility and liberty, for no love exists without them."

When we are faced with grave decisions, this experience sometimes includes austere feelings of aloneness (not loneliness), but also the sense of being dignified and treated as an adult by God. Maybe Ignatius the humanist thought the same when he spoke of the soul exercising "freely...its own natural powers" in a time of tranquillity (n. 177).

One retreatant summarized another surprise like this: "God respects me so much that my decision is not to do the best, but what the person I am can do: no more, but no less. If I do a hundred percent of what I can, that is the best, that is 'perfection' for me now; and I can't reject what I *can* do." There is a parallel to this in the New Testament, when Jesus finally asks Peter, repeating the verb used by the apostle, "Do you like (*phileis*) me?" instead of his previous "Do you love (*agapas*) me?" meaning very probably that He accepts Simon's weak love as it is. Other examples are given by Zacchaeus, who keeps *half* of his belongings and says, "*If* I have defrauded..." and Paul, who guarantees, "God will not let you be tested beyond your strength" (Jn 21:15–17; Lk 19:8; 1 Cor 10:13).

So retreatants are often surprised to discover that "perfection" is not an abstract ideal, but what *they* discern *now*, in an absolute personal way, as good *for themselves* through their *own* consolations, as "advantages" for loving and serving more in their own particular life, in "whatever state" (n. 135). The Exercises might have banished their childish dreams, but God's Word has given them the new life of a "perfection" that suits them. It also fits *their* situation: Either in their own humble Nazareth or in a more exposed environment, as the Exercises imply by starting the Election at the juncture of the hidden and the public life of Jesus (n. 135, 163).

Finally, the Election completes the process started in the Principle or Foundation, and the general question of the first colloquy: "What will I do eventually, or what must I do [for Christ]?" (n. 53). Now the retreatants' answer is specific in two senses. It is specific concerning the matter because the choice is for example, this job and not that one, marriage and not religious life. It is specific concerning the person because it is for that person only, in all that person's uniqueness. He or she acknowledges responsibility for past sins and decides to follow and obey Christ by choosing finally His Standard and companionship in his or her particular choice.

In a new job or place, religious life or marriage, another citizenship or a political career, etc., retreatants know that their words in each colloquy, "Hallowed be Thy Name, Thy Kingdom come, Thy Will be done on earth as it is in heaven," are concretely accomplished in and by them. Their praise is going to glorify God in their life in the specific "flesh" of what they have decided (Mt 5:16).

CORRECTION OF LIFE [n. 189]

At the end of the Second Week, Ignatius thinks of retreatants who have "no freedom" to change anything. I met retreatants who were "trapped" in situations they could not change; this may happen in marriage, family, or religious life; in a relationship, in the workplace, etc. At least Corrections made through prayer and discernment, with the Lord of Love, offer the retreatant the chance to put more love for self and others into the situation. Ignatius asks the retreat master to offer those people, instead of an Election, "a method or some formula" for correcting their life. He does the same for those who have no "disposition to deal with Elections about changeable things." (The A text says, more strongly, "who don't have their will really ready to do it.") Indeed, some topics of Election come back for years before they are confronted and resolved, because the retreatant's emotional state and/or circumstances of life don't allow a decision. "As long as my mother is alive, I cannot do that," a retreatant said to me.

But Ignatius' suggestion is also good for people who are not like these and are not facing a specific Election. Usually, discoveries made during the course of the Exercises impel all retreatants to correct their life. I always invite retreatants to evaluate their Second Week with the method I explained at the end of the First Week. Then, gathering together the evaluations of the two Weeks, they see more clearly their personal calls and temptations.

I have noticed that the temptations we understand in the First Week occur through our most immediate weaknesses; the ones discovered in the Second Week are more subtly related to our lust for power and the need to be Number One and to be gods (Gn 3:5). Both are grounded in our childish fears and manipulated by the ghosts of our past. God, however, calls us to a childlike acceptance of what we can bear; thus, in their decisions, retreatants are often aware that they need "a minimum of..." in order to function well; that is, a minimum of attention or financial security, success or support, etc. The "more" (*magis*) of Ignatius found in the offering of self has frequently been misunderstood: Retreatants are not called to an ideal of perfection but to discover the "one more step ahead" they can make right now (n. 97, 147, 213).

With every single retreatant, I have observed that any Election or Correction of Life is *self-centered but never selfish*. It is unavoidably self-centered since it must be the decision of a particular retreatant; this is fidelity to one's own dignity as a free and responsible human person and a necessary condition of being truly fruitful in society. Without it, we can someday expect a retaliation of the inner being who is unable to afford an unwise decision. As a matter of fact, Christian revelation is rooted in an individual person, Jesus, who freely took His responsibility for God and the world; but it was not long before He called companions.

So the retreatant's decision is personal rather than selfish: After all, it comes through the Exercises that endlessly emphasize the need to belong to a community for collective action. For instance, retreatants have a deeper sense of being part of a body of sinners, but also of being called to join a community of disciples, saints, and angels; and Jesus' mission through them concerns the whole world. The whole of human history, the cosmos, and God are never ignored in the Exercises.

Furthermore, this community (which includes the retreat master) has unceasingly taken care of the retreatant; so how could the retreatant *not* choose gratefully and freely to be one of the servants of Love, with and like Jesus (Rom 6; Gal 5:13)? Therefore, it is not by chance that the book ends with the Rules "in order to truly feel with the orthodox Church" (n. 352–370). I have also come to realize that the time of retreatants' decisions is very often the moment when the retreat master's work can be evaluated.

THE RETREAT MASTER'S EVALUATION

Here is the way I evaluate my work as a retreat master—ostensibly at the end of the Exercises, but I have actually done so at the moment when retreatants make their decisions. My first criterion is: Did the person become freer from inordinate attachments, which is the Exodus undertaken through the Exercises (n. 21)? Retreatants who have really discovered God's unconditional love through Jesus' companionship usually want to live for It and no longer under the law of *anything or anybody* else.

"Anything" means that they have uncovered more clearly their idols and that they have found an Exodus route leading out of their own Egypt of self-protection, satisfaction, and adoration through their idiosyncratic cravings for possession, reputation, power, etc. "Anybody" means that they have unveiled and exorcised enough the phantoms of their childhood and want to depend on Love's presence and energy within themselves only, and not on the parental-type law of anybody else, including the retreat master. But is the retreat master himself or herself free as well? When he or she says to a retreatant, "You should do this…" and not "It *seems* to me that as long as you don't face this…," what does that imply or reveal in terms of respect, patience, law, fears, phantoms? I know the kind of freedom the retreatants have allowed me to discover.

My second criterion is: Does the new freedom of retreatants produce the fruit of charity? I remember Paul's words about freedom for service and Matthew speaking of caring for "the least of these" as the last criterion of the Last Judgment (Gal 5:13; Mt 25:31–46). I have worked well if retreatants become more concerned in their own ways with the whole body of humankind and its poorest members (Ignatius says in n. 189, "on the other hand, how much it is fitting to disburse for the poor or devote to charitable works"; and, in Annotation 18, he includes a teaching about "the works of mercy" in the minimum given to retreatants who cannot do too much).

Finally, my third criterion is: Do retreatants become more able to forgive? These criteria test the retreat master's behaviors. If he or she has done the work well, retreatants are now ready to spread their wings for flight, because their Election or Correction of Life is decided. However, they are *just ready*, for they have not yet gone back to their everyday life and acted on their decisions (or if they are making the Exercises in daily life, they are just starting to do so). Somehow they are not *fully* ready, for something is still missing for them, which will be given them through the Third Week.

The criteria I have formulated depend on the answer to the ultimate question, "As a retreat master, have I let God be free?" (n. 15). The best example of an affirmative answer is the times when I am surprised because I don't "understand" the retreatant's decision confirmed by the Spirit and yet peacefully welcome the outcome. The Exercises cannot be programmed, for the call is heard when and how God wants to express it, and when the retreatant is ready for it. I could have said more briefly that retreat masters have just to verify if they have been "faithful servants," accomplishing at once the two commandments, "Serve God and your neighbor" (Mt 24:21; 22:36–40).

Third Week

[n. 190–217]

OVERVIEW

SUGGESTIONS

Like Ignatius, I invite retreatants to start with the Lord's Supper. I also suggest the multiplication of loaves in John 6, chiefly if a decision has been made. Retreatants can celebrate their own Eucharist with it, offering it for the service to come: "Take, this is my [new] Body, this is my [new] Blood," as the young boy with the barley loaves gave what he had to Jesus to feed the crowd. As Jesus did in the Eucharist, they have made a decision they will soon put into action.

Then I tell them to take chronologically the different scenes of the Passion, and I modify the advice I gave them when we started the Exercises. Instead of saying, "Select and only stay with Scriptures that touch you the most," I say, "Indeed, stay longer with what touches you more deeply, but pray once with *each* part of the Passion, because we don't select the times we stay with a suffering friend; we just stay with him or her." I think of Jesus yearning for His friends' presence.

Finally, I invite retreatants to focus on Christ. Could we do otherwise? If we want to know Love, here is the One we must contemplate above all (Zec 12:9–10). The Last Supper (which includes the washing of the disciples' feet by Jesus) is the only Mystery where we find the word "Love," like an overture for the whole Passion (n. 289, where *dilectionis* in our text emphasizes a choice more than *amoris* in texts A and P).

I also tell retreatants what I have observed many times:

Retreatants want to give their company to the suffering Jesus, but when they pray, it is boring, very slow going; they are distracted and often disturbed by fantasies and temptations, like the temptation to shorten the prayer period (n. 12). They end the prayer time with relief, but, strangely, they soon feel eager to go back to prayer and must make an effort to keep to the agreed-upon schedule. When the next prayer period comes, it is still boring, and the cycle repeats itself.

About this I remark, "We want to follow Jesus, but often with a romantic view of the Passion. God keeps us to our word and makes us discover that the Passion was hours of dereliction, temptation, escape, confusion. Remember when you participated in a friend's passion. If you experience what I described, you know that you are into it; just remain there. You'll experience real com-passion [*cum-patiar*: 'I'll suffer with,' see n. 203]. That is all we can do in the face of such mystery, for who could claim to understand it? Stay with Jesus and love gratis, without getting anything apparent in return. You'll live the Third Mode of Humility in your contemplations."

Ignatius gives seven days for the Third Week: I have never heard of any retreat master allotting the full seven days in a thirty-day retreat, and neither did I. Should we reflect about our option to take no more than three or four days for this Week, remembering that in the gospels the Passion is the longest part? For the Exercises in daily life, I give plenty of time to retreatants for the Passion (n. 209); it is a grace to do so once in a while, because it is there that Christian faith is grounded. However, we should keep in mind that in history these events lasted from Thursday evening to Sunday at dawn.

How to End the Third Week

When retreatants are close to the end of the Passion, I tell them not to forget Holy Saturday, a day of silence, absence, faith, and hope. The gospels say nothing about Jesus or His disciples on that day, thus making it the place of nothingness, and therefore the Holy of Holies of God's creating Love (Gn 1:2).

Then I explain Ignatius' suggestion to go back to the whole of the Passion (n. 208–209), as we often do when we reminisce and reread the story of a very painful event; thus, we better understand things that were not clear at the moment. After my brother's death, my wife and I often said, "Do you remember what he said months ago? At that time, we did not get the message. Now we see that he was already aware of the gravity of his disease." I add here the suggestion of one of my retreat masters, who followed and amplified Ignatius' words in n. 208–209: to go back to the whole with the two greatest witnesses of the Passion; once with Jesus' mother, and then with God, His Father.

Praying with Mary is not sentimentality (we learn a lot when we listen to parents who have lost a child in a senseless killing). It is to walk with the one who never lost faith, according to a very old tradition about Mary "standing" at the foot of the cross. She knew, firsthand, God's creative power, and could suspect that nothing was impossible to God (Lk 1:37, 34). Maybe, once again, she asked, "How can this be?" (Lk 1:34). She is a model for us when we are tried by an ordeal, when an Election seems to be an impossible undertaking and challenges our faith. Eventually, we must try to experience the Passion with the only One who knew what was going on, Jesus' Father. In *God's Passion Our Passion* (Liguori, Mo.: Triumph, 1994), I develop this mystery of God silently watching the new Moses leading the Exodus of all humankind.

THE FRUIT

DISCOVERIES OF THE RETREATANT

This fruit is paradoxical but freeing because it is unifying and healing. Our faith asserts that in the crucified Innocent, the compassionate Triune God of the Incarnation (n. 102) loves, forgives, and saves all the sinners of the drama and of history from Alpha to Omega—that is who have damaged and will damage Love, including the retreatants.

Centering on Jesus works like a mirror. As retreatants, we see that we have been this harmed Jesus: We see the innocent child and the grown-up person we have been. We also see that we have been childish cowards like Peter, a traitor like Judas, an opportunist like Caiphas or Pilate, hateful like the crowd, and have hurt our beauty or others'. Contemplating brings sorrow and certainty. Our sorrowful com-passion is for Love in Jesus crucified (n. 197, 203, 206) and in ourselves or others who are paying the price of sin, before and after Golgotha, and right up to Bosnia-Herzegovina, not to mention our streets, legislatures, and churches today (n. 192, 195). But because "Christ's divinity...does not destroy its adversaries" (us included, n. 196), we are certain that Jesus' love does not flinch, that God forgives us. This Week proves that we are saved sinners, that we are pardoned. This increases our gratitude and our desire to be no longer among Jesus' enemies, and to serve freely with and like Him in order to make the world a less damaging place for everyone, and especially the most innocent.

Experiencing that Love suffered and died for us, we accept the opportunity to suffer with Him for others (n. 197, 203). If necessary, we are ready like Paul to "fill up, in [our] own flesh, what is lacking in the sufferings of Christ for the sake" of all, "according to what [we] intend to decide about [ourselves] in this or that respect" (Col 1:24; n. 199).

The Election or the Correction of Life we have decided on now includes a freeing realism. The more we contemplate Jesus' Passion, the more the truth of our situation is revealed. Now we foresee that when our decision is acted upon, chiefly if it is a big and evangelical mission, we might often find ourselves as a new Jesus, rejected, disowned, abandoned, and apparently powerless. Our decision, which was rooted in the desire to be with Him, will be a Passion with Him. In the Spiritual Exercises in daily life, if such a decision is acted on immediately, the Passion of Jesus *is* contemplated simultaneously in Scriptures and in life every day (n. 203).

In our decision, we said, "I'll follow You wherever You go," and "I will lay down my life for You" (Lk 9:57; Jn 13:37). Now the Third Week brings an awareness about the death of all our godlike pretensions and gods, but such a death is a Passover for a new life. We are sure that, carrying out our decision, we will still be bought and sold, caught by compromise and human respect. But the Jesus we contemplate says to us, "Love and forgive the sinner you are going to be, the one who will deny or betray, follow from afar or run away, and do the same later for others and yourself" (n. 197).

This is not in the First Week, probably because it is a Week for all, even those who cannot make all the Exercises (n. 9, 18); maybe they would not be able to distinguish between "loving myself as sinner with compassion" and "loving myself as sinning with complacency" (for such people, when they do make the Third Week, it is just a repetition of the First Week). Thus our childish fantasies of heroism die here, and our decision is kept with the childlike simplicity of a heart that knows its permanent frailty (Gal 2:11–14).

It is also a healthy realism that pushes us to again offer our decision to God, but this time to God's mercy (n. 183, 188). It is the death of adolescent illusions about love as a romance, but it is the grown-up realism that knows that to love and serve is to give and give up our life (n. 197). Even though the death of our dreams and illusions might be painful, for we "lose" our life, it frees us from a naive and unwise heroism (Mk 8:34–37). No trumpets, no fanfares—our Love will stay in "a humble condition" (n. 144).

On the contrary, I have seen some retreatants, while looking at their decision, struggling and agonizing with the fear of being lost, "dying" during the Third Week, but comforted by the companionship of Jesus crucified. "Wherever you go, I shall go; wherever you die, I shall die," one retreatant heard Jesus say as an answer to the prayer *Anima Christi* (Soul of Christ), said there very appropriately (Ru 1:16–17). The Third Mode of Humility finds its completion here (n. 167).

I said that the Third Week unifies and heals, and sometimes, paradoxically, through a kind of death that is full of life. It is unifying because, as retreatants, we discover that we are called to love in ourselves both the sinner who can harm *and* the victim who can be harmed. No part of us is excluded from our love, exactly as nobody was or is from Jesus' mercy. This is healing because we know that we can be passion for ourselves and others, with the double meaning of the word: sorrowful passion when we hurt ourselves or others (n. 165–166), or a loving passion when we serve and forgive as Jesus did (n. 168, 197).

The Third Week makes us hope that our passionate service will counterbalance the sorrow and suffering we will cause. This will happen when we act like Mary in the Pietà, when through our decision we serve ourselves and others with the love she showed for her crucified Son. We know, realistically now, that we can be good Samaritans (Lk 10:29–37).

But sometimes such acceptance of who we are occurs through the death of all idealistic pictures of ourselves that we have previously held. This is illustrated by our decision itself: It is already a death because to choose one alternative is to renounce the other; it is more so if our decision is going to be difficult to achieve; and finally it is a death because it will never be perfectly accomplished. That is why some decisions are "bittersweet," as one retreatant characterized them. "It was so for Jesus, it cannot be otherwise for me," we say at the end of the Third Week. However, such lucidity is full of life because it prepares us to face a real life of evangelical love and service. The realism acquired in the Third Week is already a victory, for it leads to the extreme of the freedom and love of the Third Mode of Humility proven in the crucified Christ, and it anticipates the fulfillment of the promise of the King Jesus and the Fourth Week (n. 157, 199, 95).

I tell retreatants undergoing painful moments something I learned in India. As Westerners, we look at life in a linear way: We die, *and then* we are alive again. In Indian culture, if something is dying, something is simultaneously being born, and vice versa, as Jesus said about the grain of wheat (Jn 12:24). Then I invite such retreatants to keep faith in something growing up through what they might be perceiving as a death. And I have always reminded them that John, speaking of Jesus being "lifted up,"meant *crucified, risen, and in glory* all together (Jn 3:14; 12:32). My hope is that they will be ready for life while being ready to "die."

THE RETREAT MASTER'S PASSION

Retreat masters who write about the Exercises don't say too much about the Third Week, because, after mentioning the paradox I described, it is difficult for them to discern which facet of it is experienced by retreatants. Can we understand a Passion before Resurrection? (Lk 24:25–27). Often, retreat masters undergo a Passion of powerlessness, chiefly if the retreatant is "dying." Moreover, the retreat master won't live out the retreatant's decision and its consequences. "I am going where you cannot follow me," they hear from crucified retreatants who suffer and "die" (Jn 13:36). What can they say to the retreatant, who is alone? I have learned to be there, compassionate but silent, available but respectfully distant. In thirty-day retreats, the appointments with retreatants are shorter (also because the daily "menu" of prayer is obvious), but I am available ("Come and see me, if necessary"); when it is time to pray on Holy Saturday, we have no appointments or liturgy. In the Spiritual Exercises in daily life, we meet less often, but I am likewise available ("Call me, if you need me").

If retreat masters care about the retreatants they walk with, it is a "bittersweet" situation where they must accept the death of all their preconceptions about retreatants. Such a behavior reflects to the retreatant Jesus' Father in the Passion: The Father was walking lovingly but silently and sorrowfully with the One crossing the Red Sea of the Passion, because They had agreed in the Trinity to love at any price (n. 102, 108, 206). Analogically, retreatants and retreat master had agreed to pass through the Exercises, including the Third Week, and any decision to come. At least, the distance taken by the retreat master during the Third Week prepares for the separation that will occur at the end of the Exercises.

However, the retreat master still has to help retreatants to make the Exercises correctly and not to escape the Passion (n. 6, 7–8, 10, 12, 207). So if the Third Week is too easy, it is necessary to verify what is going on. Are we dealing with a sadomasochistic enjoyment that has nothing to do with the crucified One? Neither Jesus nor His Father enjoyed the Passion; but They had decided to love till the end. Similarly, retreatants normally choose to be with Christ in *any* situation since the offering of n. 95, but not suffering for its own sake, although they accept it.

The Election (or Correction of Life) and the Third Week show precisely the real or possible painful consequences of their decision if it is a big one. I have seen retreatants, because of a new call, "dying" to a great reputation, to the advantages of religious life, to the security of living in their own country. Asceticism is not a Christian goal, but it is often the result of love and service. Accordingly, in this Week, if Ignatius changes Additions 2 and 6, he does not mention Addition 10 about physical penance

(n. 206, although the Passion was mentioned in n. 87); he speaks of temperance in eating and not of penance, and he has no problem with a retreatant who would prefer "to shorten the time" spent on the Passion (n. 83, 210, 209). I think that he is cautious about any risk of sadomasochism; so must the retreat master be as well.

In fact, when retreatants are mature in their offering, they are not blindly and romantically bold like Peter, James, or John (Mk 10:35–40; 14:26–31). If they don't know all the details of the consequences of their decision, they do know that to love is to die. Nevertheless, trusting the presence and strength of the crucified Jesus within them, they say like Zebedee's sons, "We can" (Mt 21:22; 2 Cor 4:7–18; Gal 2:20; 6:14–17).

RULES ABOUT EATING

If Ignatius is silent about physical penance in this Week, he does speak of eating. Some people judge this as trivial here, even though we lose our appetite when faced with a dying friend or starving children in Rwanda, and even though Jesus said, "When... the groom is taken away, [the wedding guests] will fast" (Mt 9:15). Also, Ignatius may have had in mind Hermas' story of *The Shepherd* (around A.D. 125), which sees fasting as meaningful only if we share what we save with the poor. Classical examples of temperance or moderation, these Rules invite us to find the right measure, to master our appetite, to moderate both quantity of food and manner of eating; they illustrate the law of extremes of the Notes about scruples and the use of our body for spiritual gain (n. 83, 213, 216, 349–350, 76, 87); and, in their own field, they are tools for creating the freedom of indifference with the right balance (n. 213, 84, 15, 179, 350). I always talk about these Rules because they can be useful for many addictions, and chiefly because of their link with the Passion and the retreatants' decision.

I have been struck by the structure of n. 217 (similar to the one of n. 12–13): It is better to decide *before* the reality of the meal how much we will eat, because it will be easier to keep our decision when we get to the table; no decision is possible when a mouth-watering dessert stands ten inches from our lips. But, more important, the structure of the Rule is the one connecting the Lord's Supper to His death on the cross. Jesus had fully decided and sacramentally accomplished the gift of His life through the institution of the Eucharist. He did not back off when reality asked Him to put His decision into action. And His gift on the cross proved that His sacramental gift was total.

That is also the structure of what happens to retreatants. They make a decision, usually in a retreat house, after leaving "home… friends…acquaintances…business" with their "mind being less distracted in all directions…" (n. 20), i.e., far from the reality of their daily existence. But this decision, made before going back to their usual life, will materialize more easily because it has been seriously discerned and has come about through prayer, and because the guarantee of Jesus' companionship has been experienced. Finally, the Rules remind us that meals can be places of spiritual experiences, no less today than they are in the gospels (n. 213, 214; 1 Cor 10:31).

Fourth Week

INTRODUCTION

During this Week, retreatants pray about the risen Jesus till His Ascension (n. 299–312) and are invited to share His "joy with His own" (n. 221, 229). Ignatius also suggests two topics not found in the gospels: Jesus appearing to His mother (justified in n. 299) and the "Contemplation for stimulating within us spiritual love."

THE APPARITION TO MARY [n. 218–225]

The Third Week finished with Mary; the Fourth starts with her. I explain to retreatants that Ignatius' proposal follows the logic of the gospels and Acts (n. 299). These books show Mary present each time her Son "appears" in a new condition: She is there for His conception and birth, when He begins His public life, enters into death, and is born in His new body, the Church (Jn 2:1–12; 19:25–26; Acts 1:14). So it is logical that He would appear to her in His glorious condition.

THE CONTEMPLATION FOR STIMULATING WITHIN US SPIRITUAL LOVE [n.230–237]

Nothing says if this contemplation is part of a Week (it was the same for the Principle or Foundation). The mental re-creation of the place, the last of a series begun in the First Week, reveals where the retreatant is (n. 233). This one started, like "a common soldier (ashamed because of his wrongdoings)... in the presence of his king and the court," then made a first offering to the King's service in front "of the whole heavenly Court," and later stood before "all the saints with the desire" to find out the best manner to please God; now that this service has been specified in a personal way and tested by the Third Week, before "the angels and all saints," the retreatant asks God for this grace: "Perceiving the magnitude of the benefits He [God] has given to me, I may devote all of myself to His love, worship, and service" (n. 74, 98, 151, 232, 233).

This grace sums up the Contemplation, which is a list of God's gifts, and leads to the total offering of the retreatant to God's "love, worship, and service" through the prayer, "Take (or Receive), Lord, etc." The list of God's gifts echoes the Principle or Foundation, as does the word "worship," substituted for the word "praise," in what is called the circularity of the Exercises.

The word "love," absent in the Principle or Foundation, appears here; and the reciprocal giving by God and by the retreatant is explained by two remarks about love: Ignatius says that love consists of deeds and not words only, and of mutual exchange (1 Jn 3:18; "All I have is yours and all you have is mine," Jn 17:10). We may suspect why Ignatius has waited so long to insert love into the context of the Exercises: Retreatants have been purified by the First Week, have followed Love in their flesh as companions of Jesus, and pass through the ultimate passion and victory of Love with the Crucified and Risen One. Now they won't misunderstand what Love is all about, and, first of all, they know that it is a Person, God, experienced in Jesus.

However, the word "love" appears in these paragraphs without any religious reference; maybe Ignatius thinks that the context itself links it to Jesus' God, as it does in John's first epistle, or maybe he refuses to make love the private property of Christians. So, the last word of the Exercises is about Love. The nameless God and "man" of the Principle or Foundation are now personalized as the God of Jesus, called "Love" by John, and the retreatant (1 Jn 4:8).

SUGGESTIONS

REREADING THE WHOLE PROCESS

As soon as we start the Week, I invite retreatants to read and reread several times all their notes between their prayer periods, in order to get a sketch of their last evaluation at the end of the Exercises: thus I apply Ignatius' suggestion about the Passion to what they have written down since the beginning of their retreat (n. 208).

PRAYER PERIODS

I suggest the retreatant pray with Jesus' apparitions to His mother and other people with my advice for the Third Week: "Stay with the story touching you the most, but pray once with each apparition" (n. 226). I mention the possibility of praying with Pentecost (Acts 2; Ignatius does not go beyond Jesus' life, but he speaks of Him appearing to Paul in n. 311). I ignore n. 308–310, because they don't offer too much to contemplate.

In my second meeting with retreatants, I give and comment on the Contemplation *ad Amorem*. I invite them to use it with the method of "sandwiching" explained earlier, some prayer periods about the risen Jesus, a slice or two of this contemplation, and so on. And I say, "Slowly, pray chiefly with this contemplation while finishing the apparitions. Doing so, you are going to go back to daily life and end the Exercises as such. Once they are formally finished, you can still stay for a while with the Contemplation *ad Amorem* in your day-to-day life."

DISCOVERIES

THE RISEN JESUS APPEARS TO HIS MOTHER

This contemplation is meaningful, even without any specific devotion for Mary. The absence of a text about the event makes retreatants imagine *their own* risen Christ. Indeed, He has taken for and in them a more specific and personal face through the Exercises. With no evangelical text, do we risk the fantasies of a wild imagination? Usually, we don't, because this possibility has been reduced through the test of the Third Week (see *Contemplation* in Appendix [p. 224]).

Contemplating the Risen One with Mary implies Incarnation and Nativity, i.e., the conception and birth of a Son. Now, Mary discovers a new Son: He is the one she knew, but "reborn" beyond death. This is similar to the retreatants' situation. They now face the new Son of God they have found, and also the new son or daughter of God *they* have become. Retreatants have discovered more deeply the unbelievable Love who God is, who died and went to hell for us in Jesus. This is a brand-new God, One who is absolute and unconditional Mercy and Compassion, Forgiveness, and Love, unconquerable by sin and death.

Analogically, retreatants are no longer dealing only with the child of God they were; they are and are not the same. With Jesus, they have passed through the "baptism" of death and are resurrected as new creatures (Rom 6; Mk 10:38). For some of them, this journey included a descent into some sort of hell (n. 219). Their own love is reborn as new, purified and tested, strengthened and stimulated, by the Exercises. This is not a dream, because it is specifically incarnated here and now in a real Election or Correction of Life.

"SO I SEND YOU" (Jn 20:21)

Retreatants feel at home with the disciples' mixed feelings. Partly, this is because they may still experience some doubts and may experience yet more doubts when they put their decision into action. But also they must get used to their new forms of loving, just as the disciples had to get used to Jesus' new presence and the newness of their life in the Spirit. It will take weeks, months, or years for retreatants to integrate the new creature they are, especially if new life means changing a job or moving to another country, having or adopting a child, entering religious life or ordained ministry or marriage (2 Cor 5:17).

But they also share the disciples' increasing certainty: "It is the Lord," they say before their new love (Jn 21:7). For they "saw" and "touched" it in their contemplations through the consolations their "best friend" gave them "promptly and abundantly" (n. 224, 54; Jn 20:28). They are also sure that Jesus knows and calls them by their unique name and is with them "always [and all-ways], till the end of time" (Jn 20:16; Lk 24:36; Mt 28:20). Such certainty brings peace and joy—a "spiritual joy," as Ignatius wisely says, because it is never a noisy, excited, superficial exhilaration (n. 229, 221, 48, 93, 329).

The structure of the apparitions shows them that this new love is a mission in the world. "As the Father has sent me, so I send you...receive the Holy Spirit..." (Jn 20:21–22 justifies Ignatius' omission of Pentecost). It is time not to cling to the Jesus savored in retreat, to look up at the skies, to enjoy the security of a se-cluded place and retreat master, but to leave with their new spirit (Jn 20:17; Acts 1:11; n. 20). As the disciples did after the Ascension, as Ignatius did after a last visit to the location of this event before leaving the Holy Land, they must go back to their own Jerusalem, as Jesus' witnesses through their task. This task may be the same, but somehow *they* are changed in it, like Simon the fisherman who became Peter, "fisher of men" (Acts 1:8; Jn 21:3; Lk 5:10; Mt 4:19). There is no surprise in this, because the retreat is ending, but also because in each Week they have heard the call to serve, and it becomes clearer, deeper, and broader through the rereading of their journal (n. 23, 53, 95, 146, 197).

"HE OPENED THEIR MINDS TO THE UNDERSTANDING OF THE SCRIPTURES" (Lk 24:45)

By rereading their notes, retreatants prepare their evaluation of the totality of the Exercises for the last meetings with the re-treat master. Also, as they did with the Passion, they see new things by looking at the whole retreat. I heard remarks like, "Now I see why I was made desolate by the Two Standards"; "Do you re-member that consolation in the Third Week? It started the break-through of three days later"; "I could not contemplate the risen Christ's newness; of course, I had resisted my own Passion, the deaths I had to accept in my decision."

But now retreatants read more than their holy and sinful his-tory, as they did at the beginning. Rereading their notes, they are like the first Christians, the disciples of Emmaus, for instance (Lk 24:13–35). The early Church saw the risen Christ prophesied in Scriptures and reread them as accomplished by Him: In Jesus' victory, God had fulfilled the Covenant with Israel and with humankind (Gn 9:15–18). The Church saw itself as the new Jerusalem, where pagans and Jews were reconciled by the Emmanuel, God-with-us (Rv 21; Gal 3:28). This vocation passed through history with ups and downs, requiring the Church to offer God endlessly its own body for the sake of itself and the world, sure that "God is faithful, who called you to fellowship with His Son, Jesus Christ our Lord" (1 Cor 1:9).

Similarly, retreatants see in their notes that the "Scriptures" of their *past* prepared what the Exercises revealed. But they also read the new meaning of their *past, present, and future*, because of their discoveries about themselves, the world, Jesus, and His Father. In their renewed Christlike being, God fulfills the covenant made with them since their conception and baptism and specified now in their decisions. Their journal repeats that they are temples of a Love who reconciles all parts of their person, formerly enslaved by idolatry (like pagans) or self-righteousness (like Pharisees; Gal 3:28; Rom 1–3). Their notes teach them how to discern everywhere a call to serve , how to be freer and let Love be free in them.

Indeed, a thirty-day retreat (like the one ending Jesuits' training) and the Exercises in daily life are frequently a mystical experience influencing the whole life of the retreatant through its ups and downs. Sure of the fidelity of God, "who has begun the good work in [them, and] will carry it through to completion," retreatants know what they are responsible for: freely, to allow God to exist in the world through their personal decisions (Phil 1:6). They have only to endlessly offer themselves to the action of Jesus' God.

"TAKE, THIS IS MY BODY..."

Contemplation *ad Amorem* invites retreatants to perpetually offer the entirety of their flesh to God. This contemplation does not refer to any biblical quotes, for it is the retreatant's "text" that gives the "particular or private" examples for Ignatius' general description (n. 234).

Retreatants have offered themselves many times (n. 5, 17, 94, 96–98, 183, 188), but now they offer the whole of their new life in the world because of what the Exercises have accomplished. They give God the new creature they are, their "bodies as a living sacrifice holy and acceptable"; they don't want to "conform [themselves] to this age," for "they are transformed by the renewal of [their] mind," and they know how to "discern what is God's will, what is good, pleasing and perfect" (Rom 12:1–2). Their offering is made to the God seen through Jesus in history and in their own history, as profusely giving, as Gift (n. 234). This is the reciprocity of love described by Ignatius (n. 230–231). Finding God in all things and people impels them to give themselves back to God through everything and everybody. "A [new] body you have given me...Here I am to do your will, O God" (Heb 10:5–7).

Thus I make retreatants aware that this contemplation is structured like the Eucharist: We recognize God's gift, and we give ourselves back to God. And because this prayer is made with their life and decisions, it reveals to them that their daily existence can become eucharistic action. Jesus' God says, through *things and people*, "Take, this is my Body [of Love]"; we say in return, by our deeds *anywhere and for anyone*, "Take, this is my body [of love]."

An ordinary life in the world can be an extraordinary Eucharist, for Love is there and nowhere else. This structure also says, although the words are not in this Contemplation, that we end with gratitude and praise, as we started in the Principle or Foundation; we give thanks ("eucharisteo" in Greek). Concerning this, I mention to retreatants David's prayer (1 Chr 29:10–20) and a statement I heard years ago: "The proof that we are in Love is that we give thanks for everything and everybody."

A NEW PAIR OF GLASSES AND A NEW WAY OF READING!

Retreatants end the Exercises with grateful praise to God, which endures because they now wear new "glasses" (n. 39) and read their life in a new way. Nothing has changed, but everything is changed *for them*. It is not a transformation so much as a transfiguration. Now they marvel in front of what they see as we do in front of a simple poppy as painted by Georgia O'Keeffe. They are still a grain of sand, but they *see* the pearl God makes with it: Their history is God's history in and through them. The world is no longer just "exile," or a "valley of miseries, among irrational animals," their body is no longer "a prison," because they progressively see all things differently (n. 47).

With the Contemplation *ad Amorem*, they start to *see* that anything that could be an obstacle can be a means to meet God, that their body is God's temple and themselves God's image and likeness (n. 235). Healed by the Exercises, they are not blind about daily sins, struggles, and vanities, but they *see* more easily "God who richly furnishes us with everything to enjoy," because they are more easily "contemplative in action," as the Jesuits would say (1 Tim 6:17). It is a renewed hope in the faith that nothing "will be able to separate [them] from the love of God that comes to us in Christ Jesus, our Lord," because this God "makes all things work together for the good of those who love Him who have been called according to His decree" (Rom 8:28–39). Any event that could break the Covenant with God becomes the place for renewing it, through a loving exchange that encompasses everything (n. 39, 229). Because when we love, everything becomes sign.

THE ADDITIONS AND THE TEXT ITSELF

ADDITIONS [n. 226–229]

The climate of the Fourth Week justifies Ignatius' advice to make everything lighter, more pleasant, and freer; penance is reduced to temperance. This is a way to prepare gradually for the return to normal life, where the schedule of prayer cannot be as it was during the retreat. My meetings with retreatants become shorter: They don't have too much to learn or express, and I have less and less to do.

THE TEXT

It is certainly a text that pleases environmentally conscious retreatants, for it gives to our prayer a cosmic dimension and helps us to see God in all creatures. The verbs show also that our reason is not put aside, but is always invited to "consider" or "ponder."

In the Contemplation *ad Amorem*, however, Ignatius does not say anything about the difficulties of life, except through the words "Redemption" and "how much the most generous Lord has... suffered for me" (n. 234). Maybe he thinks that the Third Week and the Rules of discernment have made retreatants able to see God's gifts in such moments, that the Fourth Week has revealed to them that Love conquers sin and death (Jesus keeps His stigmata in His glory; so can we with our wounds); and so he prefers to emphasize the positive character of the end of the Exercises.

However, Ignatius may think of our dark days when he speaks of God "working and somehow *laboring*... for me" (Jn 5:17) because "to labor" implies pain; indeed, God's work for and in us is a labor when things are tough (n. 236). I remind retreatants that "labor" was a part of Jesus' call in the Kingdom of Christ (n. 95).

Jesus is not named in the contemplation. Ignatius probably sees retreatants as sharing the disciples' experience and knowledge after the Ascension: The individual Jesus is gone, back to His Father, but He remains present in the disciples through His Spirit, of whom they are the temple (Jn 20:17, n. 235). At the end of the Exercises, they also know that "everything comes from God who has reconciled us with Himself through Christ" (2 Cor 5:18).

Moreover, Ignatius might have read Meister Eckhart, who said that we eventually have to go beyond Jesus, to God; after all, Jesus can disappear after having accomplished Redemption (mentioned in n. 234). The retreat master, too, can disappear: "It is much better for you that I go. If I don't go, the Paraclete will never come to you, whereas if I go, I will send Him to you" (Jn 16:7).

Finally, I invite retreatants to make their own prayer ("Take...") if they are not at ease with Ignatius' scholastic expressions. At the end, I emphasize that the last phrase of the offering, "Give me only to love You with Your grace, and I am rich enough so that I do not ask for anything else," sends us back to the freedom of the Principle or Foundation, but now explicitly rooted in Love (n. 234).

THREE METHODS OF PRAYING
[n. 238–260]

Annotation 4 mentions the Three Methods as part of the Exercises. Annotation 18 includes them in the minimum of teaching; Ignatius probably did not let his retreatants go without knowing these methods, especially if they were "uneducated or illiterate." This last point may explain the absence of contemplation in the Three Methods; contemplation is always used from the Second to the Fourth Week, Weeks not made by the "uneducated." Maybe Ignatius thinks that such persons could be harmed by the risks of the use of imagination (see *Contemplation* in Appendix [p. 225]), and so he gives three methods requiring simple tools: intellect, memory, will, repetition. The methods deal with things familiar to everyone at that time (the commandments, the seven mortal sins, the usual prayers, which Ignatius recommends teaching if necessary; n. 18). The mention of the application of the five senses does not contradict what I have just said, because it is done when prayer is about sin (n. 247). "Uneducated or illiterate" persons, those sensitive to the "seductive pleasures of the flesh and of the senses," can all pray about the ways we sin with our senses (n. 314); similarly, to pray about hell with the senses might not be difficult for them, because everybody can easily imagine how we can suffer through each one of them. And if Ignatius specifies here "the five senses of the body" (n. 247; the only place in the Exercises where he use the phrase "of the body"), it is perhaps in order to be more easily understood by everyone. The use of the senses may prepare beginners and uneducated persons for eventual contemplation.

The first method is a sort of examination (n. 238–248, 18, 42), and Ignatius himself pinpoints that it "does not have so much the form of prayer as the form of a spiritual Exercise"—in my opinion, of the First Week (n. 238). It is here that we found the five senses. The second is a kind of reflective meditation on each word or phrase of a very common prayer, with the advice to stay longer with the ones that resonate for us intellectually or emotionally (n. 252, 254, which seem to imply the Rule of n. 316). The third reminds us of what is called "the Jesus Prayer" by the use of repetition. To the extent that these Three Methods might be a minimum, I think a retreat master has leeway to teach more to retreatants who are able to handle more.

THE LAST RECOMMENDATIONS

In order to prepare for the separation, the retreat master must slowly taper off the meetings, announce the coming of the last meeting, and disappear. The retreatant-retreat master relationship has lasted thirty days or, for the Exercises in daily life, for some months. It has been a very special intimacy, for only a few people hear what a retreat master hears about the journey of a human being with God. Therefore, for the retreatants, consciously or subconsciously, it might sometimes be difficult to end such a relationship. Even if the retreat master has been wise and careful, a strong bond has been created, so it is advisable to announce ahead of time that it is going to be broken (sometimes forever). This is true even in a thirty-day retreat, of which everybody knows the calendar. But we are luckier than the disciples, who did not know when Jesus was going to disappear definitively.

It is good to have a clear-cut end. This is easy in a thirty-day retreat, for there is a prearranged day of departure. For the Exercises in daily life, when I know that I will meet the retreatant again to offer spiritual help, I always maintain a significant period of time before our first reencounter.

In our last meeting, I say, "The book of your life is unfinished, but you have sown seeds during this important chapter, which contains most of the main themes of the book. So, I suggest that you save it and reread it once in a while, because your retreat is going to go on working for years, for an infinite journey." One retreatant told me that it took twenty years for him to get the last (if it is indeed the last) grace and understanding of his greatest consolation during the Exercises.

Thus I recommend keeping the whole journal for five years and rereading it once a year. I then suggest getting rid of the notes, except the evaluations, which could be read at Lent and Advent, for instance. After a few more years, we can keep only the last evaluation (and the Election, if it created a huge change in life), and go back to it several times a year. The evaluations help daily examinations, for we find in them all our calls and temptations.

In order to make the business of memory easier, I advise retreatants to see if the evaluations (or sometimes just the last one) can be summarized in one short sentence or a few words to serve as spiritual names. I remember these examples: "Backseat only," "Queen or servant," "Abandon or self-abandonment," "Nothing in myself, everything in him," "He emptied himself, behaving like a human being." The person knows all the implications, meanings, mechanisms, and details behind such a summary (the more areas of the retreatant's life are covered, the better its value). The summary often shows the two sides of the same coin, one expressing the Lord's advice and the other the Enemy's suggestions; both are frequently connected with the childlike graces or the childish risks of our own inner child. This helps our memory in daily life, for our Lord calls us endlessly and our Opponent is unceasingly "prowling like a roaring lion looking for someone to devour" (1 Pt 5:8).

I also ask retreatants to find a material daily reminder: for example, a short prayer we'll say each day, a picture on our night table or desk (Visitors to a CEO were always surprised to see a small Stop sign on his desk), a stone of the beach of the retreat house. The reminder should be something we are going to touch, see, smell, hear, or say every day. For twenty-five years, one of my Jesuit friends said, every night before falling asleep, "Take, Lord, all my freedom…" My last piece of advice always is, "And, please, never forget the 'minimum of' what you need to function in a healthy manner."

MYSTERIES OF THE LIFE
OF OUR LORD JESUS CHRIST
[n. 218–237]

These texts have created questions like: What did the word "mysteries" mean for Ignatius? Why are the Mysteries in all versions of the Exercises? How were they used with retreatants? We could answer that each event of the life of Jesus, Son of God, is an unfathomable mystery; that a traveling Jesuit would have at hand the necessary minimum for giving the Exercises without carrying a heavy Bible; that these texts are a summary given to the retreatant after the retreat master read or told the story with more details (could retreatants read, and read the Latin of Saint Jerome's translation?); that Ignatius wants to help retreat master and retreatant by dividing each scene into three points (n. 261). But I don't spend any time with those questions because we no longer need these pages of the Exercises; each retreatant can today have and read the New Testament and does not need a paraphrase of it.

I send retreatants to these Mysteries when they have to follow the chronology of the events in all four gospels (two last Weeks); what they find there is something like a synopsis of the four gospels. But a retreat master must read the Mysteries, at least once, to get some information about the Exercises and about Ignatius himself.

We don't find any parable or discourse of Jesus (except Mt 5–7, in a rather short and strong summary for the "beloved disciples," n. 278). All Ignatius' proposals are scenes that can be contemplated. Thus the retreatant is invited to be not with a message, as good as it may be, but with a person, Jesus (seen, heard, touched, smelled, and tasted through the five senses). To be with Him in such companionship makes one a disciple more than any intellectual reflection does. Indeed, as soon as the disciples appear, all Mysteries include them, the Twelve and others, like the women and Paul. It is the Church, with its message, sacraments, authorities, and community (n. 275–292, 298–312).

Of course, Jesus is the center of most Mysteries. This justifies three exceptions to what I have just said about the disciples being present in all the Mysteries: In the Passion, contemplations focus only on Jesus (the adversaries are there as unavoidable protagonists of the drama and the disciples have fled); when Jesus is tempted in the desert, nobody was present there (n. 274). The third exception is Jesus' childhood: However, here we do encounter Mary and Joseph (were they not the first companions of Jesus?).

When we look at details, we notice a few things that may help the retreat master. First, Ignatius' prudence, maybe because of the

Reformation. He wants to distinguish clearly his own words from God's Word (n. 261). He is careful when he speaks of Jesus as a carpenter, of some apostles being called three times (indeed, some vocations or decisions are discerned by degrees), of the identity of the woman who anointed Jesus, of Christ's apparition to Joseph of Arimathea (n. 271, 275, 282, 310). Some retreat masters could do the same.

Second, let's look at Ignatius' choices. Mark's Gospel is rarely mentioned, although it could lend itself better to the contemplation than Matthew's because it is more picturesque. But, maybe it is precisely Matthew's sobriety that Ignatius prefers, as it would either free the retreatant's imagination or, on the contrary, put a brake on it (also, this gospel was perhaps the most usual in liturgies, and so the best known). Sobriety reminds us of Ignatius' advice to the retreat master in Annotation 2; and maybe it is better to give biblical texts not too complicated or strange to retreatants.

Sometimes Ignatius' selection is difficult to explain, like n. 288 about Jesus preaching in the Temple and then going back to Bethany because Jerusalem did not welcome Him. Sometimes we may guess the reason for his choice: For instance, he prefers Matthew's multiplication of loaves to John's, probably because he wants to show Jesus working through His disciples (n. 283). But why did he not use John's version of the event of Bethany, which gives more details (n. 286)? This last example gives us a third aspect of Ignatius' technique, his freedom.

His text about Bethany is a mixture of Matthew and John, for he mentions Judas' reaction, related by John alone. Ignatius seems concerned not by academic points but by effectiveness: If a story works, like Christ's appearing to Joseph of Arimathea or the Fathers in Limbo, why not "piously meditate" on it (n. 310–311; n. 111 offers a she-donkey, a maid servant, an ox)? I have seen some retreatants add their own intercessors to Mary and Jesus in the triple colloquy. But Ignatius' freedom does not lose sight of wisdom, as I always point out to retreatants.

Finally, we can see here and there Ignatius' personal touch, either in the three versions of the Exercises or only in our text, as if he is making a final correction. This might be connected with his own experiences or readings (like *The Life of the Saints*, mentioned in A, n. 310, and *The Life of Christ* of Ludolph the Carthusian monk). For instance, he corrects "conception of Christ" (A, P) to "conception of the divine Word" in n. 262 (is this theological scrupulosity for the official text?); he calls "admirable" the conception of John the Baptist in the same n. 262 (in order to emphasize the miracle?); his correction "the blessed Virgin" instead of "Our Lady" (A) or "Mary" (P), is perhaps to maintain that Jesus' mother remained a virgin, according to the teaching of the Church (n. 263); in n. 280, Peter walks on water, but not because of Jesus' command (A, P); he corrects "Palm Sunday" (A, P) to "Palms Day" in n. 287 (for historical accuracy?); and in n. 290, the three apostles during Jesus' agony are of course no longer "Saint," as they were in the Autograph.

Eventually, we see Ignatius' personal touch in remarks of his own or that he borrowed. In n. 275, he emphasizes the "humble condition" of the apostles, the "great dignity" of their call, their superiority by grace over the giants of the Bible, showing that he sees Jesus' call to us as a marvelous grace (this is everywhere in the Exercises). He is sensitive about Jesus' kindness toward the sellers of turtledoves and His love for the "beloved disciples" to the point of washing Judas' feet and allowing him "to betray Him with a kiss" (n. 277, 278, 289, 291). He excuses somehow Peter's refusal to be washed (n. 289). He comments on Jesus' sweating in the Agony with a phrase from Ludolph the Carthusian monk: "one can suppose that His garments were already soaked with blood"; he asserts that Jesus "remained bound all that night"; he shows a sorrowful Mary when he speaks about "the Lord...removed from the cross...before the eyes of His very afflicted Mother," probably in order to increase the retreatant's compassion (n. 290, 292, 298, end of 208). He wants Mary to be the first consoled by her risen Son (n. 224, 299). Ignatius describes Jesus as a human God, very loving and lovable; by doing so, he reveals himself as a loving and lovable disciple of that Jesus, and invites retreatant and retreat master to be likewise.

Rules

[n. 313–370]

INTRODUCTION TO
THE RULES OF DISCERNMENT

THE ASTONISHING FACT OF THE RULES

We often take the Rules for granted; in fact, Ignatius was one of the pioneers who tried to formulate brief guidelines for spiritual efficiency. As a humanist, he trusts the human being's aptitude to discern, without denying God's necessary grace. For the retreatant *individually* uses the Rules in order to discover God's or the Enemy's word to him or her and to choose in a *personal* way.

The Rules imply obedience to God *only*, and this is part of each human being's dignity. But to obey freely *God's* insights through real consolations keeps God's word and grace first. Ignatius, a man of the Middle Ages, where solidarity was a fact of life, takes into account the emphasis on individual freedom and responsibility that began with Humanism and the Reformation; but, aware of the risks of individualism as demonstrated enough by the crisis of the Reformation, he completes the Rules of discernment with the Rules "to truly feel with the orthodox Church" (n. 352–370).

SPIRITUAL DISCRIMINATION?

I always explain to retreatants why we have two sets of Rules, which seems to imply spiritual discrimination. According to Ignatius' words, some perfect people could handle the Four Weeks and all the Rules (n. 39 for instance); others could deal only with the First Week and its Rules (n. 9, 10, 18, 19). Ignatius' distinction cannot be discrimination, because nobody knows how close to God someone else is. In the ways and words of that time, he is merely taking a fact into account: Existing *limitations* make it difficult or impossible for some persons to enter into some spiritual exercises ("limited in his capacities," n. 18).

Between persons who dislike basketball and professional players, we have a spectrum of diverse people with diverse interests or capacity for the sport; their limitations define what they can do, and it is wise to accept that. If we love our children, we respect each one's personality in what we expect from them. Analogically, because of emotional, intellectual, cultural, physical, and social limitations, all Christians don't have the same attraction for the whole evangelical message, the same capacity to integrate it, the same desire to share Jesus' mission. This was powerfully demonstrated to me and to volunteers when we started giving retreats to prisoners in maximum-security correctional facilities. I also remember a retreatant, easily able to cope daily with important responsibilities in a big firm but extremely sensitive emotionally in family life.

It is simply a matter of respect to treat each person according to who he or she is, with his or her possibilities, and this is the principle underlying Ignatius' words. Perhaps we agree about "age," "poor health," "feeble nature," and some teaching if necessary, but we don't like his distinction of the "educated" and "cultured" because it seems meaningless in God's eyes (n. 18, 19). Ignatius respects retreatants to the point of offering "all the Exercises" if they want them and only the Correction of Life if they have "no disposition to deal with the Elections" (n. 20, 189). He also lets them decide how long they'll stay with the whole Passion, and how many points they'll take for their contemplations in the Fourth Week (n. 209, 228). Different ways of dealing with different people: Jesus Himself did not call everyone to be His disciple, and He even refused some people (Mk 10:21; 5:18–19).

THE TEACHING OF OUR "GUT FEELINGS"

The Rules show that discernment is based on decoding the feelings experienced in all events, including prayer. Ignatius' words imply different levels of emotions. When he says what the *soul* feels in consolation or desolation, he does not talk about skin-deep reactions; his expression "*true* spiritual gladness" means a joy other than a superficial happiness (n. 316–317, 329).

Thus I speak of *three different levels of sentiments* that fit our experiences: We can be disturbed on the surface by an event without being destroyed and losing peace at a deeper level; we can look happy while carrying a heavy sadness in our heart. This was Ignatius' insight, too, when he was reading novels of chivalry and the life of the saints during his convalescence. I share with retreatants what I have learned: Discernment cannot be done with our superficial feelings, for they are too immediate and fleeting (n. 321 insists on patience). It is possible only through the lasting emotions we know on a second and deeper level in ourselves.

And I also mention a third level, the core of our being, to which only God has access according to the great spiritual authors (n. 330, 336). I invite retreatants not to expect this latter experience of God so that they avoid disappointment if in fact they don't experience it, and I advise them to try not to stay trapped in their most spontaneous emotional reactions. The task is to learn how to become aware of what is happening on the second level, where both the good and evil spirits manifest their impact on us. Distinguishing the levels of feelings is very difficult for some persons, who remain easily caught in their most superficial feelings; this justifies Ignatius' distinction, seen sometimes as a discrimination, that I mentioned earlier. Discovering these levels of emotions within oneself is essential for discernment.

I always point out what the Rules imply: God is met everywhere. The certainty and experience of being affected by diverse spirits in all events demonstrate that nothing in life is profane. The certitude of God's omnipresence keeps us in the world, but we maintain some distance in order to realize how and why we are affected. We must become able to feel and understand God's inspirations or the Enemy's suggestions everywhere, and not only in prayer. Everything can be a spiritual experience.

But except in urgent situations, such presence to oneself, gathering of information, and decoding require time and prayer, which are necessary to prevent us from staying with our most immediate reactions. I always hope that retreatants will master these marvelous tools, the Rules, for their future. For example, in retreat they experience an intercourse between daily events and prayer that they later recognize as occurring in their day-to-day life as well. Often, God's work in their hearts is done outside of prayer periods, when they are walking around or eating silently, and they become conscious of what happened during the day when they decode everything with the retreat master. Sometimes understanding occurs during formal prayer periods as well.

Finally, Ignatius connects the experience of those feelings with Jesus. Emotions mentioned in the Rules are related, through affinity or opposition, to the evangelical love of which Jesus is the perfection. But we can assume that, for a humanist like Ignatius, this love was available to everyone, not just Christians. Truly, *everybody* can be sensitive about such love; but some might "name" it differently, according to their religious tradition if non-Christian or value system if nonbeliever (the text speaks of a Creator, rarely explicitly of Christian faith. At Ignatius' time, of course, it could hardly imply a nonreligious belief).

This evangelical love, Agape, is service, compassion, concern for the poorest of the poor, forgiveness, and reconciliation. All of this impels Christians to sojourn frequently with the gospels, in order to increase by their companionship with Jesus their sensitivity to Christ's Spirit in themselves.

Therefore, the Rules send us within ourselves to gauge there the impact of God's Word through Jesus in all our experiences in the world.

RULES FOR THE FIRST WEEK
[n. 313–327]

DIAMETRICALLY OPPOSED

The first two Rules describe two opposite tendencies in behavior. The differences between them are clear because the description employs extremes. It is not so clear for many people who are not at either extreme of behavior; however the tendencies explained here can be applied with nuances, to everyone. I translate these two Rules this way: People are usually able to *care or not about Love* (n. 314–315). The actions of God and the Enemy are always recognized by the contrary feelings they create in us. But the picture is turned upside down according to the tendency of the person.

Those who don't (or can't) care about Love are described as sensitive to temptations of a gross greed, e.g., "pleasures of the flesh and of the senses" (n. 314, 9, 349). The good spirit shakes and awakes such people through the vigor of the law and the notions of right and wrong, without any great subtlety; it also works through reason, as if reason alone could sometimes convince someone overcome by the Enemy and perhaps behaving like an "irrational animal" (n. 47. Humanists were starting to believe in the sciences). Among people who "cannot" care about Love, I recall a prisoner who said, "I can't stand religious meetings where it is always a question of Love; I have always lived in hatred!" I also think of sharks at high levels of the financial, political, or religious world who know well what they are doing against Love. In 1 Timothy 1:8–11 and Romans 8:5–6, Paul seems to have in mind similar people.

Sometimes this tendency can be present in certain persons because of their very rudimentary religious and ethical background. This explains Ignatius' concern to teach during the First Week about examinations, Commandments, mortal sins, confession, the five senses, and the works of mercy (n. 18). I always warn retreatants that *we can all* fall into that tendency for a while or remain habitually in it in some specific areas of our life (this is one more reason for refusing any spiritual discrimination).

Therefore, it is important to know ourselves, in order to interpret correctly our consolations or desolations. For instance, if I am aware that I don't usually care about justice in my business, I can't interpret the sting of my conscience about it as the Enemy's attack. Of course, the retreat master must be able to figure out what kind of person the retreatant is, one who cares or doesn't about Love, in order to be really helpful to him or her.

The opposite tendency is characterized by a care, search, and struggle for Love that the Enemy tries to disturb. If the evil spirit "instills troubles, scruples, sadness, false reasons" (n. 315), the good spirit does everything possible to comfort and console, confirm and strengthen, the persons who want to devote themselves to "the divine service." The following Rules refine the sketchy description of real and apparent consolations and desolations we have here.

CONSOLATION AND DESOLATION

Thinking of people who care about Love, Ignatius describes the two fundamental spiritual experiences, consolation and desolation (n. 316–317). As a "translation," I speak of feelings *enlivening or stifling* our being. I always point out that the Rules emphasize emotions, but that we shouldn't forget intellect, as it is proven by the words "ethical and rational judgment," "false reasons," "any increase of faith" (n. 314–316). Powerful feelings can "obscure" our reasoning (n. 317); in the Bible darkness is often God's adversary.

But our feelings can also "enlighten the mind" (n. 315); for instance, when serenity calms down our "passions" and makes us capable of clarity and objectivity, as classical authors and modern psychologists would say. This experience has been named "intellectual" consolation: When, more clearly than usual, we suddenly understand something about ourselves, Jesus, our journey with God, etc., without any systematic reasoning. Often we can't articulate well our new knowledge ("increase of faith") to ourselves or others, although it is crystal clear to us and solid in terms of coherence with dogma or Scripture.

This sort of consolation explains Ignatius' desire to teach important matters to retreatants who need them: He wants to give them tools to verify any intellectual inspiration provoked by consolation, with the lessons about faith of the best minds. This justifies his advice to "kindly correct" the retreatant and try "to make him [or her] sound of mind and free from error" (n. 22). I always insist on this kind of consolation because it is too often forgotten; and I have always seen the dogmatical balance of a retreatant's report as a sure sign of God, because God cannot mislead our minds as many gurus have done since Christ (Mk 13:21–23). In this regard, I think of Sister Pascale: Each time in her retreat that

I would connect her name with a sign of resurrection, she would say, "Yes, but Easter implies Good Friday"; and when I would pinpoint a painful moment for her, she would reply, "But Easter is coming through it."

In summary, I have this to say about consolation and desolation: "A thought giving consolation is a green light; it is from God and we can follow it. A thought that creates desolation is a red light; it comes from the Enemy, and it is better not to follow it" (n. 313, 199). I also point out that a consolation is not a narcissistic enjoyment, for Ignatius uses the word "motion," which means "movement toward"—God and others, as we know (n. 316). It reminds us also that, each time the Risen One gave His disciples the consolation of seeing Him, they were sent to others. The following paragraphs of the Rules give more details about what to do in time of consolation or desolation.

How to Behave in Time of Desolation

N. 318–319 allow me to tell retreatants that the Rules often express a wisdom we forget in our relationship with God. Common sense says that when we are feeling down, it is wise to avoid making big decisions and that we would do well to shake ourselves. That is Ignatius' advice for times of desolation, and he suggests stimulating ourselves by three actions: prayer, self-examination, and penance (n. 318–319, 321).

Desolation often evaporates when we go back to our usual "diet," our ordinary fidelity to small things in any task, like making our bed or washing ourselves each day, eating meals regularly, and following the daily schedule in a retreat (Mt 25:21–23; Lk 16:10). Many people tempted by despair in prison or concentration camps have verified that truth. However, today, with someone in deep emotional depression, while we would retain the advice about not making big decisions, we would be leery of "shaking" the person; instead, we would invite him or her to get professional psychological help.

Two Kinds of Consolation and Desolation

I always tell retreatants that there are *apparent or authentic* consolations and desolations. The Rules for the First Week already deal with both kinds. When the Enemy presents "seductive pleasures of the flesh and of the senses," like the prospect of a robbery, violent revenge, or profitable embezzlement, for instance, this is an apparent consolation for those "who easily sin mortally" because it is pleasurable (n. 314). But it is not from God, for it produces bad fruit for the perpetrator and victims if the temptation is acted upon. Another apparent consolation is explained in the Rules for the Second Week.

N. 314 also includes an apparent desolation, when "the good spirit assiduously stings [the] conscience" of people tempted to sin, because the fruit is good if the temptation is rejected, although the feeling experienced is not pleasant. N. 322 is about a desolation that is apparent, for its outcome is good for us if we understand its meaning and act accordingly (the passive form of the verbs could suggest God's action). One reason to be sometimes "rightly deprived of divine consolation" is our spiritual laziness (n. 322); this is somehow an apparent desolation because it disappears quickly if we react according to the Sixth Rule (n. 319).

For me, the other reasons for desolation given by Ignatius are based on what the Seventh Rule says: We are tested and taught (n. 320). It is an apparent desolation because it teaches us beneficial lessons: We can resist "our enemy with our natural forces" because God does not abandon us, even if we aren't aware of the divine presence (n. 320). We see how generous we are without reward; we discover that any consolation is God's gracious gift, and fortunately not under our control or we would be tempted by the sin of pride (n. 322).

Some retreatants dislike the notion of a God depriving us of dessert if we don't behave or sadistically "sandpapering" us in order to test and teach us (but we might instead see God as a good training coach rather than a sadist). I prefer to talk about Passovers we face in our life, when we confront some deaths, inevitably with difficult feelings, which are apparent because we reach a new life if we agree to pass through them (only true desolation leads to a dead end if we follow the thought causing it).

With Ignatius' text, I tell retreatants that we must die to the seduction "of the flesh and of the senses," to the idea that God abandons us, to our reluctance to work gratis for God, to the pride of claiming "as our own" any spiritual consolation, in order to grow spiritually (n. 314, 322). I have seen retreatants who had to die to the spoiled or fearful child, the movie star or the self-righteous despot, the insecure macho man or the masochistic slave, the demanding bleeding heart or the self-defeating imprudent teenager, still present in themselves. It was often the retreatant who said to me, "I feel that I must stay with that," the prayed text or the wound revealed by it, and asked for time, because only time shows the trajectory of what is going on. Finally, Jesus' words can be applied to consolation and desolation: "You'll recognize them by their fruits. A sound tree bears good fruit, but a rotten tree bears bad fruit" (Mt 7:16–17).

HOW TO BEHAVE IN TIME OF CONSOLATION [n. 323–324]

A retreatant told me, "I can't expect to enjoy a permanent orgasm; our body's lessons fit our spiritual experiences." Seasons follow each other, and Ignatius asks retreatants to act like squirrels during the good time of consolation and "store energy and strength of spirit" in order to anticipate intelligently and face victoriously the winter of desolation to come. Finally, he summarizes his teaching: To stay humble in time of consolation, because past desolations have proven how weak we might be, and to believe in God's grace and its efficiency in time of desolation.

THREE USUAL TACTICS OF THE ENEMY

The description of a woman in n. 325 does not give credit to Ignatius; it is surprising because he admired and spiritually helped many women (but, in n. 326, the Enemy is compared to a man). My summary of the Rule is: "The sooner, the stronger, the faster we react against the Enemy, the better." There is an old spiritual saying, "Never discuss with the Devil." Jesus did not discuss Peter's reaction about the Passion to come; He strongly rebuked him: "Out of my sight, you Satan!" (Mk 8: 33).

However, I have met a few persons for whom such vigor backfired, creating a lust for compensations or preparing a subtler way for the temptation to return. A friend of mine used diplomacy: She gave herself three minutes to cry when she felt down; it was long enough to discern what was going on, and short enough to keep her in control of the situation.

The Rule of n. 326 asserts that openness is always good, at least in sacramental confession. Maybe Ignatius is specific because he knew the custom of knights confessing to each other before a battle, as he did himself once in Pamplona (see his *Autobiography*, n. 1). Thus I invite retreatants to have a spiritual helper, and not necessarily a priest or even a man, for our Latin text says "*spirituali homini*," translatable as "spiritual person" (as we see in A and P) because "*male* person" would be "*vir.*" I remind retreatants that Ignatius helped people before he became a priest, that the gift of discernment is not a priestly privilege, and that churches have had many excellent spiritual advisers who were women or laymen.

I also warn them about "our noisy devil and our mute one" (Mt 9:32; Mk 9:17): "If you hear, in one corner of yourself, a devil making great noise about obvious temptations, check in the opposite corner of your life to see if there do not exist temptations or behaviors more reprehensible than in the first corner, which you are hiding beneath a silence." In the last century, the European churches were noisy about sexuality but mostly silent about social justice. One retreatant I worked with was very concerned about social involvement but absent at home as a father.

The Fourteenth Rule is common sense. Most of the time our wrongdoing occurs through our weaknesses (n. 327). Retreatants discover that it is important to face and know their weak areas, and the ways to deal with them (to react strongly, to use diplomacy, to avoid situations favoring mistakes, to refuse glib excuses like "I am not worthy; it's just human...").

They also see that, through their "less fortified and guarded" parts, they learn lessons and experience graces of salvation, forgiveness, and gratitude. At the end of a retreat, I return to this Rule, with Jesus' parable about an evil spirit coming back to a "house well swept and tidied" with seven worse companions; this might help retreatants during the following weeks (Mt 12:43–45). And if retreatants say, "With my education, I cannot commit such a major sin," I always remind them that we must remain on guard in all our behaviors, because even stars have fallen from the sky. I also remind readers that the Third Week helps us to discover compassion and forgiveness for our greatest weaknesses (one retreatant who had prayed with Matthew 9:9–13 after confession said, "With Matthew, his friends, and Jesus, I had a party about my wounds!").

RULES FOR THE SECOND WEEK
[n. 328–344]

THE USUAL SIGNS OF THE PRESENCE OF GOD OR OF THE ENEMY

Thinking now of those attracted by Love as Jesus always was, Ignatius refines the Rules "for a more complete discernment of spirits" (n. 328). In the new set, "spirits," but also "angels," and even "God," are responsible for our emotions. This change of vocabulary may suggest that retreatants who can make the four Weeks of the Exercises are more aware about the spiritual, and even divine, dimension of their feelings.

The principles found in n. 329 and 335 were not in the Rules of the First Week, probably for two main reasons. First, n. 335 speaks of "disposition" and n. 329 does not link gladness with deeds, as n. 315 does. I believe that Ignatius describes a *state, the usual state* of those he now has in mind. So I say to retreatants who make the four Weeks, "When we *usually* care about Love, we must *usually* feel *content*." I prefer the classical notion of "contentment," because joy often suggests feeling merely happy, and because "contentment" fits more exactly the constant peace experienced by faithful people. If, however, we meet some persons asserting too loudly that they feel something of that sort, they may be barricaded behind fears, or excuses that they misname reasons, and so deaf to God's Word. Such people don't usually make directed retreats (faithful Christians might be that deaf for a while, but God easily breaks down their barricades). I tell retreatants that contentment is normally what people concerned with Love experience *first* (the Rules always rank consolation first, n. 317). After all, if they are faithful to the Spirit of the risen Christ, whose joy is to console His own, they must usually savor the signs of the presence of the Kingdom: "justice, peace, and joy brought by the Holy Spirit" (Rom 14:17; n. 224).

I end my comments about the state of contentment with, "So, as soon as you feel troubled, it is probably a signal, a flashing light, telling you that something might be wrong." Following Ignatius, I insist on the fact that, since God is simple, each time we hear too complicated discussions within ourselves ("sophistic arguments" in n. 329) for doing or not doing something, we must be on guard.

Another reason I see for the principles to be here, and not among the Rules for the First Week, is that Ignatius is preparing us for the main Rule of the Second Week (n. 331–334). He speaks of "true spiritual gladness" and "semblance of truth" because we are going to hear about a fake consolation and a fake angel of light (n. 329). This latter matter is not for anyone easily tempted by "seductive pleasures of the flesh and of the senses" (n. 314); such a person may benefit from the Rules of the First Week but "derive harm from those of the Second, because the subtlety and sublimity of their object is over his head" (n. 9).

CONSOLATION WITHOUT PRECEDING CAUSE [n. 330, 336]

This description is classical (text P quotes Thomas Aquinas), although it creates a question: Nothing in our senses, mind, and heart explain why we are consoled, so what is left that could? I merely tell retreatants that it is a sudden awareness of a very deep level of our psyche: A wound, a sensitivity, has been touched in us by something we can't clearly identify, and reacts. This experience is not in the Rules of the First Week, maybe because it supposes people free enough that they can talk from their inmost depths without fear, and sufficiently trusting Love as God present in themselves.

Our innermost being either exults or attains unfathomable stillness or welcomes Love without restraint; our body frequently shares such a climax, and the word "orgasm," mentioned earlier, fits the experience, which is so strong that it often colors the next hours or days (n. 336). This event is rare in a lifetime, and we ought not to expect it in order to avoid disappointment or spiritual greed. There is no need for discernment here, because the message, if understood on the spot, is crystal clear, although it may take years for it to become integrated into our intellectual responses or ethical behaviors. Ignatius precisely distinguishes the moment of the consolation, where there is no doubt, from the times that follow, when what we might "feel or resolve" is not guaranteed because it might not be "directly from God" (n. 336).

A SUSPICIOUS KIND OF CONSOLATION [n. 331–334]

N. 330 implied that our emotions usually have a cause. Ignatius goes back to that and refines the Rules for the First Week. He warns us that the bad angel, too, can give consolation, which I call "apparent" because it is not the "true spiritual gladness" brought by God or the good angel only (n. 329), and because it pushes "the soul [to] do evil and perish" (n. 331). This is the temptation under the appearance of good that afflicts essentially generous people (n. 10, 14, 15). It is usually rooted in greed, not for "seductive pleasures of the flesh and of the senses" (n. 314), but for power or adoration, the need for security or self-esteem, through more or less conscious very *subtle* ways. Ignatius describes what I call "deviation of trajectory" and its applicable discernment in n. 332–333.

Quoting Paul, spiritual writers say that the evil spirit transforms "himself into an angel of light" in order to succeed in the process of the temptation (2 Cor 11:14). At the beginning, the thoughts and feelings about a desired goal are or seem good; but the next steps reveal a succession of distortions that create increasing degradations in thoughts, emotions, and deeds.

I spoke earlier of apparent desolations as Passovers leading to a new life; here it is an apparent enjoyable consolation leading to ruin if we let ourselves be taken in by the Evil One's deviations. In my books, *Discernment, The Art of Choosing Well* and *The Hungry*

Heart: Answers to the 20 Most-Asked Questions About Prayer, I apply this analysis specifically to the decision-making process and to prayer.

I usually add a few things to Ignatius' words. First, I invite retreatants to see if these temptations follow some patterns: "When you started an undertaking that sounded good but deteriorated and ended badly, was it usually about the same kind of people (authority figures, the other gender, your children) and/or of things (money, your own stuff or habits), and/or something at stake for you (reputation, security, self-image)?" Then, with Ignatius, I recommend rereading the event in order to discern, with the tools of the mind and heart, the successive degradations in thoughts, actions, and feelings.

But I suggest making this examination *backward,* from the end of the process to the beginning. This technique makes the work easier, for we go upstream from thoughts, deeds, and emotions that are obviously bad toward some that are less and less clearly so. This latter point gives the other reason for my reversal of the process. I have noticed that the closer we get to the beginning, the more difficult it is to understand what happened, because the cause of the first deviations, which frequently sets off the whole process, is often rooted in the unconscious, e.g., some childish fear or greed. Sometimes it might even be genetic. The only retreatants I saw going very far backward were people who had been psychoanalyzed. Of course, I emphasize that, knowing our Enemy's "deceits through such experience, we will more easily be on guard against them in the future" (n. 334).

I have to say to some retreatants, "When you start flying too high, you might create an increasing tension with your inner being, unable to handle such altitude; at the climax, you risk a terrible crash landing!" In *The Hungry Heart,* I mention a priest who spoiled one full day of retreat by fasting too much. Another retreatant used to verify during several yearly retreats, if she was called to "martyrdom" by staying with a very difficult husband, although even their children advised her to leave him (this was for me a good illustration of Ignatius' caution when he says that "true and actual poverty" can be embraced only "if the reason of divine obedience and a choice from above would lead to it," n. 146).

Regarding Ignatius' words about the Enemy's "sophistic arguments that present themselves with the semblance of truth" (n. 329), I think of the justifications for torturing prisoners I heard as a soldier during the war between France and Algeria (1954–1962). Another example is the excuses often given us in our democracies for political measures that eventually hurt the poor.

HARMONIOUS KINSHIP

Finally, I leave retreatants with the principle of discernment of n. 355. If we are in harmonious kinship with a spirit, it comes easily to us. If, on the contrary, our usual tendency is to be in disharmony with a spirit, it is experienced as a disruptive intrusion. Here is my summary of this Rule in the usual situation:

For people who want and try to be faithful to Love:

1. *True consolation is given them by the good spirit*: It is there or comes without a clash; it will be good for the person to follow the inspiration that caused the emotion.
2. *True desolation is given them by the bad spirit*: It happens with a disturbing clash; it would be bad for the person to act according to the suggestion that provoked the feeling.

For people who don't want or try to be faithful to Love:

1. *Apparent consolation is given them by the bad spirit*: It is there or comes without a clash, and suggests that it will be pleasurable to act according to the thought that caused the emotion.
2. *Apparent desolation is given them by the good spirit*: It is an unpleasant, disturbing clash, calling the person to change according to the inspiration that provoked the feeling.

But another situation may happen for people who want and try to be faithful to Love:

1. *Apparent consolation is given them by the bad spirit*, and to accept the suggestion that provokes pleasant feelings would be damaging. Flying too high will end in a crash landing.

2. *Apparent desolation is given them by the good spirit*: Those temporary troubling thoughts are a call to face and pass through something difficult but leading to new life.

A symmetry exists in the first case between the two different kinds of people; it disappears in the second instance. Does that mean that persons who do not care about Love may *usually be* subject to *apparent* consolations and desolations; that they would experience the true ones only if they change? Maybe, because Ignatius' picture of them, as "easily sin[ning] mortally, and add[ing] sin to sins" (n. 314), corresponds in Scripture to people with "hardness of heart," who need a strong shock to turn their hearts back to God; Pharaoh in Exodus and Saul were such persons. And logically, those persons could not be often tempted under the appearance of good since their tendency aims at "seductive pleasures of the flesh and of the senses" and "inferior or earthly things" (n. 314, 317).

Finally, some people might be like that because they are extremely disturbed or have been severely injured by social or emotional wounds. With such people, the wisest course is to abstain from any judgment and to entrust the person to God, a course I have followed with some prison inmates. And let me repeat that we can *all* ignore Love for a while or in some sectors of our life.

NOTES ABOUT SCRUPLES
[n. 345–351]

I comment about these Notes here because I always mention some of them when I speak of discernment. I rarely had to explain n. 346–348 about scruples themselves; they only helped me sometimes to "kindly correct" the retreatant's thoughts when they were far from everyday wisdom and Christian revelation (n. 22). This minimum of teaching worked when the retreatant trusted me and allowed me some moral authority, for spontaneous obedience and confidence in clerics or their equivalents are not the norm today (n. 18, 22). I also tried to do it when I supposed it could be effective: I did meet a couple of retreatants so incapable of changing their mind that I did not allow myself to risk disturbing them by taking "every suitable way to make [them] sound of mind and free from error" (n. 22); their behavior seemed to require the skills of a professional psychotherapist. These two occasions arose only in short retreats open to anyone.

Regarding scruples, I always highlight that their main characteristic for spiritual authors is the troubling and endless fluctuation between the thoughts "What I did is a sin!" and "No, it is not a sin!" I advise people afflicted by that spiritual disease to work on it with a very good spiritual helper; if they have recently started to live in tune with Jesus' message, I tell them that this torment could for a while refine their fidelity, as Ignatius says, because he experienced it after his conversion (n. 348).

BETWEEN TWO EXTREMES

I always speak of n. 349–351, because they explain *the temptation of the extremes* that we face in spiritual growth. This temptation is so important and frequent that the Exercises often deal with it in different ways and invite us to keep or build a balance between two contrary exaggerations. When the retreat starts, Ignatius asks retreatants to make efforts toward "the opposite direction" of a personal inclination they might already be aware of (n. 16); this anticipates the Rules inviting us to fight the Enemy in temptation, desolation, and consolation by taking the opposite way (n. 319, 323, 325–327). Then the Additions relate how to avoid extremes in penance (n. 83–86, 89, 214, 229). In n. 129 and 205, the retreatant is asked to take a lighter schedule if the normal one has been too tiring. While correcting their lifestyle, retreatants are advised to discern how many of their possessions they should retain for themselves and how many can be given to the poor. Implicit in the text is the idea that extremes of either kind (extravagance or excessive renunciation) are to be avoided (n. 189). Concerning alms, Ignatius counsels not to give too much to ourselves or people we love, and not to forget the poor (n. 338, 342–343). Finally, in the Rules about feeling with the Church, he recommends keeping a balance between two extremes (and his opinion is justified by the excesses of the Reformation): e.g., to praise positive *and* scholastic theology, to assert the efficiency of God's grace *and* of our free will in our good deeds, to see both faith *and* good actions as necessary, to keep together the filial fear *and* the servile one (n. 363, 366, 368–370).

The real goal of Ignatius' advice is to go back to equilibrium, midway between something *too* good and something *too* bad. In my comments about Ignatius' example, I remind delicate persons of this: Anyone who has seen glassblowers at work has learned that stretching glass makes it thinner and thinner...till it breaks. But the desired middle is not the one of the Latin saying "*In medio mediocritas*" (In the middle, mediocrity); it is where equilibrium gives lucidity, objectivity, and freedom.

However, does Ignatius not twice recommend that we desire an extreme? In the Two Standards, we are invited to pray that we be chosen for spiritual and even material poverty; and in a following note to beg for "perfect poverty" (n. 147, 157). But in the first case, any attraction to total poverty "by deprivation of things" must be carefully examined, in order to verify if it is a call from God. In the second case, if we pray "to God to elect us" for perfect poverty, it is above all in order to distance ourselves from the opposite attachment and become free.

This last point evokes indifference, which is reached when we stay distant from the extremes of situations. Health or sickness, wealth or poverty, honor or contempt, long or short life, are the words heard by retreatants with the Principle or Foundation, after they have been advised to practice Annotation 16 (n. 23).

The same search for a point of equilibrium between two possibilities is found in the third of the Three Kinds of Men, in the method for an Election in a time of "tranquillity" (n. 155, 179). Some people have seen here a similarity with the main Note about scruples: For, choosing something that is not for us would lead us to a situation as damaging as if we had chosen an extreme. Proverbs already gave a warning: "Give me neither poverty nor riches; lest, being full, I deny You... or being in want, I steal, and profane the name of my God" (Prv 30:8).

Thus I invite retreatants to practice the Note about extremes according to their personal tendencies: "Intellectuals" have to accept and learn from their feelings; loners, to be more cooperative with others in collective action; followers, to take some responsibility and risks; rulers, to become servants; workaholics, to acquaint themselves with leisure, etc. If I emphasize this, I do so also because such tendencies are often connected with the wounds, fears, and greed we experienced in our family and social circle during our childhood, and that have created weaknesses in us.

The Enemy can graft onto these frailties childish temptations to look for power or satisfaction, affirmation, or recognition in the wrong ways. We have already seen this in the temptation under the appearance of good (n. 332–334). If we have been too spoiled or ignored, too protected or neglected, etc., we can easily be led to an extreme; and sometimes from one extreme to the other: from fear of rejection to self-rejection, from not feeling trusted to not trusting, from having been molested to molesting. We and others pay the price. Therefore we must learn and practice this Note, so that "by avoiding the dangers of both extremes," rooted in our more or less conscious selfish motivations, we can remain "continually in a kind of quiet middle and secure state," free (n. 350).

RULES ABOUT ALMS

[n. 337–344]

Attachment to Human Persons

These Rules are valuable for people who, for instance, want to give to charities, financially help relatives or friends, or write their will. One retreatant, an aging businessman, the creator of a successful and efficient firm, had to discern about handing the business down to his son. We are advised to discern, when beneficiaries would be "people related [to us] by blood or friendship," to avoid inappropriate generosity (n. 338).

Through these Rules, Ignatius nuances more than ever his observations about attachments. Here, he clearly implies or says that some are good; for example, four times he specifies with adjectives, more clearly than in texts A and P, that an attachment is bad (n. 150, 154, 155, 157). And, it is only if the attachment is "strong*er*..." or "inclining *more* toward..." that discernment is required (n. 338, 342). So discerning is not necessary if the attachment "for such persons" is just normal, good, or "directly from God's love." One Rule about Election, phrased like n. 338, even speaks of "the attachment infused from heaven by God's love"; such an attachment is certainly laudable (n. 184). But formerly some people would say, "I love you in the Lord," "I love you because of God" (as the description of consolation implies, n. 316); this often meant, "I don't love you very much."

In order to avoid misunderstandings with retreatants about Love, I always speak, as soon as possible, of Agape, the Love we encounter in the New Testament. I explain that this love means to serve someone else, *whatever our feeling* for that person may be. Thus the first Rule becomes, "Verify if you have, above all and as much as possible, the desire and the will to act for the growth of people you have in mind, whether you like them or not." Of course, more than my explanations, praying with the Third Mode of Humility and Jesus' Passion makes retreatants understand what Agape is all about (n. 167). Therefore these Rules about alms, like the ones about temptation under the appearance of good (n. 332–334), protect people from generous inclinations that could eventually favor injustice and nepotism.

FREE FROM HUMAN BONDS, FREE FOR LOVE

N. 342 adds something that is nowhere else in the Exercises, even though it has some similarities with the behavior of the third of the Three Kinds of Men (n. 155). The Rule invites us, when we discern, to forget the object of discernment, "the alms or…the way of distributing them," and to focus on where the problem might be: our attachment to those who could benefit from the alms, especially if "I feel my attachment inclining more toward persons related to me by a human bond." It is difficult to say where the emphasis is, whether on "inclining more toward" or on "by a human bond"; it may be on both, since common sense says that the more we are attached to someone, the more difficult it is to remain free for Agape, and Agape alone. Money and passion often hurt Love when they work together.

This is the strongest and only text in the Exercises about *indif-*

ference applied to a relationship: It counsels us to stay free, to let no human bond and attachment drive us away from evangelical love. This might seem excessive for a question of alms, but let us remember that Jesus, at twelve, put God's service before His parents; He also often asserted the absolute priority for His disciples that they follow Him in spite of any human bond that might dissuade them from doing so (Lk 2:41–50; Mt 19:29; Lk 14:26).

Then Ignatius advises those whose ministry is to manage ecclesiastical goods—and therefore, to some extent, alms—to follow the Rules in order to avoid scruples about "the just portion for their own expenses" (n. 343). Jesus and Paul have already said, "The worker deserves his wages" (Lk 10:7; 1 Tm 5:18). But Ignatius invites those persons, and anybody else, to demand more for themselves, and always to keep something for the poor (n. 344).

RULES FOR TRULY FEELING WITH THE ORTHODOX CHURCH
[N. 352–370]

Understanding these Rules requires that we keep in mind a few things, in order not to project onto Ignatius' words notions or realities, problems or expectations, of our own time. One, these texts belong to the epoch of Humanism and of the crisis of the Reformation. Two, Ignatius was himself still a man of medieval traditions, and with his contemporaries was far from any concept of what today we call democracy. Three, while speaking of the Church, Ignatius uses general terms for its leaders, and never the words "pope" or "bishop" (he had problems enough with the authorities for not being naive about Church leaders' limitations). Finally, all Rules except the first deal fairly directly with *speaking* (most of the time publicly) about things of the Church; this is typical of Ignatius, who was so concerned with communication that he insisted on an exchange of mail within the Society of Jesus.

Ignatius asks us to praise, recommend, and approve practices that had been and were still attacked by some partisans of the

Reformation: e.g., confession to a priest, entering religious life, holding special devotions to one saint or another, ornamentation in churches, and so forth (n. 354–360). Ignatius then speaks of precepts and decrees, orders and traditions, rites and theological systems, and says that they must be supported, defended, approved, and esteemed (n. 361–363). In passing, he praises attending the eucharistic liturgy (and receiving frequent Communion, which was unusual at that time; n. 18), the monastic tradition of the Office and religious life (he kept the latter but never wanted the former for the Society of Jesus).

Ignatius also maintains, in opposition to the Reformers, the classical notion of religious life as somehow more perfect than marriage (even though, as we saw, he keeps some nuances about that when he is dealing with Elections). Realistically, he asserts that criticism against leaders is not the solution, when "integrity of conduct is not found"; but he invites us to act privately in ways that can be efficient (n. 361–363, and previously n. 41–42, 351).

Some people see Ignatius' Rules as characteristic of a court-bred Basque man with a medieval background and southern European sensitivity. This is true in part, but the First and Thirteenth Rules (n. 353, 365) show that his rationale is based on his faith. He believes, as many do, that the Spirit of Jesus Himself inspires the orthodox, Catholic, and hierarchical Church, and that the God of the Decalogue is the One instructing and governing the same Church.

Therefore, two consequences come from this faith. First, exactly as he did with the Election, Ignatius invites us here "not to be inclined either toward accepting or rejecting the debated thing," and "to remain in the middle and in equilibrium, ready in [our] mind to bring immediately all of [ourselves] to the side that [we] will recognize as conducing more to the divine glory and [our] salvation" (n. 179); he recommends here that "having put away all our own judgment, we must always keep our mind prepared and quick to obey the true Spouse of Christ" (n. 353).

The second consequence is very carefully phrased in the Thirteenth Rule: "In order that we be totally unanimous and in accordance with the Catholic Church itself, *if* the Church *defines as black* something *that appears white to our eyes*, we *must* in like manner *declare* it black" [emphasis mine]. The italicized words help us to understand Ignatius. First, he is not at all rejecting the respect he has shown for the individual conscience through the Exercises, for he does not ask us to modify what we might think or believe in conscience. He says that we *must speak* according to the word of the Church ("declare" translates the Latin *"pronuntiare"* which means "to make publicly known"). For Ignatius this is a duty for preserving communion with one another and with the Church.

I don't think we will have a problem with Ignatius' point if we remember that he was neither shaped by nor lived in a democracy, and that disaster and bloodshed were the fruits of the divisions created by all parties during the Reformation. Moreover, Ignatius remains prudent, for the Church's word has to be followed *if* it *defines* something (as different from what we *see*). Eventually, as scholars have noted, Ignatius' last remark alerts us not to give total credit to our *individual* perception of reality, because it is never perfect. But this Rule answers a famous saying of Erasmus. The great Christian Humanist said that white would not be black, even though the pope were to decide so ("a thing I know he will never do," was the end of his sentence). Some very analytical commentators have even noticed that, if Erasmus seems to talk about the substance of black and white, Ignatius speaks about the color *of* something, which for philosophers of that time was only an "accident," and not about the "substance" of the object. We cannot say that Ignatius is not careful.

Finally, Rules Fourteen to Eighteen deal with some specific questions debated because of the theological positions of Reformers: predestination, faith and deeds, grace and free will, filial and servile fear. In each case, Ignatius advises that we avoid extremes while preaching about these subjects (n. 366–370).

I have never had to deal with these Rules in retreats, essentially for one main reason. The years of most of my retreats, the ones I have made and the ones I have given, have been impregnated with the spirit of Vatican II: before 1962, indirectly, through the influence of some of the theologians whose thoughts prepared and fashioned the Council; and from 1962 on, directly, by the works of the Council and their realization. As we know, the

Council, which was not called to combat any heresy, sent the faithful back to the most important aspects of faith. The points emphasized by Ignatius were not treated because the tendency of the Council was to emphasize that which united Christians, and not what divided them, as Pope John XXIII said in a unique spirit of ecumenism.

This aspect of Vatican II reinforced for me the great respect Ignatius wants the retreat master to have for each retreatant, and made my job easy with retreatants of other Christian churches (even more so because we never find any word about a specific Christian denomination throughout the Exercises themselves). I saw God asking a Lutheran minister to be a better Lutheran, a Baptist preacher a better Baptist. However, with the same ecumenical mind, I have always mentioned the Twelfth Rule (n. 364), which I just enlarged by inviting retreatants never to make comparisons. Any comparison is always detrimental to someone, at the very least because everybody is absolutely unique and in a unique relationship with God, of which Ignatius once again asserts the ultimate extension at the end of these Rules, as he does at the end of the Exercises: The "union of love with God" (n. 370).

Just a Daily Rendezvous

The insights shared in my commentary are not usually perceived all at once by all retreatants or retreat masters. Also, each person tends to discover first what is relevant to his or her situation; sometimes these discoveries are made in the midst of the Exercises. One man suddenly realized that his love for a woman was a pattern for *all* his relationships; another said at the end of our meeting, "Wow, we are both men, and we have just now shared the experience of Mary and Elizabeth!" (Lk 1:39–45). However, despite the individual variations during the retreat, years later most retreatants find themselves on a common path, the characteristics of which I will now summarize.

The retreatants I meet after their retreat are back in their "own country"; like the Queen of Sheba or the eunuch of Candace, they have heard the "good news of Jesus," "surpassing all the reports" they knew before (1 Kgs 10; Acts 8). In their usual situations, they remind me of two persons who marry each other after having assessed the gaps between themselves, found some means to narrow them, and taken the soundings of their mutual love.

The Exercises have paved the way for retreatants to set free their own truth and God's, and they want to say "yes" to it. They know well which sins will still tempt them and which "minimums of…" they need in order to prevent the Enemy from playing with their weaknesses. They also see how to use God's gifts and which ways to take or avoid in order to stay free and to serve. They have learned to say to their ghosts, "It is not for you that I have started this, it is not for you that I will end it" (n. 351). But above all, they have taken a sounding of their love. They know that God's Love is stronger than any word, thought, deed, however deadly, because they contemplated It in the risen Jesus, and also in their own renewal, because this Love belongs to them through the Spirit.

Aware of what they can or cannot do, retreatants are also fully convinced that "nothing is impossible with God" (Lk 1:37; Mk 10:27). So, with the tools they have acquired, consciously and efficiently, they allow the Spirit of Love to be present in this world through their flesh. Therefore they see and accept more easily their place and role in history, as the Bride of the Song of Songs, faithful to her Bridegroom.

But what is progressively more important for them is the grace given to Ignatius in the vicinity of Rome in 1529: Jesus' companionship.

Through "the synagognes, the villages, and the towns" of their own (n. 93), they go, "walking, traveling, and [sometimes] running" with Him. They walk with him, He walks with them (n. 1, 71; Mi 6:8; Is 43:1–5). They share everything with Him, even "daily labors, night watches" (n. 93). And they carry within themselves day after day what they practiced during the Exercises: a fellowship with Jesus and a friendship with His Spirit, a conversation with Christ and a recourse to His Love in them. They want to be united with the Trinity. And so they keep returning to God's Word, for they know it is never fruitless, even though it might sometimes be a "two-edged sword" dividing "soul and spirit" (Is 55:10–11; Heb 4:12). They become like a permanent prayer, "God-Love, fill me *so much* with You, that I won't resist You to empty me for others." They no longer say, "I want but I can't, I am too weak" or "I can but I don't want, I am afraid to lose my life." They enter the *second conversion* described by the masters of spiritual life, for their heart says with the "humble" Love discovered in Jesus (n. 144) and tested through the Passion, "Do it in me, for You, You want it and You can do it."

Moreover, they know that in their freedom they have to let Love overflow from themselves. "Thy will be done *in me*," "Your Kingdom come *in me*" becomes their prayer, with the addition "and wherever I am." And like each Person of the Trinity for the Others and all Three for us, they live for others. Somehow they cannot help it, but "there is no evasion from [their] neighbor" (Dt 22:1–4). They share Ignatius' concerns, "to help the souls" for "the most universal good." Their enlightment came through a man who lived at a time of major historical events, like the discovery of America by Christopher Columbus, the revolution in astronomy made by Galileo, the Reformation and Counter-Reformation, but usually they live it out in the most ordinary life. All possible Love was in Nazareth, and is now in their own Nazareth. A French poet said, "To peel potatoes for God's love is as great as building cathedrals." Through potatoes or cathedrals, retreatants I have known enter more and more into the world with others dedicated to living for the sake of Agape. They even know that as soon as they serve, they accomplish something evangelically cosmic, as they learned through the Contemplation *ad Amorem*.

Each one of us becomes aware that he or she is called "by name" to behave in a new way, to compose and play with God a cantata of Love for others (Is 43:1). "The Son of Man has not come to be served but to serve" (Mk 10:45). The musical instruments change according to the place, but it is always the same Song of Songs. With God we play violin and harp in our family life, oboe and cello in our workplace, French horn and trumpet in our neighborhood. We may sometimes hear a wrong note in the duet, but, finally, "Everything is grace."

It might be in an abbey or a garage, an office or at home, in a political career or as a volunteer, in Andorra or Zaire, but it is our personal place, the one to which we are called. There, God accomplishes the promises made through Haggai: "I will shake the heavens and the earth, the sea and the dry land. I will shake all the nations and the treasures of all the nations will come in. And I will fill this house with glory....Mine is the silver and mine the gold....Greater will be the future glory of this house than the former....And in this place I will give you peace" (Hg 2:1–9).

Called by His companions, Jesus said, "Let us move on to the neighboring villages so that I may proclaim the good news there also. That is why I came out" (from the Trinity?). And so He left off praying in a "lonely place in the desert" and went to "the synagogues, the villages, and the towns and other places" around (Mk 1:38; n. 91). In the same way, the retreatants leave the Exercises and go back to the world, the shrine of God's *daily rendezvous* with the Love in us.

APPENDIX

ANIMA CHRISTI
(SOUL OF CHRIST)

The complete text of this prayer is:

Anima Christi, sanctifica me	Soul of Christ, sanctify me.
Corpus Christi, salva me.	Body of Christ, save me.
Sanguis Christi, inebria me.	Blood of Christ, inebriate me.
Aqua lateris Christi, lava me.	Water of Christ's side, wash me.
Passio Christi, conforta me.	Passion of Christ, strengthen me.
O bone Jesu, exaudi me.	O good Jesus, hear me.
Intra tua vulnera, absconde me.	Within Thy wounds, hide me.
Ne permittas me separari a te.	Don't allow me to be separated from Thee.
Ab hoste maligno, defende me.	From the malignant enemy, defend me.
In hora mortis meae voca me,	At the hour of my death, call me,
Et jube me venire ad te,	And enjoin me to come to Thee,
Ut cum Sanctis tuis laudem te	So that, with thy saints, I praise Thee
In saecula saeculorum. Amen.	For ever and ever. Amen.

CONTEMPLATION

Let us speak first of the "mental re-creation of the place," which sets the stage for the prayer period. The more literal translation, "composition of the place," suggests that retreatants act like artists, i.e., "composers." Composers adapt to themselves the rules they have learned in order to express their deepest unique mental and emotional idiosyncrasies, and make their own creation. Thus, imagining allows retreatants to let rise to the surface what is within themselves, including their picture of God. So, the "mental re-creation of the place" is really a prerequisite deed, a prelude; because if we cannot sufficiently liberate what dwells in us, nothing will happen in our prayer about the story—which is always an interplay between God in Jesus and human beings—to make it our own. And the word "prelude," from the Latin verb *ludeo,* to play, invites us to use our imagination with pleasure, as athletes

221

or artists enjoy their passion (and not with the tense meticulousness I saw in some retreatants, afraid to be free).

For many psychologists, imagining is a good tool to make what lies deep within us emerge. Does our imagination risk getting wild here? Not too much, for the "composition of the place" must follow the story given to the intellect (the streets of Jericho are not New York City's) and the grace desired, which is specified by the Week. This prelude starts the encounter with God in a very personal way, much as the setting, with all due respect to Shakespeare, gives a specific touch to *Othello*.

When the stage is set, from the Second Week on, contemplation blossoms. To contemplate, to see, is to enter the story as if we were at least spectators; it makes us contemporaries of what happened between Jesus and So-and-so, and we share the witnesses' experience. It is more powerful if, by grace, we become one of the characters (n. 114); for this time it is the story that is contemporary to us; the interplay *is between Jesus* (or His God) *and us*. The truth is, that right now in our life, we *are* (or feel it is difficult to be) this character. Our current relationship with God is revealed and benefits from the specific Good News of the story (Meister Eckhart said that contemplation, in the monastic sense, realized a sort of incarnation of God's Word in us, so much so that we could say, "I am the Son of God." Indeed, we may be for someone else God's Love present in flesh and blood at this time of our life).

So contemplation evangelizes us, even probably at our unconscious level. Risks of daydreaming exist despite the limitations mentioned above, and I remember some "movie-making" during retreats; but it never lasted, because of the kind of retreatants I worked with. One retreatant's reports were always like a fireworks display of images; but, even so, he and I were able to connect some pictures with the story. This man taught me that we can trust our imagining power *as long as we complete it with discernment*. Is it not a blessing that artists don't repress their imagination (even about religious things)? Without such freedom, we would have today no masterpieces, and probably no art at all.

Does seeing the Holy Land help contemplation? It does, because it asserts Jesus' historicity: He walked and ate here, died there, etc. The specific landscape limits our imagination: Judea is not the Alps, the old Jerusalem is not the old London. But what we remember of that objective land is what touches us subjectively: We make in ourselves our own Holy Land with the one we see. The real sacred ground for us is not Palestine, which is no longer the way it was two thousand years ago; it is in ourselves, it *is* ourselves. There we meet the Jesus who is our own, His God who has become our own, the Spirit we house: The Holy Land is where we fight, love, suffer, and wait, with the situations and people we carry in our hearts today. The evangelists and Paul described the same Christ, but through their own perception. Painters, sculptors, and other artists have done the same. Finally, another geographical landscape may give us the same grace: I "saw" in Algeria the twelve disciples walking through a field of wheat, I "met" in India the man born blind.

Finally, in my opinion, contemplation reaches its zenith in the application of the senses. This method invites us, at the end of the day, to involve the whole of ourselves in the evangelical story (see also *Structure of a Retreat* [p.228]) and to let all our being absorb through all its pores the contemplated mystery "to impress more strongly on the soul the three contemplations made during the day" (n. 227); this method is the one that emphasizes the most that our body is part of all our spiritual experiences (n. 66–70). In *The Hungry Heart*, I develop ways of praying with our senses, because many possibilities exist: One retreatant finished each day of her retreat by painting; another made discoveries through different styles of music—the challenge was to decode their experiences. No contemplation is given in the First Week, perhaps because some retreatants might practice it with the wrong kind of sensuality (when we pray about hell, the application of the senses does not favor lust, unless we are sadomasochists!). But also, God became accessible to our senses only when Jesus appeared; so this might explain why we don't start to contemplate until the Second Week.

DESIRE

I agree with those who think that, for some retreatants, we have "a Week before the Weeks" of the Exercises. Before starting, retreatants who want that journey "with great and generous spirit" are already inhabited by "the desire of the soul" (n. 5, 2). Often, we can perceive an immeasurable hunger behind their first answers to a question like "Why are you here?" Ignatius mentions desire, and it means a fundamentally good thirst in us, always connected with God's views about us (n. 2, 16, 23, 98, 130, 146, 151, 155, 157, 199). For me, its best summary in Ignatius' words is "to know more clearly" God's incarnate Word "in order to serve Him and to adhere to Him the more willingly" because of "His incredible goodness toward me" (n. 130). It goes as far as wanting to follow Jesus for God's glory, even in humiliation (n. 155, 146). Desire seems linked to some relationship with Jesus, His God, and others (through service, for instance); some psychologists have seen here the desire of the other, in a perfect, respectful exchange, well phrased in Ignatius' description of Love (n. 230–231).

However, for believers, it is deeper than what we may perceive through our psyche, so much that it is not fully satisfied by intellectual means (n. 2). In n. 157, it even seems beyond our availability for perfect poverty, because we are invited to keep it free in spite of the extremely generous offering of ourselves. This means for me that the deepest answer to our question "What am I looking for?" is not accessible to us, and that we would be wise to let the only One who knows it, God, reveal it to us (Jn 1:38). Paul said, "The Spirit too helps us to pray as we ought; but the Spirit Himself makes intercession for us with groanings that are unutterable. He who searches hearts knows the Spirit's intent [in some translations, "desire"], for the Spirit intercedes for the saints, according to God" (Rom 8:26–27). Beyond our fears and greed, our generosity and dedication, our specific hopes and decisions, Jesus' Spirit of Love in us desires God's intimacy, God's Name sanctified, and God's reign in us.

In the Exercises, Ignatius speaks of the Enemy's desire to destroy us (n. 169, 325). This does not contradict the previous analysis, because he uses the phrase "perverse desires" in n. 332 (*perversa* in Latin literally means "turned upside down"). At Ignatius' time, the image of the Devil was one who had been first among angels, dwelt and inhabited by the desire for God like all creatures; but Lucifer had turned upside down this desire, was "changed from grace to wickedness and thrown from heaven to hell." And the fallen angel, working against God and us, wants to drag us into the same downfall (n. 50). This picture fits some people we see today, whose best desires are turned upside down, or perverted, and whose love becomes hatred.

Of course, such a desire is at the root of the "searching" (and "finding") so often mentioned through the Exercises. It has some bond with our body: Our way of dealing with our body may help it to come out, or it may help our body to make discoveries (n. 73–90, 130, 214). This is not surprising, because nothing in us is real without the cooperation of our body (we speak of a "platonic desire" when it does not take shape).

It seems that the desire in itself is never bad (except when perverted in the Enemy); it is good and aims at goals ordained by God; some people would say, "Of course, it is God's mark within us." But it can be more or less perverted, and emerge from us distorted by our childish, selfish tendencies or denied by the refusal of our will (after all, though everyone may desire to love, how many really want to "lose" their life?). That may explain why the word "desire" is never used in the First Week; maybe people "who easily sin mortally" and are tempted by "seductive pleasures of the flesh and of the senses," although they are inhabited by the same desire as others, have difficulties getting in touch with it; or, if they do, they "mistranslate" it in their deeds (n. 314). William A. Barry, S.J., has written very helpfully about desire in *Allowing the Creator to Deal with the Creature* (Mahwah N.J.: Paulist Press, 1994).

FACULTIES OF THE SOUL

Ignatius uses the classical notions of his time, memory, intellect, and will, from the First Exercise to the last (n. 45, 234). The first two are quite close to our current notions of those concepts.

Memory helps retreatants to recall what they have been asked to pray about, and also what might come back from their past through the topic of their prayer; "re-membering" often connects and puts things together. Intellect makes retreatants understand the Mystery they pray with and reflect about it; but in the Exercises the intellect applies the story to the retreatants themselves in their own situations.

The will must be explained to retreatants today: It is, of course, our ability to will and make decisions, but for Ignatius and scholars of his time, it also meant our deepest emotional capacity to feel, as Annotation 3 shows. This will is also a special sort of knowledge. Today, we would say "memory, intellect, and heart," if we keep in mind that it is our heart that eventually gives the last push for acting or choosing. Paul said, "May the God of our Lord Jesus Christ, the Father of glory, grant you a *spirit* (*pneuma* in Greek) of wisdom and revelation to know Him clearly. May he enlighten the eyes of your *heart* (*kardias*, in Greek) that you may know the great hope to which He has called you, the wealth of His glorious heritage to be distributed among the members of the church, and the immeasurable scope of His power in us who believe" (Eph 1:17–18).

FEELINGS

Discernment is based on the decoding of our feelings. Therefore it is essential for us to *accept, name,* and *understand* them. Accepting our emotions supposes that we face them, without denial, fear, scruples, or rationalization. Then we must identify them: At what level within us do they happen, and are they authentic or apparent consolations or desolations? Finally, decoding their meaning tells us to follow or not follow the thoughts that provoked them. All of this is possible if we have learned and practiced the methods given us by the Exercises; and we are supposed to make "efforts" to do so (n. 5, 16, 107, 116, 189, 206). That is why the retreat master's essential task is to verify if Ignatius' methods, and specifically his methods of discernment, are used correctly by retreatants (and to teach them, if necessary).

This centering on methods essentially asks any retreat master not to rule retreatants, as a retreat master who had never been a Jesuit tried to do with me in my first encounter with the Exercises. This is one dimension of the retreat master's respect for the retreatant, so "that our Creator and Lord Himself can act more surely in His creature," and that this latter can answer freely to God (n. 16). My strongest experience about that was made with two women, both dealing with their bodies, one in pregnancy and the other in menopause; Ignatius' concern for retreatants' freedom allowed me to help them, although I could never understand firsthand their physical and cultural experiences (n. 14–15).

Thus retreat masters must work as all good psychotherapists do. In fact, some people have said that past spiritual masters like Ignatius were the first psychologists, or even psychoanalysts; it is true, for they tried systematically to understand the events occurring in the human psyche with the tools of their time. However, some differences exist. When people work with psychologists, they try to discover what is revealed about their psyche, in their thoughts and feelings, words and deeds, and mental images, even the religious ones; and with such knowledge they hope to become freer in their behavior. When they work with spiritual helpers like retreat masters, they decode the same things, looking again for more freedom, but freedom to integrate all their discoveries into their journey with their God with a new meaning. If Jeremiah was a crying baby and Ezekiel a man with an astounding imagination, Peter a loudmouth and Paul a creature of passion, God integrated their personalities into their testimonies very well! Another big difference is that retreatants (and retreat masters) believe in the Spirit's presence in themselves, which is not the realm of any psychologist as such. Further, unlike a psychologist, the Spirit can always work in and with someone whose wounds cannot be cured. Therefore, if retreat masters work with a psychological system of reference, and especially if they have professional training and experience in psychology, they must remember that spiritual help is not merely psychotherapy.

Eventually, because our feelings must be remembered to bring them to our meetings with the retreat master, a minimum of a daily journal is necessary, and seems implied by Ignatius (n. 6, 17, 62, 122, 227, 334). He clearly says so in his draft for a Directory (n. 8).

STRUCTURE OF A RETREAT

THE WHOLE RETREAT

Ignatius' calendar for a retreat is quite loose. He never says if and how long retreatants have to stay with the Principle or Foundation. *One* full day seems to be alotted for the First Week (n. 72), *one* for the Kingdom of Christ (with two prayer periods only, n. 98), and *twelve* for the rest of the Second Week. In these, the fourth day is for the Two Standards and the Three Kinds of Men (n. 148). In the fifth begins the process of Election, which requires one day devoted to the Three Modes of Humility before it is started (n. 163–164). So, the fourth day includes the Two Standards, the Three Kinds of Men, and the Three Modes (two of these Exercises are just a "consideration"). But this schedule confirms that the Two Standards, the Three Kinds of Men, and the Three Modes of Humility go together. The Third Week lasts *seven* days. No indication about the Fourth, except that the first Exercise is probably made in *one* day. Nothing is said either about the Contemplation *ad Amorem*. The total is twenty-one days, which leaves nine extra days. We don't know exactly what these days are for. But I have never heard of a retreat master following Ignatius' schedule literally.

The totality of the Exercises can be made in daily life without problems, if we agree to take sufficient time and respect the retreatant's pace; I see them lasting six to seven months and meet retreatants every two weeks (less often during the Third and Fourth Weeks). In a thirty-day retreat, we may make all the Exercises, but I remember a few retreatants who left the retreat house at the beginning of the Fourth Week and finished it at home. In shorter retreats, the whole is rarely done. If retreatants have already made the whole of the Exercises, whatever can be done is good enough, because the time spent with the Principle or Foundation and the First Week may be shorter.

When the retreat is around one week long, new retreatants end, at most, with the first contemplation of the Second Week. When the retreat is just a weekend, it is something like a First Week. In both cases, I often invite retreatants to finish by contemplating the Last Supper. For instance, in prisons we had an equivalent of the First Week, an at the end we washed each other's feet and celebrated the Eucharist (the equivalent of the encounter with the retreat master was offered through possible meetings with each volunteer or small groups for sharing and "decoding"). Some retreat masters find short retreats frustrating, but people do what they can according to their desire, available time, and financial means, and God still works efficiently. I have also noticed that, through the years, some retreatants make an equivalent of the whole of the Exercises, each retreat starting more or less where the one before left off.

ONE DAY OF RETREAT

In a thirty-day retreat, Ignatius sees five prayer periods a day, each one an hour long: at midnight, at dawn or on rising, the times of around Mass and Vespers, and before supper (n. 12, 72, 99, 128). This schedule is like that of a convent (where Mass and Vespers can be attended, n. 20), and not like the one most of us follow in our usual life; however, it may be adjusted to the retreatant or the Week (n. 129, 227). Two examinations also take place daily (n. 25–26, 160, 207). The schedule of the prayer periods usually consists of two meditations or contemplations, two repetitions, and the application of the senses.

Repetition is an essential technique in the Exercises. Through it, retreatants come back, not to the whole previous Exercise, but only to what they have "noticed" as affecting them; it allows them to pray with that "longer and more diligently," and "treating [it] with more attention." Ignatius calls the repetition "a kind of rumination" that permits the intellect, helped by memory, to stay longer "without digressions" with what has made a strong emotional impact on us (n. 62, 64, 118).

I summarize the method by saying, "Stay with what is touching you, chiefly if the feelings are strong" (n. 227). "For how long?"

retreatants sometimes ask. I often say, "Till you get bored, or if nothing really new comes out, because this is probably the proof that we have to move on." This prevents retreatants from flying around in all directions, from flattering their intellect with many new thoughts, from escaping what they must hear. It gives God's message *time* to sink into retreatants and impregnate them, while unfolding all its potentialities; it gives retreatants *time* for absorbing and assimilating, clarifying and understanding, what is said to them. If the feeling experienced is a desolation, repetition helps us to discover if it is a real one or a Passover. Finally, the two daily repetitions prepare us very well for the application of the five senses (see *Contemplation*). Repetition in the Exercises also prepares retreatants to be enriched by an experience many people have often known without being trained to deal with it. A text might attract us, haunt us, question us for months or even years, showing obviously that some message is there for us. I think of someone who was attracted for one full year by the call of Abraham, and for three years by Jacob struggling with the angel (Gn 12:32); trained by the Exercises, this person was eventually able to decode the experience.

The Kingdom of Christ is an exception (prayed only twice during the day). I suspect that, as is done in many thirty-day retreats, Ignatius probably gave the retreatant a sort of break after the First Week, with a lighter schedule (n. 99).

ADJUSTMENTS

Ignatius often recommends adjusting the Exercises to the retreatant (e.g., n. 4; even the way of eating and sleeping, in n. 89); the problem is to adapt them without betraying them. My first way of doing that is to let retreatants make their own daily schedule, which we go over together in order to see if break times, prayer periods, daily appointment, meals, Eucharist, etc., are distributed during the day at reasonable intervals. In a thirty-day retreat, I always invite retreatants to see if they can pray, once in a while, in the middle of the night—with one criterion of discernment: "This is probably okay for you if you can go back to sleep easily."

I want to mention two opportunities that taught me a lot. For reasons I don't have to explain here, I said to a retreatant, "For the day to come, let us try this: Let us forget the schedule. Pray when, how, and as long as you want"; to another, "Maybe we have to forget everything. Do what you want for twenty-four-hours. Go to a movie, visit some friends, or whatever." I added in both cases, "But it must be a *decision*, so, before doing this or that, verify if it is really what you want deep down in yourself." In our next meeting, we saw that the permission to use their freedom without restraint had made miracles happen, in terms of discoveries! Another retreatant I knew said to an excellent retreat master the first day, "I am sorry, but I have to prepare some lectures I am supposed to give next week. How can I manage that?" The answer was, "*Schedule* one or two hours for that preparation every day. Before and after that time, forget about the lectures." Relieved, the retreatant made a good retreat and gave good lectures.

In all retreats, it is important to schedule break times. In a thirty-day retreat, it might be one full day at the end of the First and Second Weeks, half a day after the Third Week. I also routinely invite retreatants to relax through mild physical exercises.

BIBLIOGRAPHY

The 500th anniversary of Ignatius' birth has yielded a new crop of articles and books. Among an embarrassment of riches, I think it sufficient to send readers back to two books that, in my opinion, will be the most informative and helpful. The second is for those who read French.

— *Ignatius of Loyola, The Spiritual Exercises and Selected Works*, in the series the Classics of Western Spirituality. George E. Ganss, S.J., ed., with the collaboration of Parmananda R. Divarkar, S.J., Edward J. Malatesta, S.J., and Martin E. Palmer, S.J. Mahwah, NJ: Paulist Press. 1991. 503 pages.

We find in this book both commentary and some of Ignatius' works: the *Autobiography*, the *Spiritual Exercises* (based on A), the *Deliberation on Poverty*, selections from the *Spiritual Diary* and *Constitutions of the Society of Jesus*, and ten selected letters.

— *Ignace de Loyola, Écrits*, traduits et présentés sous la direction de Maurice Giuliani, sj, par un groupe de pères jésuites: Jean-Noël Aletti, Adrien Demoustier, Jean-Claude Dhôtel, Gervais Dumeige, François Évain, Édouard Gueydan, Antoine Lauras, Luc Pareydt, Claude Viard, avec la collaboration de Pierre Antoine Fabré (chargé de conférence, EHESS) et Luce Giard (CNRS, Laboratoire d'Histoire des Sciences). Collection Christus N. 76, Textes. Paris: Desclée de Brouwer, 1991. 1109 pages.

We find in this book both commentary and, from Ignatius himself: the *Spiritual Exercises* (the three versions A, P, V), notes for a Directory, documents about the founding of the Society of Jesus, the *Deliberation on Poverty* and the *Spiritual Diary*, the *Constitutions and Rules of the Society of Jesus*, some letters and Instructions (236 texts), the *Autobiography*, and a letter about Ignatius' death by his secretary.

I have already spoken about the Exercises in two of my own books:

— *Discernment: The Art of Choosing Well.* Liguori, Mo.: Triumph, 1993. 145 pages. This book focuses more specifically on treating the process of making decisions. Grounded in the Exercises, it unfolds the method in a systematic and simple way to guide the reader who has to make a decision, whether that choice is to be made by an individual or a group.

— *The Hungry Heart, Answers to the 20 Most-Asked Questions About Prayer.* Liguori, Mo.: Triumph, 1995. 173 pages. In this book, I apply many aspects of the Exercises specifically to prayer life.

About the Author

B orn in Marseille, France, Pierre Wolff is a former Jesuit priest with advanced degrees in Philosophy and Theology who now ministers to the Episcopal diocese in Wallingford, Connecticut, where he resides. A popular retreat director and seminar leader in the United States and France, Wolff is also a noted teacher of discernment and Ignatian spirituality.

Wolff's previous books include *The Hungry Heart: Answers to the 20 Most-Asked Questions About Prayer*; *God's Passion, Our Passion*; *Discernment: The Art of Choosing Well*; *Is God Deaf?*; and *May I Hate God?*